JOSEÑO

Joseño

Another Mayan Voice
Speaks from Guatemala

Narrated by
IGNACIO BIZARRO UJPÁN

Translated and edited by
JAMES D. SEXTON

UNIVERSITY OF NEW MEXICO PRESS
ALBUQUERQUE

Library of Congress Cataloging-in-Publication Data

Bizarro Ujpán, Ignacio.
    Joseño : another Mayan voice speaks from Guatemala / narrated by
Ignacio Bizarro Ujpán ; translated and edited by James D. Sexton. — 1st ed.
    p. cm.
English translations of unpublished Spanish diaries.
Includes bibliographical references and index.
ISBN 0-8263-2354-5 (cloth : acid-free paper)—ISBN 0-8263-2355-3
    (pbk. : acid-free paper)
    1. Bizarro Ujpán, Ignacio—Diaries. 2. Tzutuhil Indians—Biography.
    3. Tzutuhil Indians—Social conditions. I. Sexton, James D. II. Title.

F1465.2.T9
972.81'00497415—dc21

                                    2001001511

All photographs by author unless otherwise noted.
Book design: Mina Yamashita

Contents

About the Authors

JAMES D. SEXTON has been working in Guatemala for the past thirty years. Among his publications are *Education and Innovation in a Guatemalan Community* and numerous articles on modernization and cultural change in highland Guatemala. Since receiving a Ph.D. in cultural anthropology from the University of California, Los Angeles (UCLA), in 1973, Sexton has been teaching at Northern Arizona University (NAU). In 1982 he received the NAU President's Award for excellence in teaching, research, and service. In 1991 he was named Regents' Professor, and in 1997 he was selected as the NAU Phi Kappa Phi Faculty Scholar. He is past president of the Southwestern Anthropological Association and currently serves on the editorial board of the Internet journal *Delaware Review of Latin American Studies*. Sexton has traveled extensively throughout Mexico, Central America, South America, and the Caribbean. He and his wife, Marilyn, a medical social worker, have one son, Randy, a graduate student.

IGNACIO BIZARRO UJPÁN is a *principal,* or town elder, of San José la Laguna. He has held several religious and civil offices in San José, including *alcalde* (head) of the *cofradías* (religious brotherhoods) of María Concepción and of San Juan Bautista, the two most important *cofradías* in his community, and *síndico* (town syndic), the second-highest elected office. Bizarro writes in his spare time, when he is away from his cornfields and coffee groves and when he is not helping his wife, a Tzutuhil Maya Indian, with her weaving projects. Bizarro and his wife have eight children and three grandchildren. Their eldest daughter and a younger son are among the few Indian students of San José who have attained their teaching credentials.

Illustrations

Maps

Figures

Introduction

THIS IS THE STORY of a Tzutuhil Maya elder who grows crops on the semitropical land bordering the western shore of Lake Atitlán, a majestic expanse of water that laps the feet of three mighty volcanoes. To protect his privacy, we shall call him Ignacio Bizarro Ujpán and his town San José la Laguna.[1] In 1972, at my request, Ignacio wrote his autobiography and began to keep a diary of what he considered to be the significant events of his life, town, and country. This volume, which covers his life from 1987 to 1998, is the fourth and final one in the series.

In the past thirty years, there have been a number of changes in the towns surrounding Lake Atitlán. There are more Maya Indians wearing western-style clothing and speaking Spanish, and more of them are becoming members of Protestant denominations. There are more paved roads connecting towns and more buses, carrying more people, running on these roads; more motorized launches than canoes carrying people across the lake; more schools with more grade divisions; more people competing for scarce land and jobs; and more new office buildings and homes, especially vacation houses of Ladinos (non-Indians) on or near the waterfront. Many of the new homes, as well as a number of the traditional ones, have running water, electricity, and modern furnishings. Although newspapers are still an important source of information for those who are literate, more homes have radios and televisions that carry both local and global channels, which expose residents to national and international events.

Ignacio's chronicle is unique in that it documents cultural change, as well as cultural continuity, from a personal perspective for a period of more than a quarter of a century.[2] It offers insights into what has taken place among the present-day Tzutuhil Maya and their neighbors during this turbulent time. Also, a number of general themes emerge from Ignacio's account that help us to better understand the human condition of the highland Maya. These themes include alcohol abuse and civil violence, as illustrated by Ignacio's best friend breaking a shaman's collar bone in a bar brawl; community solidarity, illustrated by Ignacio's townspeople coming together to help one another after a severe earthquake killed and injured thousands of their countrymen; political violence and turmoil, exemplified by the machine-gunning of Señorita María Luisa by a death squad in Ignacio's town of San José; and resistance to repression, portrayed by *Joseños* (people of San José) cursing Ladino army officers in Tzutuhil for forcing them to attend classes on how to handle and shoot a Mauser rifle. Finally, the theme of campesinos caught between "two fires," the army and the guerrillas, is documented by the burning of public buses and murder of the drivers and their assistants in the department of Sololá by guerrillas and the subsequent killing in retaliation of sixteen Maya Indians, including women and children, by the army.[3]

These themes continue in the present volume, although the intensity varies with the period in question. For example, in 1988 Ignacio reports an unresolved massacre of Cakchiquel Indians in El Aguacate. It was not until 1999 that a truth commission revealed that guerrillas were responsible, although they had publicly blamed the army. In 1990 Ignacio provides a perceptive account of the army's blatant massacre of Tzutuhil Indians in Santiago Atitlán. By December 1996, however, political violence diminished with the signing of peace accords by the guerrillas and the military. Communal resistance to unwanted outside pressure is illustrated when Ignacio, toward the end of this volume, reveals how the *Joseños* refused to report one another to the army or to the guerrillas. Alcohol abuse is still a major problem for some, but Ignacio now drinks only moderately. The most prominent new theme that emerges is propriety and cultural revitalization, especially the reinforcement of both traditional and modern religious values in the community. Ignacio plays a major role in this revitalization as *alcalde* of the *cofradía* of San Juan Bautista, the patron saint of the town.

Background to Ignacio's Story

My graduate studies in anthropology at UCLA were interrupted when the U.S. Army called me to active duty in May 1968. I resumed my studies in October 1969, after a tour of duty in Vietnam, participating in a war that I thought was a mistake. In spring 1970, before I could complete the academic year, demonstrations against the Vietnam war shut down the university. As I was eager to make up for lost time and long had been intrigued by the Maya Indians, it was not difficult for

1. *Guatemala with political boundaries and location of Lake Atitlán.*

Professor Clyde Woods to persuade me to join his field school in Guatemala, which was to be directed that summer by Professor Peter Snyder.

I met Ignacio in June 1970 when I began my first anthropological fieldwork in San José as a member of the team of researchers studying development and modernization in the fourteen towns surrounding Lake Atitlán. Ignacio lived across a rocky, unpaved street from the small, one-room house I was renting. When I asked him to be my research assistant to help collect a random sample of interview schedules, he agreed.[4]

In 1972, during my third season in Guatemala, I decided to approach Ignacio about keeping a journal of his life. Initially, I had two main goals in mind. First, I wanted to give Ignacio something to do for which I could pay him a reasonable wage. Second, I wanted to stay in touch with what was happening in the area while I was back in the United States, completing my dissertation and teaching at a university.

I asked Ignacio to write about his family, town, work, religious activities, and dreams. My instructions to him were to record accurate dates and times of events. Following Walter Dyk (1938), I asked Ignacio to first write an autobiography and then to keep a diary, and following Leo Simmons (1942), I encouraged him to record mundane as well as extraordinary events.

By fall 1974 Ignacio had given me the first draft of his story in Spanish. And by summer 1975 I had completed the first English-language version. There were, however, some voids and confusion in the material. In 1975 and 1976 I again traveled to Lake Atitlán to ask Ignacio questions about his story. Some of our conversations took place in San José; others, in the quiet privacy of my rented house in Panajachel. In total, over the past thirty years, I have made fifteen field trips to work with Ignacio in Guatemala. We published *Son of Tecún Umán* in 1981, *Campesino* in 1985, and *Ignacio* in 1992.⁵ The present volume is appearing in 2001.

In translating and editing the books, I stayed as close as possible to Ignacio's own words to retain his patterns of speech. For example, I translated such expressions as *debajo de la lluvia* and *debajo del sol* as "under the rain" and "under the sun" rather than "in the rain" and "in the sun." In most cases, grammatical and stylistic concerns dictated a free translation. For instance, I insured that there was subject-verb agreement and that verb tense was consistent within paragraphs. I deleted trivial episodes and asked Ignacio to clarify or expand on others. In the latter cases, my questions appear in italics, as do occasional editorial interpolations. If an Indian or Spanish word appears in *Merriam Webster's Collegiate Dictionary, Tenth Edition,* with the same meaning intended here, it is not italicized. If there is more than one definition for a foreign word, such as *muchacho, campo,* and *quintal,* and *Webster's* provides only one, I have used italics. In Ignacio's diary, my explanations and definitions appear in brackets; parentheses are retained for Ignacio's explanations.

All but a few of the subtitles of episodes in the texts were added by me. I first inserted the subtitles of specific episodes to help me locate repetition. I deleted most of the repetition but retained some repeated material, such as adages that Ignacio uses for emphasis. For example, as a way of introducing two boating accidents and one car accident, Ignacio uses a variant of the saying, "We all know where we were born, but we don't know where we are going to die."

2. Lake Atitlán with surrounding towns and villages.

The inserted subtitles are, in effect, mini-themes that give greater structure to the story (Daily 1971), and they often are specific to Ignacio's personal life. These mini-themes often occur in a cultural context shared by other Maya and to some extent by Ladinos. Like John G. Kennedy (1977), I attempted to place the entire story and the subject in their historical, political, and cultural context in the introductions, notes, and appendices to the books.

The Historical and Political Context of Ignacio's Story

Before the Guatemalan revolution of the early 1940s that overthrew the thirteen-year dictatorship of General Jorge Ubico, the backward state of the country was most acute in the countryside, among the Indians, who made up more than half the population of Guatemala. Malnutrition was endemic, because 80 percent of the land that surrounded their overpopulated towns and villages was owned by large plantations and was lying fallow. Indian life expectancy was forty years (compared to fifty years for Ladinos), and more than 90 percent of the Indians were illiterate. In short, there was extreme peasant poverty, underutilization of labor and resources, and an economy that was almost wholly dependent on the U.S. banana and coffee markets (Gordon 1983:48).

In 1944 Dr. Juan José Arévalo, a teacher living in exile, was elected president by an overwhelming majority—the first candidate to be elected under a democratic constitution in more than a century. He inaugurated political and economic reforms, but there were no serious attempts at land reform until his successor, Jacobo Arbenz Guzmán, a reform-minded colonel, was elected in December 1950. Arbenz introduced an agrarian reform measure that targeted lands or farms of more than 223 acres for appropriation. The owners of the land were to be paid the same value that they had declared on their May 1952 taxes. Even Arbenz and his foreign minister had hundreds of acres of their own land expropriated.

One of Arbenz's goals was to break the grip that foreign corporations such as the United Fruit Company had on the Guatemalan economy. However, the Boston-based company had powerful friends in the United States, including the Republican senator Henry Cabot Lodge. In 1952 the Arbenz government legally recognized the Communist Party, called the Partido Guatemalteco de Trabajo (PGT, Guatemalan Labor Party), and labor unions began to exert greater influence. The death knell was not sounded for the reform government of Arbenz, however, until it began the expropriation of 240,000 acres of the United Fruit Company's holdings on the Pacific Coast and 173,000 acres on the Atlantic Coast. The Guatemalan government offered the company compensation of $600,000 based on its declared tax value, but United Fruit insisted that the Pacific Coast land alone was worth more than $15 million. Ultimately, the company was able to convert what was essentially a business dispute with Guatemalan officials into an ideological conflict between the United States and countries of the Soviet bloc (Simons 1983).

In 1954 the Central Intelligence Agency (CIA) sponsored a coup, led by Colonel Carlos Castillo Armas, that successfully overthrew the Guatemalan government. Under his direction, the government made a sharp turn to the right, reversing revolutionary change and initiating three decades of direct or indirect military rule.

In 1960, when the new president, General Miguel Ydígoras Fuentes,

1. *View of the eastern side of Lake Atitlán, near the village of Godínez.*

allowed the CIA to train Cuban expatriates in Retalhuleu to overthrow Fidel Castro, dissidents within the barracks threatened a coup. The dissidents admired Castro for standing up to the United States, and they were opposed to training foreign insurgents on Guatemalan soil. The coup was thwarted with a show of force by the U.S. aircraft carrier *Shangri-la,* but not all of the rebels submitted to the punishment of a demotion and a reprimand. Two leading rebels fled to the mountains and eventually organized a guerrilla group. One of them, Marco Antonio Yon Sosa, was a twenty-two-year-old lieutenant who had been trained by the United States in the Panama Canal Zone; the other, Luis Turcios Lima, was a nineteen-year-old lieutenant who had been trained as a ranger at Fort Benning, Georgia.

Turcios operated in Izabel, in Alta Verapaz, and occasionally in Guatemala City, and Yon Sosa struggled among the peasants of the Sierra de las Minas region. They participated in some joint actions but eventually went their separate ways. Yon Sosa's group, MR-13 (13 November Movement), began to follow a Trotskyist orientation. Turcios's group, Fuerzas Armadas Rebelde (FAR, Rebel Armed

Forces), was initially aligned with the PGT but then broke off from the PGT and realigned itself with MR-13. Shortly afterward, a second guerrilla group surfaced, led by a former Arbenz minister of defense, Carlos Paz Tejada. Both guerrilla groups tried to organize Ladinos with a *foco* strategy (i.e., small groups established themselves in the countryside and tried to radicalize the people by confronting the army, thereby setting an example of resistance).

In 1966, according to Elisabeth Burgos (1999:53–54), Luis Turcios Lima led a Guatemalan delegation at the Tricontinental Conference she was attending in Havana. The goal of the conference was to coordinate an armed struggle on three continents of the Third World— Asia, Africa, and Latin America. Also attending the conference was a Guatemalan couple, Ricardo Ramírez and Aura Marina, who were leaders of the PGT. Marina, an anthropologist, argued that the participation of Maya Indians was crucial for the insurrection to succeed in Guatemala and that the most suitable model for Guatemala's armed struggle was that of the revolutionary war that developed first in China and then in Vietnam.

Burgos (1999:54) recalled that she met Marina again in 1969 when Marina arrived in Europe to organize support networks for a new phase of guerrilla war in Guatemala. Ramírez had returned to Guatemala to help organize the Ejército Guerrillero de los Pobres (EGP, Guerrilla Army of the Poor).

The Guatemalan military and its U.S. advisers, however, were determined not to have another Vietnam in Guatemala. They initiated a counterinsurgency campaign, dubbed Operation Guatemala, that lasted until 1970. Operation Guatemala was similar to the infamous Operation Phoenix in Vietnam, which lasted until 1971. Both programs were conceived by the CIA, and both claimed the lives of innocent civilians— Operation Guatemala an estimated 2,800 to 10,000 and Operation Vietnam an estimated 20,587 to 60,000 (Sexton 1985:411). With U.S. assistance, General Ydígoras's forces decimated the rebel bands of Turcios, Yon Sosa, and Paz Tejada. In the process, governmental forces killed and jailed hundreds of students, labor leaders, peasants, professionals, and former soldiers. The guerrilla war, having flared up in 1962 and peaked in 1966, did not subside until 1973. Although the army crushed armed opposition to the government, it failed to completely eradicate it.

Discouraged with the lack of progress in the urban areas and with the *foco* theory of revolution, the EGP had a new goal, to win the support of the Indians (Sexton 1985:412). In 1975 it initiated another cycle of insurgency and counterinsurgency. Thus, following Marina's earlier advice, the guerrillas focused on the Maya Indians of the west rather than the Ladinos of the east. In the department of El Quiché, the EGP executed a landlord named Luis Arenas Barrea, who had been called the Tiger (Jaguar) of Ixcán. According to Mario Payeras (1983:266), a member of the EGP, Arenas had been linked to land seizures and crimes, and he had been given this name by campesinos because of his cruelty. The temporary and permanent workers on Arenas's plantation, however, did not cheer the landlord's execution and the subsequent bankruptcy of his plantation. They lost their source of wages, and they had to deal with the reprisals of governmental forces in the region.

On 7 February 1982 the guerrillas stated that their four separate organizations—the EGP, the Organización del Pueblo en Armas (ORPA, Organization of the People in Arms), the FAR, and the PGT—were fighting under a united command called the Unidad Revolucionaria Nacional Guatemalteca (URNG, Guatemalan National Revolutionary Unity). Within hours after the declaration, a series of bomb blasts almost blacked out Guatemala City. This action suggested that unification might have strengthened the estimated three thousand to five thousand armed guerrillas (Rohter 1982). The main objective of the unified command was to improve and consolidate its presence among the Indians in the western highlands, which it had code-named "Vietnam" and where it had set up liberated zones (*Latin America Regional Reports Mexico & Central America* 1982).

As the guerrillas seemed to be growing in military strength and popular support, the Reagan administration grew alarmed that Guatemala rather than El Salvador might be the next domino to fall in Central America. In early February 1982 the Reagan administration decided to test Congress by requesting $250,000 in military assistance for training in Guatemala. The request noted that Guatemala was facing a Cuban-supported Marxist insurgency whose goal was to overthrow the government and that Guatemala's challenge was to respond effectively to the guerrilla threat without the indiscriminate violence to which some segments of the security forces had resorted (Sexton 1985).

Unfortunately for the guerrillas, the second cycle of civil war peaked in 1983, when the Guatemalan army gained the upper hand. During this period, the army admitted that it had destroyed more than 440 towns and villages in an attempt to "rid the water in which the guerrilla fish swam" (Sexton 1992:288). It was estimated that from 1981 to 1983 between 500,000 and 1,500,000 were displaced internally or externally. The guerrillas, however, did not immediately settle for peace, perhaps influenced by their North Vietnamese predecessors who negotiated with the United States in Paris for nearly five years. During the next thirteen years, the URNG bought time by engaging in a low-intensity conflict with the army. Although for all intents and purposes the guerrillas had lost the shooting war at home, by prolonging it they won an important psychological victory abroad.

Finally, in December 1996, the URNG's leaders signed peace accords with officials of the Guatemalan government, having obtained what they considered to be "peace with justice." They complied with the terms of the treaty and disbanded as a guerrilla army, but they won the right to organize as a political party and officially did so two years later, on 18 December 1998, as a revolutionary party of the "democratic left" (*Latin American Caribbean & Central America Report* 1999a:3). Other terms of the peace accords were a one-third reduction in the size of the Guatemalan military, sanctions for a Mayan cultural revival, and the establishment of a commission to document human rights abuses during the civil war, with the proviso that the commission would not publish the names of perpetrators of either side. The commission was to be called the Comisión para el Esclarecimiento Histórico (CEH, Commission for Historical Clarification).

In April 1998, however, Bishop Juan Gerardi Conedera, working on behalf of the Catholic Church and apart from the CEH, released a report titled *Guatemala: nunca más* (Guatemala: Never Again), which blamed 80 percent of the killings on governmental forces, including the civil defense patrols that were composed largely of local Indians. Unlike the commission, he provided the names of individuals responsible for human rights abuses. Less than two days after he released the report, he was assassinated at his residence in Guatemala City. As of January 2001 the official investigation of his murder is not close to resolution. It has led to the arrest of four people and one dog, gone through eight judges and prosecutors, and sent at least twelve people into exile (Garvin 1999; Darling 2000).

From early 1997 until late 1998, Christian Tomuschat, Otilia Lux de Cotí, and Alfredo Balsells Tojo (1999a:1) directed the CEH (Rohter 1999:1). Without identifying the culprits by name in a report titled *Guatemala: memoria del silencio* (Guatemala: Memory of Silence), the directors and their assistants documented 42,275 victims of political violence, 21 percent of the estimated total of 200,000 victims, including men, women, and children. Eighty-three percent of the fully identified victims were Maya, and 17 percent were Ladino. According to the commission, elements of the Guatemala state (army, civil patrols, military commissioners, and death squads) committed 93 percent of the atrocities, the guerrillas 3 percent, and unidentified forces 4 percent. Although most observers had long ago concluded that governmental forces were responsible for most of the human rights violations, it may never be possible to determine exactly how many of the confirmed 132,000 people who lost their lives during the thirty-six-year conflict (*Central America Report* 1992a:3) were the responsibility of each of the two forces.

The commission concluded that the cold war played an important role, especially since "anti-communism and the National Security Doctrine formed part of the anti-Soviet strategy of the United States in Latin America" (Tomuschat, Lux de Cotí, and Balsells Tojo 1999a:3). It also concluded that the influence of Cuba and its promotion of armed struggle had a bearing on these processes as much in Guatemala as in the rest of Latin America. Reacting to a repressive state in Guatemala, Marxist leftists adopted the Cuban perspective of armed struggle to take power and secure the rights of the people.

Although the commission assigned responsibility to the army for the vast majority of the atrocities, it stated, "[T]his disparity does not lessen the gravity of the unjustifiable offenses committed by the guerrillas against human rights, including arbitrary executions, 'revolutionary justice' (the executions of members of the insurgent groups themselves), massacres, forced disappearance and kidnapping, and forced recruitment of even minors, which was an offense against personal freedom" (Tomuschat, Lux de Cotí, and Balsells Tojo 1999a:9–11). For such tactics, Jorge Ismael Soto, a leader of the URNG, apologized to the survivors of victims (Associated Press 1999a:17).

Also, the commission confirmed George W. Lovell's (1988) accusations that the guerrillas had applied the tactic of "armed propaganda," military occupation of towns and farms to force local people to listen to political talks to gain supporters or to demonstrate their strength (Monsanto 1983:263). Once they withdrew, however, they left the communities defenseless and vulnerable. This was the case especially among the Mayan peoples, where the army exacted a high civilian death toll. In some cases documented by the commission, whole towns were razed just days after the guerrillas withdrew. "Caught in the middle, scores of Mayan communities paid dearly for their affiliation, whether direct or indirect, real or imagined" (Lovell 1988:47). While the army clearly committed the violations, the guerrillas' actions had a bearing on the way these events unfolded (Tomuschat, Lux de Cotí, and Balsells Tojo 1999a:7).

Unfortunately, the acute social and economic conditions in Guatemala that fueled the flare-ups of civil insurrection in the 1960s and again in the 1970s persist in the year 2000. The population has more than doubled and now stands at more than 12 million souls (*World Factbook* 1999), the vast majority of whom live in poverty. Although the private sector of the agricultural economy grew by about 4 percent in 1997, with coffee, sugar, and bananas being the leading exports, but with products from *aquila* (assembly operations) gaining in importance, a marked disparity in the distribution of income still exists, as does pervasive poverty, especially among the Indian community. Eighty percent of the population lives in poverty, and per capita income in 1997 was $1,650 (U.S. Department of State 1999:1). While the rate of illiteracy has dramatically declined since the early 1940s, at 44 percent of the population, it is still the highest rate in Central America.

The presidential election of 6 November 1999 reflected the surrealism of the civil war from which Guatemala had emerged. The candidate who won the most votes (47.8 percent) was Alfonso Portillo, a former law professor who unabashedly confessed that in self-defense he had fatally shot two men in a brawl in Mexico seventeen years earlier. His campaign for the presidency was affiliated with the party Frente Republicano Guatemalteco (FRG, Guatemalan Republican Front), which was headed by General Efraín Ríos Montt, whom human rights groups have accused of genocide in the early 1980s and who was the president of the National Congress in 2000. The candidate with the second most votes (30.3 percent) was Oscar Berger, running on the platform of the ruling Partido de Avanzada Nacional (PAN, National Advancement Party). Alvaro Colom, representing the interests of leftists and former URNG guerrillas under the banner of the coalition party Alianza Nueva Nación (ANN, New Nation Alliance), gained only 12.2 percent of the vote (Kovaleski 1999). Because of the high turnout (54 percent of the voters, compared to only 35 percent in the previous election of 1995), Portillo became the first presidential candidate to earn more than a million votes, although he barely failed to secure a majority. In addition to being the party that won the most presidential votes, the FRG gained control of the 113-seat congress, with 64 seats to the PAN's 36 and the ANN's 9 (*Latin American Caribbean & Central America Report* 1999c:3; *Central America Report* 1999c).

It is noteworthy that nine members of the Guatemalan congress belong to ANN, which represents former guerrillas. Having members of the Left and of the Right settle their differences in the political arena is certainly preferable to having them do so on the battlefield. Costa Rica has long permitted members of the Left and the Right to coexist politically, and it is the epitome of democracy in Central America.

In the runoff election held on 26 December 1999, as predicted by the polls, Portillo won with an overwhelming majority of the votes (68 percent). Voters were more interested in his promise to curb rampant crime, to reform the corrupt judicial system, and to improve dire social and economic conditions than in his political ties to Ríos Montt.[6] Before the election, Portillo had reassured the weary by declaring on public radio, "Neither the Congress will rule the presidency nor the presidency will rule the Congress" (Associated Press 1999b:A27; *The Arizona Republic* 1999:A16).

Ignacio Bizarro Ujpán and Rigoberta Menchú

Son of Tecún Umán was the first full-length life history of a Maya Indian to be published (Sexton [1981] 1990). Two years later *Me llamo Rigoberta Menchú y así me nació la conciencia*, an account edited by Elisabeth Burgos-Debray, was published in Spain. It was the second full-length life history of a Maya Indian. A year later an English-language version, translated by Ann Wright, *I Rigoberta Menchú: An Indian Woman in Guatemala*, appeared. The basic material for Rigoberta Menchú's story was taped in Spanish for one week in Paris in 1982 by Burgos-Debray, then a student from Venezuela who was writing a dissertation in comparative ethnopsychiatry (Stoll 1997). According to Burgos-Debray's dramatic introduction, Rigoberta had been speaking Spanish for only three years when she rendered her eloquent account. "Rigoberta learned the language of her oppressors in order to use it against them. . . . Spanish is a language which was forced upon her, but has become a weapon in her struggle" (Burgos-Debray 1984:xii).

I Rigoberta Menchú is a narrative by a Quiché Maya that focuses on the violence in Guatemala in the 1970s and early 1980s, especially in and around Rigoberta's highland village of Chimel, near the administrative municipality of San Miguel Uspantán. *Uspantecos* (people of Uspantán) were once the main inhabitants of this region, but they largely have been displaced by Ladinos and Quichés. In the opening paragraph of her life story, Rigoberta (1984:1) states that her testimony is the story of all poor Guatemalans and that her "personal experience is the reality of a whole people." As Stoll (1999a:xi) writes, the book "used the compelling story of one family to personify the moral dualism of a society at war with itself. With its noble Indians and evil landlords, ancestral ethnic hatred and revolutionary martyrdom, Rigoberta's story became a deeply influential portrait of the violence in Guatemala." Although at this time Rigoberta seemed to be trying to distance herself from the URNG, her story provided an iconic face for leftist sympathizers abroad to associate with the embattled revolutionaries. While she provided the image that validated the URNG's claim that it represented the Maya Indians, the URNG's European representative coordinated the campaign that won her the Nobel Peace Prize in 1992 (Taracena in Aceituno 1999).[7]

According to David Stoll (1999a:179), in 1966 Burgos and the Marxist philosopher Régis Debray received military training in Cuba with the intent of joining Che Guevara at an unknown location and creating one or more Vietnams. Che was killed in Bolivia by the army, however, and Régis was captured and imprisoned. To gain visiting privileges, Elisabeth married Régis behind bars and led a successful international campaign for his release. Although Rigoberta's story captured the essence of the period of violence of the area in which she lived, Rigoberta did not witness or experience some of the episodes she claimed to have witnessed, such as working on the coastal plantations (Stoll 1999a:25), seeing soldiers burn her tortured brother alive in a village plaza (Stoll

1999a:63–70), and having little prior exposure to Spanish before relating her story to Burgos-Debray. In fact, according to Stoll (1999a:161, 163), from 1976 to 1980 (six years before she met Burgos-Debray) Rigoberta had advanced from the third grade through the sixth grade at the Colegio Belga, a Catholic school, and she had received some advanced schooling at the Colegio Básico Nuestro Señor de Candelaria. Another brother told Stoll that on a visit home in 1978 she spoke Spanish well and reprimanded family members who did not.

Rigoberta has responded that the omissions in her story were "conscious omissions" to protect certain individuals from retaliation by the security forces. She also said that she indeed had spent time at the Belgian school as a servant and that the nuns there protected her and taught her many things. She said that her story was not one of personal memory alone but of "collective memory" (Menchú in Burt and Rosen 1999:8) and that her town's story was her own story. For example, the important point was that her brother died. It didn't matter that her mother had told her about it, because she trusted her mother (Menchú in Aznárez 1999:2). Nevertheless, Rigoberta dramatically and repeatedly described this episode in the first person (Burgos-Debray 1984:172–82), just as she described her experience on the *fincas* (farms) in the first person (Burgos-Debray 1984:86–90). She admitted that she did not witness some of these events herself only after Stoll's exposé (*New York Times*, 12 February 1999).

Although eyewitness accounts have a more profound impact in testimonial literature, and they carry more weight with the reader (just as they do with a jury in a court of law), Rigoberta's story still would have been compelling had she been careful to say where she had obtained her information. Few readers doubted that these kinds of atrocities were occurring since there was so much other corroborating evidence. And although both the guerrillas and the army were guilty of carnage, no one questioned that the army was responsible for most of it. Unfortunately, the glaring inconsistencies that Stoll (1999a) has uncovered will cause some to doubt her whole story.

Ignacio Bizarro Ujpán wrote about the same period in Guatemala from the perspective of a Tzutuhil Maya on the southwest shore of Lake Atitlán, some seventy-two miles southwest of Uspantán. Both Rigoberta and Ignacio described numerous atrocities committed by the army and by paramilitary forces. Ignacio, however, also described atrocities committed by the guerrillas, internal conflicts in his town, and problems arising from the abuse of alcohol, whereas Rigoberta did not. Both learned a Mayan language (Ignacio learned Tzutuhil and Rigoberta, Quiché) in their homes as their first tongue and both have little formal education (Ignacio three years, Rigoberta perhaps eight years), but both are obviously intelligent and have learned Spanish as a second language. While both told their story to anthropologists, Ignacio wished to remain anonymous, but Rigoberta did not. And most significantly, Rigoberta joined the EGP, a guerrilla group active in her region of Uspantán, after members of the security forces had killed three members of her family. None of Ignacio's family was killed by right-wing forces, and, according to Ignacio, neither he nor his fellow townspeople joined the ORPA, which was active in his region of Lake Atitlán.

Ignacio explains toward the end of the present volume that both the army and the guerrillas were responsible for spilling blood, especially the army, but that he and his fellow *Joseños* were on neither side. They never considered being servants or supporters of either group because both factions were led mainly by Ladinos who were using the Indians as pawns.

Because Ignacio's perspective differed considerably from Rigoberta's on a number of points, it was not long before scholars were comparing their stories (Smith and Boyer 1987; Sklodowska 1991; Zimmerman 1992, 1995; Stoll 1999a). I have not interacted with Rigoberta Menchú for the last thirty years, as I have with Ignacio, and I do not know her personally. I did read her gripping life history when it was first published, however, and since then I have read various pieces about her by journalists and academics. It appears that Ignacio initially was more exposed to Ladinos than Rigoberta was, but not now. Still, both strongly identify as Maya Indians, although as Ignacio mentions, they come from different subcultures. Both are deeply religious and proud of their Mayan heritage, but while Ignacio and the wife he married in 1962 have eight children and three grandchildren, Rigoberta and the husband she married in 1995 have one adopted child. Rigoberta fled to Mexico in 1980 in fear of her life when the Guatemalan army identified her as a revolutionary, and she did not return to live in Guatemala until 1994. In contrast, Ignacio and his family remained in Guatemala throughout the turmoil of the 1980s and 1990s. Finally, Ignacio continues to live the life of a rural campesino, like most other Maya Indians. As a *principal* (elder), he is an informal leader in the religious, social, and political activities of his town. In contrast, Rigoberta lives in Guatemala City where, with funds from her Nobel Prize, she has established the Rigoberta Menchú Tum Foundation, which is assisting in reconciliation and reconstruction and which is promoting political participation on the local and regional levels (Menchú in Burt and Rosen 1999:10).[8]

Neither Ignacio nor Rigoberta may be representative of all Maya Indians in the sense of an "everyman" or "everywoman."[9] While present-day Maya Indians share a general Mayan cultural heritage, including learning a Mayan language as their first tongue and sharing values and beliefs, and while they generally have suffered from social, economic, and political repression, there is wide variation within and between towns with regard to particular behaviors and beliefs (Sexton and Woods 1977, 1982; Sexton 1978; Sherman 1997).

Life histories of real people, such as those of Ignacio Bizarro Ujpán and Rigoberta Menchú, have much to tell us. Rather than rely on the point of view of prominent people whose perspective is from the top down, it is important to understand the point of view of common people, who look at life from the bottom up. We need to be aware of as many voices as possible, especially those of individuals who live in cultures different from our own.[10]

Like Rigoberta's story, Ignacio's diary is best classified as a life history, because the final product is neither an autobiography nor a biography but a blend of the two. As L. L. Langness (1965) and Robert B. Edgerton and Langness (1974) have pointed out, life histories have a long tradition in anthropology. Ignacio's and Rigoberta's stories are intensely personal accounts of their own lives, and at the same time they are first-person accounts of the history of their towns and country. When life histories are put together with the collaboration of editors who are anthropologists, they also are anthropological studies, because special attention is paid to cultural aspects and because the life story is placed in a cultural context.

What makes life histories so appealing in general is that readers of different ideological orientations may find material of interest to them. Most life histories can be considered literature as well as testimony, because they are in a readable narrative form and the narrator portrays his or her own experience as an eyewitness rather than as an interpreter of the collective memory of a group (Beverly and Zimmerman 1990:173; Yúdice 1996:44; Sklodowska 1996:86). Because the story is also original data, the reader can analyze the results any way he or she wishes, regardless of his or her academic perspective or personal view of life. A great strength of life histories is that they can appeal at once to anthropologists, sociologists, historians, political scientists, cultural geographers, humanists, literary critics, and general readers.

Academics in the field of literary criticism often examine works from a secondhand perspective. Because they have not directly interacted with the subjects of the works, they may ascribe motives to them that they do not have. Furthermore, literary critics' personal philosophies may permeate their analyses to the extent that they are incapable of understanding fully or writing objectively about subjects who do not share their own beliefs.

Although testimonial literature may be propagandistic, each testimony has to be evaluated on its own terms. For example, regardless of how much we admire Rigoberta Menchú for her struggles and empathize with her for having lost her father, mother, and brother, her views, as Marc Zimmerman (1995) notes, were obviously biased in favor of the guerrilla movement with which she identified at that time.

One has to consider both the personal and the collective aspects of testimonial literature. It is often difficult to ascertain the extent to which the subject of the testimonial is typical or atypical of his or her own culture or subculture. There is some self-selection toward atypicality in the sense that it is uncommon people whose life stories are documented. If, however, a person were too representative, or typical (average), readers would find them boring.

In *Rigoberta Menchú and the Story of All Poor Guatemalans* (1999a:236–37), Stoll elaborates on the issue of academics and other political activists wanting the subjects of their causes to fit simple, preconceived images. He points out that although human rights is a legal discourse, what drives "its application around the world is solidarity— political identification with victims, dissidents, and opposition movements." While the eradication of the abuse of fellow humans in the world is a worthy cause, campaigns to support indigenous rights tend to play off the exotic side of indigenous life, and international support becomes conditioned on images that have little to do with the actual lives of the native people in question. Thus Stoll (in Dudley 1999:9) believes that the reason that Rigoberta Menchú claimed she was un-educated and knew only Quiché until just a few years before telling her story to Burgos-Debray is that her audience expects Indians to be bare-foot, preliterate, and traditional. Whereas natives who satisfy such an image are considered authentic, other natives who are literate, who wear modern clothing and accessories, or who are financially success-ful, are not considered genuine.

Ignacio's Motivation and Character

Ignacio said that he writes in order to record the good and the bad that there is in his life. Thus he documents both the harmony and the conflict. In this respect, one could not level the same kind of criticism at Ignacio that Oscar Lewis (1951) leveled at his mentor, Robert Red-field (1930), who described the people of Tepotzlán, Mexico, in the Rousseauian sense of being homogeneous and harmonious. In contrast, Lewis described the *Tepotzlanecos* (people of Tepotzlán) more in the Hobbesian sense of being heterogeneous and discordant.

Ignacio also said that he writes so that other people will be aware of the marginalization and contempt that the Maya are subjected to by the more powerful Ladinos. He said that he has not been remarkably influenced by external ideologies (such as capitalism or Marxism). His main intellectual influence is the Bible, which advocates that people work hard and eat bread earned by the sweat of their brow until they return to the dust from which they were made. Furthermore, Ignacio rationalized his lack of interest for material rewards by quoting the lamentation of Job, "Naked I was born, and naked I will die." Ignacio realizes that there are other people who want to learn about the life of a man who is not formally educated—a campesino who daily forges the pickax and swings the hoe and who reflects the heritage of his Maya ancestors.[11] Although he refused to speculate on how useful his writing is for others, he stated that each person can think for himself or herself. Neither did Ignacio wish to speculate about the personalities of the people who read his books. To this query he responded with the proverb, *Comida a fuerza cae mal* (Food by force displeases), and he said that is the way it is with books. "We people look for books that are useful, fascinating, or critical. As we Maya say, *Tortillas con sal, corazón contento* [Tortillas with salt, happy heart], and so it is with the books."

Ignacio went on to say that he had not personally met Rigoberta Menchú, nor had he had any communication with her.

I only know that she took refuge because her life was threatened because of her participation with the *guerrilla* [guerrilla movement]. She is an indigenous person like me, only she is of another culture; she is from the Quiché [people], and I am from the Tzutuhil [people]. There is no doubt that we are different.

What I know of Rigoberta [is that] she had the luck to arrive in Europe [France] and that with the help of Elizabeth Burgos[-Debray] she published a book that speaks of many things.[12] And that book brought her acclaim. Now she has the Nobel [Prize] for peace. She is the best remunerated indigenous woman because by earning the Nobel Peace Prize she became a millionaire. That is to say, for her participation as a guerrilla, she is now worth millions of dollars.

It seems to me that she herself is deceptive by saying abroad that she has fought in order to obtain peace in Guatemala. It [peace] is a lie; we every day are exploited and marginalized, and the land that truly belongs to us Guatemalans is in the control of the millionaire. Mostly for this reason there is much unemployment, lack of education, and poor health.

Those who indeed live peacefully are those who are in the government: the president, the ministers, the deputies, and the military. Why aren't the politicians saying [there is poverty]? All of them live in peace because they have all the money of Guatemala while the poor [person] continues to walk barefoot without having [money] to buy a pair of shoes to cover his calloused feet and continues to beg for bread every day. That is why I say that in Guatemala there is no peace.

When I asked what he thinks about the delegates for the campesino committees who were fighting against the oppression of the Maya Indians, Ignacio responded:

As far as my thought about the delegations of rural committees, the truth is that they are fighting so that the country will have a change, so that we Guatemalans will have equality and the same right[s]. But this is difficult because the representatives of the Comité de Unidad Campesina [CUC,

Committee of Peasant Unity] are carried in the hands of Ladinos like newly bought pups. They come to manifest their feelings for an opportunity for the campesinos; then it is misrepresented by the Ladinos, or guides, as they call them. From Europe and from [North] America, they send commission[s] to investigate how the situation in Guatemala is. They come to chat with the members of the government, or, better said, they come to sit down a while in the congress with the deputies, and then they go to the more luxurious hotels. And when they return to their country, they say that in Guatemala everything is changing, without knowing how the people of the towns and of the provinces live.

When asked his opinions about the extent to which religious and political propaganda had affected Guatemala in the last few years, Ignacio responded:

The religions have not had much impact on the country. They are constructive in the sense that they teach proper deportment. What I don't like about the religious groups is that they don't behave well [toward one another]; the Catholics hate the evangelicals, and the evangelicals despise the Catholics because they respect and revere the saints. Each group wants to win over more people, without following the words of Lord Jesús: "Love one another as I have loved you." This is a great truth because God is for all and all are for God, if we are obedient to him.

As for the politicians in Guatemala, they are corrupt. When the big rich people launch [their careers] as politicians and file the papers to be the candidates for presidents and deputies, they begin to swear by heaven and earth that they are the ones who are the most honorable. But everything is to the contrary when they win and assume power—they change. When they come face to face with money, they forget the people who elected them. And they begin to steal the money of the people and to carry off millions of quetzales, despite their salaries. The people are the ones who pay the high tax.

This is clearly the case with that gentleman who was said to be a prophet—the evangelical Jorge Serrano Elías. He deceived all the evangelicals and a good number of

2. *Women of Santiago Atitlán marching in a religious parade.*

the Guatemalan Catholics. In his campaign he talked about many ways to improve the country; he even said that he would do it with the power of God. But it was just a lie, because it is known in Guatemala that Serrano Elías is the biggest thief in Guatemala. There is a phrase in the Bible that says [to beware of false] prophets, which come to you in sheep's clothing, but inside they are predatory wolves.

As far as new ideas about the world and about society, it is important and interesting, not only for me but for the majority, to raise our consciousness for change to a better way of life. I like the cooperatives and the organized groups, but I [now] am not able to participate in them for lack of time; I have a big family and a big commitment. To be in an organization, time is lost.

For many years I belonged to a political party of Guatemala—PID [Partido Institucional Democrático, Institutional Democratic Party, which was the party in power at the time]. I know how the politicians are. Mainly we Maya only serve

3. *Women soldiers marching as a show of strength, carrying automatic weapons during Army Day in Guatemala City.*

as a stairway [for them]; they offer education, health, and a change of life for the people of the provinces. They said, "Many will have employment." But when they take power they forget all the promises. The salaries of the military go up, the price of the medicine remains high, and the tax on electricity goes up.

This is the kind of dirty politics the government did with the Comité Coordinador de Asociaciones Agrícolas, Comerciales, Industriales y Finacieras [CACIF, Coordinating Committee of Agricultural, Commercial, Industrial, and Financial Associations]. Instead of us receiving a benefit, they extract more from us. For us poor people who don't have a salary, it is worse. We eat [bread earned] by the sweat of our brow, working daily under the sun, eating tortillas with salt and drinking a jug of water. Meanwhile, they are wasting good money in the better restaurants, driving the best, latest model cars, and they still are not happy. They go to the foreigner and ask for charities so that they can become millionaires. Meanwhile, every day the poor person gets poorer and the rich person gets richer. As I see it, we poor people are always the turkeys of the party, and the politicians are the vampires sucking our blood.

Conclusion

Although critical of the treatment the Indians have received from the government, Ignacio is not oriented to the Right or the Left. He is a centrist who desires progressive material change in his community. He does not attack the ideology of the guerrillas or the army, but he does criticize the arbitrary way in which they proceeded; above all, they acted in their own interest, regardless of the outcome for the Indians. Both groups had a tendency to exploit them. Ignacio realizes that neither the extreme views of the Right nor those of the Left are in his best interest or the best interest of his family and town. Ignacio favors democracy, and in his story he describes his efforts to bring about improvements for his town. Although in his latter years he is partial to traditional Mayan elements in the *cofradías,* he seems open to the goodness that can be found in other religions. When he is critical of pastors or priests, his criticism focuses on their hypocrisy and insensitivity.

When it became clear to North American intellectuals who were sympathetic to the Central American Left that the guerrillas were not going to triumph in the civil war, some of them began to search for explanations in published material that had been relatively ignored or misinterpreted. Quoting Lovell, Zimmerman (1995:89) pointed out that the question of why the guerrillas failed catastrophically to rally the Indians to rebellion would "consume the energies of the left for many years to come." He (1995:88) stated that Ignacio, as a centrist, might have more to tell us directly than Rigoberta about the Marxist ideology of consciousness raising; that is, whereas Rigoberta may represent the "potential consciousness" of the Maya Indians of Guatemala, Ignacio may represent their "real consciousness."

Although Ignacio's plight is not as well known as Rigoberta's, there is no evidence that Ignacio claimed to witness or experience events that he did not, regardless of whether such events could be construed by intellectual supporters as a "collective experience." One could not say that Ignacio's style "favors impassioned subjectivity over documentary accuracy," as Victor Perera (1993:116) has proposed for Rigoberta's style. No doubt influenced by our long relationship, Ignacio, like a trained anthropologist, makes it perfectly clear when he did not see something happen with his own eyes. In this respect his story is closer than Rigoberta's to the canons of testimonial literature as defined above by John Beverly and Marc Zimmerman (1990) and by George Yúdice (1996).

In any case, Ignacio's account, like Rigoberta's, is important and captivating. It is another voice that describes the condition of the present-day Maya in Guatemala, sometimes from the same perspective and at other times from a different perspective. We are indeed fortunate to have had such an articulate spokesman as Ignacio to share with us his Mayan life and culture over the past three decades.

Ignacio's Diary

Danny Hi, Guerrilla and Assassin
July 1987 to 5 August 1987

In Pachichaj, an *aldea* [village] of my municipality, live the Tuc brothers and sister who have a lot of money and land. These siblings don't know what it means to be poor, although it is true that their parents are good workers. But the siblings do not get along with one another because of their inheritance. They just have one problem after another.

Their parents, Don José Plinio [Tuc] and Doña Mónica [González] Jiménez, came from San Cristóbal Totonicapán, and they exploited many *Joseños*. Don José Plinio took advantage of knowing how to speak Castilian [Spanish]. He got involved with lawyers and took possession of many pieces of land to the point of falsifying deeds. Since the *Joseños* didn't know Castilian, they couldn't recover their lands. José Plinio did what he wanted to do with the ignorant people.

Until he died in 1953, José Plinio was the Father and Lord of the village of Pachichaj. Since at that time there was no cemetery in Pachichaj, the body of José Plinio was buried in the cemetery of Patzilín [a village of the municipality of San José]. I was a little boy, but we indeed went to see the grave of this man because he was famous.

When José Plinio died, he was survived by his children, Warren Tuc González, Ignacio Tuc González, Zamora Tuc González, and Tanya Tuc González. Warren was the oldest of the brothers, and his father left him thousands and thousands of *cuerdas* [areal measures, each equal to .178 acre] of land. He gave little to his other sons. When they saw that the inheritance was not divided as they thought it should have been, they were always mad at Warren. They fought in the court of first instance, but as Warren always had the astuteness of his father, he beat out his brothers and came out ahead.

Warren Tuc had children who are named José de León Tuc, Eduardo Tuc Pérez, Hugo Zamora Tuc Gómez, and Rita Tuc Gómez. In the last four years to 1987, Rita Tuc was the biggest enemy of her father, going before the court of first instance of Sololá, fighting for her inheritance.

Rita wanted the biggest part of the land, but her father, Warren, didn't want to give it to her. They say that Rita swore that her father was going to die by a gun or by a knife, that he wasn't going to die of a sickness from God.

Rita's father despised her, and for that reason she went to live in Mazatenango. In Mazatenango she continued her suit against him. When he died, her brothers suspected that she had paid to have him killed, but Don Warren Tuc's children now know who the real assassin of their father was.

Hugo Zamora Tuc, Warren Tuc's son, sent a daughter, Roana Nilda Tuc, to study in the institute of Sololá. Sometimes fathers try to do well by their children, but it is the children who cause the problems. Hugo Zamora's Nilda quit her studies and married a man named Danny of the Hi family, owners of some buses that run from Los Encuentros to Chichicastenango.

When Roana got married, her parents got angry with her and didn't want their daughter to come anymore to Pachichaj. Relationships are never free of problems, however, and who knows why Roana and Danny separated.

Since Roana didn't get along with her father, when she left her husband she went to live with her grandfather, Warren Tuc. Then, the story says, her grandfather told her that she could live with him but on the condition that she would not go back to her man [husband].

"Very well, Grandfather," she said. And she lived with her grandparents, because these old folks also needed someone to take care of them.

That's how it was when the husband found out that his woman [wife] was living with her grandparents. Then he went to ask her grandfather to give his woman back to him. But the grandfather rebuffed the man, telling him that he didn't want to see him in his house, a man who wasn't able to take care of his two children. Danny became angry when he was thrown out of the house of the grandfather of his woman.

They say that Danny missed his two small children and wanted very much to be able to live again with them and his woman, but she didn't want to go back to him because her grandfather had told her she would have everything she needed, that he could feed her and her two children. So the woman stayed with her grandparents.

Roana's husband became angry and went to get mixed up with the guerrillas in the mountains, since the village of Pachichaj is surrounded

4. *The departmental town of Sololá overlooking Lake Atitlán.*

by mountains, where, they say, there are camps of guerrillas. Without doubt the man went to get involved with the subversives for revenge, or, better said, to get arms.

The twentieth of July of this year [1987], Danny Hi, the guerrilla, approached Warren Tuc's *sitio* [place; homesite] about 7:00 P.M. When Roana went outside, Danny captured and carried her away. When her grandparents realized that their granddaughter had disappeared, they informed the auxiliary tribunal and the patrolmen, but nothing was done to rescue the woman.

When the woman was kidnapped by her husband, he took her in the night to a mountain. She says she wasn't familiar with the place, but she saw many paths where bad men passed. He constantly threatened her with a knife, telling her that if she preferred to live with her grandparents, either she or her grandfather was going to die, that she should stay with him on the mountain. He said he was a guerrilla and that his companions were near.

The woman was scared because she didn't know where she was. In secret she prayed to God.

At sunrise on a mountain that Roana had never seen before, Danny told her, "Let's go up to see if my *compañeros* [companions] are there. I have told them our story. If we find them, they will tell you not to live with your grandparents or they will kill you. If they ask about your grandfather, tell them you are not going to live with him anymore, so they won't kill you. And if they ask about your grandfather, tell them you agree that they should kill him. Tell them yes so that nothing bad will happen to you."

"Very well," said the woman.

But they didn't find the group that the man was looking for. They were there the whole day, and the woman was worried about her two children who had been left with her grandparents. Night fell and she told the man, "Our children are sad because they always sleep with me."

"Don't worry," said Danny. "They are not going to die in two or three nights."

All day and night on the twenty-first, the two were on the mountain. When dawn broke on the twenty-second, they were already near the house. The man said to his woman, "We're here again at the *sitio* of your grandparents. Now we are going to carry out the operation. If you really don't want to die, you have to live with me. Stay all day in the house of your grandparents; don't tell them what we have done or what you have seen or what I have told you. Tonight we are going to get our two children and go to the mountain. Don't worry. I'm going to the *finca* Los Horizontes on a mission, and during the night, I will arrive close to your house to wait for you. But if you make me mad, well, you already know that you are going to die for sure."

"Very well," said the woman, "I'll go with you for sure, but be patient with me. Don't kill me."

"Well, I'm not going to kill you, but you had better comply with the promise."

"Very well," said the woman. She waited, and the man left for the *finca* Los Horizontes.

But, according to the story, when the woman entered the house of her grandfather, it was strange because the patrolmen and auxiliaries had already known that the woman had been kidnapped. Then the grandfather took this woman to the auxiliary tribunal and presented her to the patrolmen to give them information about all that had happened to her. When the patrolmen and auxiliaries were informed of all these things, they armed themselves with machetes, sticks, and stones and headed toward the farm Los Horizontes, which is about ten kilometers from Pachichaj in the department of Suchitepéquez.

But the patrolmen didn't wait for the man to arrive in the night in Pachichaj as they had told the woman. They thought that it was already very dangerous for them because this man could have many companions.

When the patrolmen arrived at Los Horizontes, they looked throughout the whole *finca*, but they didn't find the said Danny Hi. They put out a notice in all the houses, but the campesinos of the farm informed them that this man was unknown and never came there. The men got tired, and everything was futile. They headed back to Pachichaj. They had walked about two kilometers from the *finca* by the place called Chi Horizonte, where one of them noticed Danny Hi hiding in the hollow of a tree. He called all of his companions, and they captured him.

They brought him back, tied with lassos around his neck, waist, and legs, punishing him until arriving at the village. And when they arrived, they called the woman to see if she recognized if this was the man who had kidnapped her. She told them yes, that this man was her former husband and the same person who had kidnapped her and taken her to the mountain of Pancoy. The woman said in front of Danny Hi what he had told her on the mountain, and he just listened and said nothing.

The patrolmen and the auxiliaries took the man to the jail of the town. Not until they put him in jail did they untie him. When the man was in jail, the woman presented herself in the office of the *alcalde* and said that the man was a guerrilla and that he should be conducted to the prosecutor's office. The woman told the prosecutor all that Danny had told her on the mountain and that she saw many roads where the guerrillas traveled. Also she asked the mayor for protection, because, she assured them, someone was going to die, be it her grandfather or herself, because this is what the man had told her on the mountain.

But the mayor was not competent to conduct the investigations, or, better said, they say he was bribed by the uncle of the guerrilla and also by the military commissioner of this town so that they would not inform the national army. That is to say, they concealed this bad man. They brought him to San José the twenty-third of July of this year, and they only handed down a sentence of Q50 [50 quetzales]. They set him free on the twenty-fifth of July of this year, 1987. There was a lot of criticism in the town. Also, the same woman, Roana Tuc, complained that she was not free, nor was her grandfather free, because her ex-husband had told her that he was going to kill one of them, either her grandfather or herself. But they say that the mayor thought that the woman was falsely accusing her ex-husband, and he told them to reconcile. The woman, however, was sure something was going to happen. Still, the disagreeable mayor, Benjamín Peña, didn't administer justice well. They say that in the afternoon when they freed this man, he said in the hallway of the municipality that he was not going to delay his revenge for all he had suffered by the grandfather of the woman. The same *alguaciles* [municipal policemen, aides, and runners] and municipal guards heard these things, and they commented a lot about it when the elder, Warren Tuc González, later was assassinated. But the comments blamed the mayor and the military commissioner.

After they set this man free, nobody knows where he went. It's only known that he left on the road that leads to Pachichaj, but they say that he didn't go to the house of the woman.

The information I have comes from one of the grandsons of the fallen Warren Tuc González who always came to see me because we had been family friends since we were in the PID. Warren Tuc González was the secretary-general of the subbranch of the *aldea* of Pachichaj and his own sons were the other directors, and, for that reason, I know their story well. They, for their wealth, always commanded respect from the people, who obeyed them a lot. Warren Tuc, during the times that we chatted, always rejected communism and is very much an enemy of the subversives. He told me that since 1951 he had come to condemn communism. But finally, he lost his life.

In order to write these things, I had to talk to a person who had witnessed these events. Also, I talked to the *mozos* [helpers, servants] of the deceased and with the grandsons in order to write an accurate episode. And I also asked Cleta Tuc if it were true what the people were saying—that Roana Nilda Tuc was kidnapped. She told me the same things that I have written here. I had to wait in order to have concrete information. Everything that these pages say is true.

Warren Tuc González, on 3 August 1987, arrived at the house of his son Eduardo Tuc Pérez to ask him how things were going with his work in the *campo* [field, countryside]. After the chat, they say that Eduardo offered a meal to his father. The two dined together happily.

After the dinner, Don Warren said good-bye to his son Eduardo to return to his house. Warren's house is a kilometer from where his children live. They say when he returned to his house, two of his grandsons of eighteen years of age went with him to accompany him home. When passing by a *tienda* [small store], the grandsons asked their grandfather to buy them some sodas and sweets. The grandfather gave them the money to buy what they wanted. Then he told them, "Children, take your time drinking the sodas. I'm going ahead because I walk slowly, and when you finish drinking, run to catch up with me."

"Yes," said the grandsons, and they stayed in the *tienda* while their grandfather went on ahead. When he was about three *cuerdas* away, the children heard shots. They thought they were firecrackers, however, and they continued drinking their sodas. Then they continued on the road, running to catch up with the grandfather, but when they caught up with him, they saw that their grandfather was stretched out where a small river flows. They thought the señor had fallen, and they ran to pick him up. When they realized that he was covered with blood, the children ran to tell their father what they had seen and heard. When they ran back to the body, Warren had already died. They just examined the body and informed the auxiliary tribunal.

The auxiliaries and patrolmen came to San José to call the justice of the peace, who is also the mayor, but these persons arrived when it was already night, since the event had taken place at five in the afternoon and the distance from Pachichaj to San José is twelve kilometers and it was raining.

When they informed the justice of the peace, he said, "It's already night. I can't go. It is very dangerous to walk at night." He gave the order to bury the señor without an investigation, without taking the body to Sololá, and to say that the señor died of old age.

The commission returned again to Pachichaj. But when they arrived, the children didn't accept what the judge had ordered. Then, on the same night, another commission came to tell the justice of the peace to present himself at the place of the bloodletting to investigate the cadaver because it was an assassination and certain people had cause to take action.

The commission arrived in town when it already had dawned Tuesday. The justice of the peace went when he realized that the children of the dead person had influence. He left San José at seven o'clock in the morning and arrived at ten o'clock at the site.

Only then was it realized that Señor Tuc González had been killed with two shots. He was first shot in the back, which tore out his heart. That is to say, the impact came through the chest and took out his heart. The other shot was near the knee, in the thigh. Not until 11:00 A.M. did they carry the remains to the hospital in Sololá for the examination according to the law. The cadaver was carried *cargado* [on their shoulders] six kilometers to Patzilín, where there is a road. Since these men have a car, they took the body of their father in the car and returned on the night of the same day.

All the people of the *aldeas* of Patzilín and Pachichaj and some of the people of the pueblo were indignant about this bloody deed. It made them sad and talkative, because, as I said earlier, Señor Warren Tuc was like a great *principal* of the two *aldeas* and they treated him like a father. With the great expanses of land that he had, he had rented to the poorer people of the two *aldeas*. Also, he was the owner of big mountains where many groups of lumberjacks earned their living by the sale of timber.

Although we didn't see it, they say that much earlier Don Warren was bad to the poor people. When we knew him, however, he behaved better toward the poor. During each fiesta of San José, the municipal corporation [town council] always invited him because they took him as one of the better *principales* of the town, and he remained for three or four days sharing with those of the town. For that reason, when he died sadness was felt in all the homes, as well as much fear, because the subversives were beginning to kill the working people.

The burial was Wednesday, 5 August. I was sad, but I didn't go to the funeral. I respected Warren Tuc a great deal, and he respected me. When he came to visit me, sometimes he would spend the night when it was raining because he did not wish to risk returning. He would stay either with me or with my wife's father. I thought a lot about going to the funeral, but I was afraid because the subversives control things a lot and they pay attention to those who pay their respects, and, for that reason, I didn't go.

One certain version is that the death of Don Warren Tuc was caused by the said guerrilla, Danny Hi, but who knows on what mountain he is? They tried to look for him, but it was impossible. For this assassination not one person is in jail. The sons of the deceased are conducting

5. *A woman vendor and her daughter in Panajachel. Photo by Randall Sexton.*

their investigations to find this man. They are doing this with the help of lawyers, but it is difficult for them. They are spending a lot of money, but I think it is wasted because they are not carrying out the investigations in the right way.

What do you mean?

No one would say for sure that they saw Danny do it because they were afraid they also would be killed. They say many saw him do it, but no one would testify.

Problems with the Mayor Continue in San Martín la Laguna

24 August to 27 October 1987

In the last episode of Ignacio: The Diary of a Guatemala Indian, *Ignacio wrote about Bartolomé Yac, the socialist mayor of San Martín la Laguna who was struggling to stay in office. In the November 1996 elections, of the 326 municipalities of Guatemala, San Martín la Laguna was the only town in which a socialist became mayor.*

As Ignacio described the situation, Bartolomé is a Tzutuhil who cannot speak Spanish well. He wears the typical shirt and pants and generally goes barefoot, although he occasionally wears caites *[typical,*

Indian-style sandals]. His behavior is Indian. He is a very simple man. For these reasons, many Mexican journalists came to congratulate him when he won the election. From the day he took office, however, Bartolomé's political enemies were determined to remove him. In the episode that follows, Ignacio brings closure to the story of Bartolomé Yac.

Indeed, Bartolomé Yac usually prevailed over his enemies in the municipality. They tried to throw him out once, but he appealed to the higher authorities and won. His enemies were determined, however, and didn't give up. His outspoken critics in the corporation were Ciro García, the syndic, Alberto Vásquez, the first councilman, and José Xicay, the second councilman. They collaborated with members of other political parties to accuse Bartolomé before the tribunals, but the councilmen's main interest was to remain in the municipal administration.

Finally, they achieved their objective. On 25 August I went to Sololá, and an uncle of the ex-treasurer told me all that had happened.

On 24 August the municipal treasurer, Juana García [who had been appointed by Bartolomé], was captured by the national police of Sololá [and accused of financial improprieties]. She remained in jail for twenty-four hours, and she left under an Q800 bond. After her arrest, Señorita Juana García wanted to continue performing the duties of treasurer, but no one would deal with her. She had to accept it [not being able to do her job].

Then the councilmen wanted to select a new, capable treasurer, but Bartolomé disagreed. He wanted the treasurer to be named by himself, not the councilmen. The dispute was between the mayor and the councilmen, and neither side wanted to lose.

Exercising his prerogative, the mayor named Julia Cuc Bolaños, a *perito contador* [qualified accountant], treasurer. Unlawfully, the councilmen named Juan Herberto Cojox Puzul, a *bachiller* [secondary school graduate].

The twenty-first of September, Monday, at 11:00 A.M., I returned to San Martín, after running an errand to Panajachel, to attend a meeting presided over by the Señor Governor of Sololá. The meeting had been going on for about twenty minutes before I arrived. I witnessed the following events.

With Bartolomé there was a group of persons but of very low status. With the councilmen were the people with money, members of other political parties, who had more experience as politicians. And the evangelical pastors, teachers, and students were against Bartolomé.

Poor Bartolomé wanted them to respect his choice of treasurer, and he was verbally abusing the members of the municipal council, saying:

People of San Martín, we are the people. No one can tell us what to do. I am the mayor. I have to name the person of my confidence. No one can order me, neither the councilmen nor the other parties nor the governor. The governor can govern in Sololá [the departmental capital] but not in San Martín. The councilmen don't have any taste, neither bitter nor sweet, nor sour, nor salty. They are rotten thieves and drunks. In the future the people need to elect a corporation that is capable of governing the town's destiny. Moreover, the syndic is a thief, because he asked for Q135 as a loan from Señorita García and he robbed the municipality of two hundred writing pads. Moreover, he owes Q500 to a family, whose name I will not reveal.

The person in San Martín who doesn't owe five centavos to anyone is I, Bartolomé Yac García, who can face his enemies in any tribunal and who will still be mayor. The governor is a Ladino, who can't threaten the indigenous people. The people are a socialist's army, and a socialist isn't afraid of the military.

Immediately Ciro García, the syndic, spoke:

I don't want Bartolomé to be mayor anymore because of his ignorance. I don't want to be at the side of a crazy or demeaned mayor. The councilmen only took possession of the tribunal when the mayor neglected them, and the councilmen and mayor never had a camaraderie worthy of the dignity of the corporation. The mayor does everything his own way. Never does he want a piece of advice.

Then the governor spoke:

I am the departmental governor. I'm not threatening anyone as the mayor claims. I only want to intervene in this serious problem of the people of San Martín la Laguna, so that the citizens who agree with the works that are going on can see them be accomplished. It's known that the construction on the new municipal building has been suspended for three months and it hasn't been possible to pay the masons or the municipal workers, and it's because the money, that is, the monetary flow, has been suspended. To end this foolishness, none of these persons is going to be treasurer, neither the person named by the mayor nor the one named by the councilmen. It's better to have a hundred aspirants for this post and select the one who has the best qualifications. Each applicant should present his or her application to the civil department of the government of Guatemala to avoid future problems. I'm not in favor of the mayor or of the other group. I'm neutral. And for that reason, I do what the law says. Let's forget the foolishness.

When Bartolomé heard what the governor said, he became belligerent. The public meeting had no value. It was seen that the governor had more contact with the group of councilmen. Together they went to eat lunch and left the mayor with his group. And the people dispersed murmuring, small groups against the mayor and small groups against the councilmen.

The new building under construction, as mentioned by the governor, was for the municipality. Bartolomé's enemies went to Guatemala [City] to accuse him before the office of the comptroller of the nation. This office ordered an audit, but they didn't find deficits. The audit came out well for Bartolomé—the books were in good order. Bartolomé's enemies could not have him jailed for embezzlement.

Afterward, Bartolomé was even more macho. He thought that the councilmen had forgiven him, but on the contrary they became more infuriated. They looked for other improprieties and, it is said, used dirty politics. They say that when Bartolomé, the mayor, planned the construction of the new building, he did not have an engineer estimate the cost and put it out for competitive bids. The mayor himself looked for masons. That was when his enemies contracted an engineer to give an appraisal. But as in this world everything is possible when there is enough money, they say that Bartolomé's enemies paid an engineer a bribe to condemn the mayor. When the engineer came accompanied by other functionaries of the government, they counted all the material used in the work. The information that the engineer gave the functionaries claimed that Bartolomé was short of money. But, to be more exact, it is said that this was a paid deal by the enemies of Bartolomé to look for a trick to put him in jail.

When Bartolomé realized that the situation was already serious, he then sent to call the ex-treasurer, Jaime Ixtamer Cojox, to immediately occupy the office of the municipal treasury. This Jaime Ixtamer Cojox had been discharged by Bartolomé Yac when he took possession of the mayorship. That is to say, Jaime Ixtamer was the treasurer during the time of the de facto mayor. Bartolomé, instead of looking for help, handed over the treasury to his own enemy. Jaime Ixtamer took possession of the municipal treasury on 17 October 1987.

Bartolomé didn't have any other recourse for the report of the deceitful engineer. The twenty-sixth of October of this year, the mayor, Bartolomé, and the councilmen received a summons from the judicial tribunal for Tuesday, the twenty-seventh, to present themselves in Sololá, where they were imprisoned the same day. But the councilmen were able to leave jail within twenty-four hours, paying a fine of Q200 each. They were able to get out of jail because when the mayor planned the work, they didn't sign it. Just the signature of the mayor was there. For that reason he was charged with the crime.

Now Bartolomé Yac García is in the men's prison in Sololá. There is a lot of criticism. Some say that he will spend seven years in prison; others say three or four; still others say he will only spend some months. Until now, no one knows the truthfulness of this case. But the socialist party is not lending itself to help him. He is forsaken. It's true that he has some friends, but they are lacking in legal knowledge and in financial resources.

Truly, Bartolomé would not have ended up in jail if he had accepted the corporation's naming a treasurer. But he had a lot of machismo. They told him many times that they didn't want him. He should have presented his resignation and allowed the others to govern the town.

I'm not against or in favor of him, but indeed I saw that he behaved very rudely. Although he didn't know Spanish, he thought he was the only one [for mayor]. In the end he lost.

These things will serve as a lesson in the life of a man. In all of Guatemala, Bartolomé is the only mayor who belongs to the socialist party, because San Martín is the only pueblo of Guatemala where the socialists won. Also, he is the only mayor who is imprisoned. He is a discredit to his party.

The Violence Continues in Santiago Atitlán
9 November 1987

A group of well-armed men went out to where the Rebuli bus of Santiago Atitlán passes on its way to the capital of Guatemala. The bus left Santiago Atitlán at 6:40 A.M., and when it passed by the place called Cerro de Oro, it was attacked by these bad men. According to the news, all the passengers were taken off the bus by force of arms. When the passengers left the bus, they put them in a file behind the bus and asked each to identify himself according to his *cédula* [national identification card].

On this bus there had been a military commissioner by the name of José Eduardo Yotz Quinto and also the political director, Raimundo de Dios Ramírez Ralón. The armed men robbed the majority of the passengers of their money and then told them to take off running without the commissioner and the political director. At the moment the passengers ran to hide, the military commissioner and Señor Raimundo de Dios Ramírez Ralón were shot. The killers left the cadavers lying there and left quietly. It is more certain that the killers are subversives.

Señor Raimundo de Dios Ramírez Ralón was a mayoral candidate of Santiago Atitlán for the PID, but he didn't win the elections. In the previous [national] elections of deputies of the constituent assembly, Señor Ramírez was also a candidate for deputy for the department of Sololá, but the outcome was the same. He lost the election. In the past general elections, in November 1985, the said señor also was a candidate for representative for the department of Sololá. Due to bad luck, he also lost the election. He struggled a lot to occupy the said post, but it was all impossible for him.

It is because the Partido Institucional Democrático is suffering a lot from the time of the coup d'état led by General Ríos Montt. The party remains poorly viewed by the majority, especially the youth. They say that the secretary-general, the *licenciado* [counselor, graduate] Donaldo Alvarez Ruiz, caused many deaths in Guatemala, and, for that reason, the people don't like this party anymore. Don Raimundo [Ramírez] wanted very much to restore the said party but couldn't. All the secretaries-general of the municipalities now didn't want to collaborate with the ex-candidate, Ramírez.

On previous occasions, the ex-director [Ramírez] arrived at the towns to try to convince the people, but he could do nothing. One time he arrived to tell me to continue as a director of the said party, but I told him I didn't want any more politics. "I have a lot of work, and I don't want to lose time." The now-deceased Raimundo became angry with me and said that in the future he would not do me a favor when I have some need. I told him that I respected him a lot as a friend but not as a politician. I also told him that I am tired of the lies of the politicians. The now "disappeared" friend then saw me with bad eyes.

One time we met in Panajachel. He threatened me, telling me that all the PID secretaries-general of the towns would be kidnapped and drowned in Lake Atitlán. It was a revenge because I didn't want anymore to help the party that in past times had a lot of fame but now has none. I asked him, "Who's going to do these things?"

He told me, "The directors of the party Movimiento de Liberación Nacional [MLN, Movement of National Liberation] and the high directors of the PID are going to do it."

I told him, "Very well, if God thus permits it, and if something bad has been done or if [there is] something I owe the party; well, very well, they can do with me what they wish." I told him, "Thanks a lot for the news," and I walked away.

[Despite his threat] I was truly distressed when we heard on Radio Fabulosa what had happened to the person who once had commanded a lot of respect and confidence. Sincerely, he once had been a friend of our house, and when he came to San José, he always had visited us. When we were still friends, I always had visited him when I went to Sololá. But I had decided not to help his party anymore. I had already seen that it was viewed unfavorably by the young people. For that reason, I had backed out and said no more politics with the old parties, because the truth is they only used us Indians to fight and confront our own people. For the Indian it was nothing more than a lie. The Ladinos were the ones who made a lot of money. Thus, for these reasons, I had said no.

A Strange Case: A Suspected Intelligence Operative Assassinated
30 November 1987

In Santiago Atitlán in the *cofradía* of the said town, a fiesta is always celebrated in honor of San Andrés Apóstol. The news reports say that the members of the *cofradía* and the rest of the people were enjoying themselves, dancing to tunes of the Sol y Mar Marimba of San Martín la

Laguna, when a man entered looking like a tourist with a camera for [taking] photographs. The man acted as if he were really drunk, and he also began to dance with the indigenous people. But he took photographs of those who were dancing in the house of the *cofradía*. Who knows who discovered that he was a member of army intelligence. After this man left the *cofradía,* his enemies followed him. About four *cuadras* [linear measure; 1 *cuadra* = 275 feet] from the military detachment, Pijuy, a kilometer from the town, he was shot dead. When the forces of the detachment left to look for the assassins, they weren't able to do anything because, they say, the assassins disappeared in the town. Thus came the suspicion that the *Atitecos* [people of Santiago Atitlán] are members of the rebels. But who knows the truth. What indeed is known is that a lot of people of this pueblo are dying.

The Insects Also Do Justice
5 to 9 December 1987

This case is of Jerónimo Quiacain of the *aldea* of Tzancuil. He went to San Martín to sell ripe coffee. After selling the coffee, they say that he peacefully entered a cantina to drink his brandies. Somewhat drunk, he crossed the lake in his small canoe and arrived at the *aldea* and went to drink more. When he got home, he wanted to kill his wife and children, but by the grace of God, they were able to defend themselves; that is to say, they hid in a neighbor's house.

Then Jerónimo went to get a stick to break open a box for keeping bees. He wasn't able to do anything with the stick, and he ran to get a machete and began to tear open the hive. The insects became angry and rose up against him; thousands and thousands of bees attacked him until they killed him. Without doubt the sting of the bees was unbearable. Poor Jerónimo fell dead and jammed his head in a fork of a coffee tree.

Not until the middle of the afternoon did his family realize that the man had died. Then they informed the auxiliary tribunal. But, lamentably, the justice of the peace didn't show up until the next day at noon. Monday, 8 December, they sent the cadaver to the hospital of Sololá. They didn't bury him until Tuesday, the ninth. The case was purely the result of a drunken bout.

6. *Young woman picking ripe coffee near the shore of Lake Atitlán.*

Bones of Three "Disappeared" Appear
December before Christmas 1987

Bones of three cadavers were found buried without a coffin in a coffee plantation in San Martín la Laguna where previously there had been a military detachment in a place called Chuanup. They say that two of the cadavers still had gold teeth in place and that one of them is the cadaver of either the "disappeared" José Bizarro Có or the ex-mayor, Juan Sicay. In this discovery silence was maintained. No investigation was made. The bones were buried in the cemetery of the town.

The First Auto Accident in My Pueblo of San José
24 December 1987

For the first time since the inauguration of the road in 1960, an [auto] accident was registered, which took place right in the middle of the town. At 9:15 P.M. on 24 December (Christmas Eve), Señor Mario García Ixtamer was driving his truck accompanied by his assistant, Abraham Méndez. Together they went into a cantina to drink some *tragos* [drinks, shots] for Christmas Eve, but it turned out bad. When the driver of the truck left the cantina, he asked the assistant to guide him to back up the truck, but because the effect of alcohol was overwhelming, who knows how the assistant fell and the tire ran over him, destroying his head, without even a shout, leaving his cerebrum outside his skull?

Nearly the whole town was alarmed because there are persons who had never seen a vehicular accident. Many condemned the driver, stating he should be jailed once and for all because it was he who caused the death with his truck. There was a lot of criticism by my indigenous people. We went to visit the driver when he was in the jail of San José, but most of the people didn't want to talk to him.

A Bloody Case in Santiago Atitlán
28 December 1987

[This is] news given by Radio Fabulosa by means of the program "Patrullaje Informativo" [Informative Patrolling], of the day 29 December at 3:00 P.M. It says yesterday [28 December] in the night two women were shot by heavily armed men. It only gave the name of Dolores Ajcabul. It says that the two women, accompanied by their husbands, went to a meeting of an evangelical church on Monday night. Then violent assassins took them from their husbands and machine-gunned them a half-*cuerda* [away]. Dolores Ajcabul fell dead with her baby in her arms. The baby was lying in the blood of her mother, but nothing happened to her.

When the judge arrived, they cleaned the baby and saw that it had not been hit by a bullet. This caused indignation among the indigenous people, condemning this bloody act. The assassins don't even respect a mother. There are many cases, graver than this case, that are not in these pages.

Rain Was Scarce in 1987
June to December 1987

This year of 1987 rain was scarce. It only served to erode the land. In the month of June, it only rained a few times, but heavily. In July the *canícula* [dog days, a relatively dry period, July and August, between the two periods of maximum rainfall, June to September] began soon, and in the month of August it hardly rained. Not until September did it rain again, but it was little. And then it was summer again. In the month of September we planted chickpeas on a piece of land, but because of the scarcity of rain, they didn't grow.

In the month of November began the harvest of corn, coffee, and other crops, but this year there wasn't much to harvest. The corn was very little, and there were hardly any chickpeas. There wasn't even enough for seed. Well, we who are in the highlands produced a little corn, beans, and coffee, but those who suffered more were my people of San José, San Martín, Santiago Atitlán, and other parts, who went to the coast to rent land with the *finqueros* [owners or administrators of *fincas*]. It was misery for nothing. Nothing was gained. They lost money by going to the coast, that is, the cost of travel, food, the bad treatment of the *finqueros,* the cost of the fertilizer, and, as if that weren't enough, the great sickness of malaria. They only extracted three or four arrobas of corn.

In these contracts with the *finqueros,* the renter has to pay the rent by planting grass on the cattle ranches whether he has a harvest or not. The contracts state that the *finquero* will rent part of his land to the poor people, who must pay for the two crops of corn they extract by cleaning well the land where they had planted corn and then planting it in pasture. The renters must hand the land over to the *finquero* after the second harvest, in the month of December. If the renter doesn't want to plant a second crop, he still has to go clean the area and plant the grass for the *finquero*. If the renter doesn't show up, the *finquero* demands it in court. The species of grass they plant is *Estrella africana* [African star], which is the best pasture for the livestock.

For that reason, the poor person is always exploited by the rich. Three of my *Joseño* countrymen didn't want to fulfill their obligations, but they had to go by the law of the authorities. That is to say, in this year the harvest was lost. In these pueblos when coffee was planted, they had little harvest; it hardly was of any use since many owed the banks for the cost of the fertilizer. But it was due to the scarcity of rain. With regard to the big agriculturalists, they didn't lose anything because their farms are well mechanized and irrigated, and for that reason they succeed. But also it is a favor, because what they harvest is for everyone.

Story of a Shaman
A Day in the Month of January 1988

On this day we went to look at a piece of land in Patzunoj. [We met] my friend Félix Quiché Cakay, a shaman who has always lived performing *costumbres* [customs, rituals] for the sick people. He told me that indeed he has the power of a shaman, but certainly he has to behave honorably, without seeking money or things that can deflect his luck.

Félix is a Cakchiquel of San Miguel, but he said that when he was small he was taken to the *fincas* because his parents were poor. He felt a power and always dreamed that he would cure the sick by means of herbs. The dreams taught him which herbs to use for each illness and which days to perform the *costumbres* to ask for the health of the ill.

When he was young, he had to look for a way to make a living, and he came to live in San Martín la Laguna. He was working with persons who gave him work as a campesino, and they only paid him twenty centavos a day.

This is the way it was for many years until Félix found himself a woman in the same town. He told me that he had been living for eleven years with his father-in-law. It was in this house where he did the first *costumbres* as cures for the sick. But he said that his father-in-law and mother-in-law were bad, just fighting at home. A dream told him he had to leave. He had to accept his dream, and he went to the coast to work as a guardian of a *finca*. But he said that the parents became angry and went to get their daughter. He remained living alone on the *finca*, sadly, because they had taken his woman.

On this *finca* he knew many herbs used to cure sicknesses. Also, the people were aware that he indeed was able to cure, and he did *costumbres* for the sick people in order to win back their health. He became famous there for curing those who were ill.

He had the desire to return to San Martín, however, and he had to leave the *finca*. When he arrived at this town, [he discovered] his woman already was living with another man. He couldn't live with her.

What he did was to obtain a woman by the name of Melinda from San José. Then they went to live on the *finca* La Memoria, planting corn, beans, tomatoes, and watermelons. He cured patients by performing *costumbres*, but he didn't make his living doing this because it was only a favor that he did for the poor people, since he said that in a dream they told him that he should not take money because the *suerte* [luck, ability] he enjoyed was not something that he had bought. It was just a gift from God. When the people of the other *fincas* received the news that he didn't charge money for a cure, they came from all parts of the coast. When the other shamans realized that Félix had a lot of fame, they did a lot of *costumbres* to kill him, but they were unable to do anything bad. However, Félix always performed *costumbres* to defend himself from his enemies because there were three strong shamans who wanted him dead. He told me, "For a man to defend himself, he first has to have faith in God, obeying and doing his will, and also respecting the powers of *el [santo] mundo* [the lord of the world, earth].[13] It's certain that God is the *dueño* [master] and creator of all the visible and invisible. This same God permits the powers of the *mundo*. If a person says that he believes in God but doesn't respect the things of the *mundo*, this person isn't worthy."

I asked him how he knew the names of the herbs that he used to cure the ailing. He told me he didn't know the names of the herbs. He just knew them because in his dream each herb appears for each sickness, and the next day he goes to the rivers or the mountains to look for them.

I asked him, "What do you do to perform a *costumbre* to heal the ailment?"

"The *costumbre*," he told me, "is done according to the *nagual* [spirit and animal forms of humans, especially witches; soul] of the person. Each *costumbre* has value when the patient and the family have faith in what is going to be done, if the shaman is good. But if inside the house there isn't faith, the remedies and the rituals lose their value."

Félix told me that he receives notices from the birds and the other animals of the *campo*. When an opossum, fox, or wildcat crosses the road, that is where the shaman goes in search of the remedy in the fields. Something good or bad is able to happen to the sick person. If it is difficult to find the herb on the mountain, one only has to take into account when an animal crosses from left to right. This is bad for the patient, and he can die. Or say the shaman spends a lot of time to cure him, or better said, it's difficult for the shaman to find the medicine (herb) or reeds, or if a snake is found coiled up inside the grass, it is a sign that the patient is going to live only for a few days and it isn't worth the effort to be losing a lot of time trying to cure him. It is better for the shaman to advise the kin to prepare to buy a coffin and other things for the burial.

Now, when an animal crosses the path of the shaman from right to left, it is a good sign that the sickness has been conquered by the good luck. The herbs will be found, and the sick one will be cured. Then the shaman returns with joy and tells the kin that the patient is going to recover, and he begins to perform the *costumbres* by day and at night.

Also, he said that the woodpecker is the *alguacil, mayordomo* [low-ranking officer of a *cofradía*], and *comisario* [commissary] of the *mundo*. When this bird sings, he is advising something on the paths of life; something good or something bad can happen to the man. When the woodpecker sings on the left side of a person, it is a bad sign, indicating he will lose something, there will be sickness in the family, or there will be a death of some brother or some child. When the woodpecker sings on the right side, it is a good sign, that there will be a good future in work or in business or good luck in the family. But also it advises that one has to take care to respect the things of God and the *mundo*. The person or the shaman is well able to live a lot of time on the earth because he respects the things of God in heaven and the powers of *santo mundo*.

I asked him, "Why do you believe that the animals or the birds indicate something if they cross the path of a man and that they advise something when they sing on some side of the shaman or of the person?"

"It's that animals know what we suffer in our works and in our sicknesses, and also they have to see with us the good or the bad luck. The animals are our brothers," he said.

I replied, "Why does the woodpecker predict the good and the bad for human beings?"

"Well," he told me, "this bird is sacred because he doesn't eat the things that we eat like tortillas, salt, and chili. The woodpecker just eats the insects that are found in the trees. The same with the animals such as the opossum, fox, and the wildcat. They don't commit sins; for example, the animals don't mistreat or gossip. They're not liars and they're not drunks; they're not egotistical or arrogant. More for that reason, these animals are more sacred than we. And thus they are able to see of us what we can't see of ourselves."

I asked him, "Is it true, sometimes, to have positive indications from some animal?"

"Many times," he told me.

"Tell me one," I said.

"Very well, Ignacio, I'll tell you what happened to me ten years ago when I was on the *finca* La Memoria, on the coast of Mazatenango," and he told me what I'm going to write.

Félix was famous on this *finca* for curing, but his harvest turned out well, and the curing was just a favor he did for the people. On this *finca* lived a shaman who also was famous, but he charged a lot for the cure and performing the rituals. He tried many times to do something bad like bewitching and killing his rival, Félix Quiché, but he wasn't able to do it to him. Félix was content with his crops and did not pay attention to the witchcraft that the other was doing.

One time he went with his wife to the field to pick tomatoes and watermelons to sell in the market of Río Bravo. When they were happily picking tomatoes, on his left side a woodpecker was singing. Félix kneeled in this same place saying these words, "God of heaven and of earth has ordered you *alguacil* . . . you *alguacil, mayordomo,* and *comisario* of the world, to give me some evil that is happening or is going to happen to me and my woman." He says that after saying these words he got up and said to his woman to go home because something bad was happening.

"Yes," she said, and she went home. When the woman arrived, the house was open, and a thief already had robbed her and her husband's clothing and Q143. The woman returned crying to advise her husband what they had suffered. The two left sad for the *rancho* [hut]. Félix was left with only the pair of trousers and the shirt he was wearing; his woman was left with only the *corte* [native skirt] and blouse that she had on. The two kneeled to pray before the image of San Simón inside the rustic house. After the prayer, they followed the footprints of the thief that led to the back of the house of the *brujo* [witch] who so hated Félix. Then Félix spoke to the administrator of the *finca* to have the daughter of the *brujo* return the clothing that she had filched.

"Yes," said the administrator, and he went with Félix to tell her to return the clothing of Félix and of his wife. But when the administrator and Félix arrived at this *sitio,* the daughter of the witch threatened to kill the administrator and told them to leave immediately before they leave dead from this *sitio.* The administrator and Félix could do nothing to recover what had been looted.

The shaman, Félix Quiché, remained in poverty because it was difficult to earn money. Not until later was he able to buy clothing for himself and his wife. But he developed resentment for all that had happened. He planned then to buy a lot of candles to perform a *costumbre* for the saint of San Basilio. When he arrived at the church of San Basilio [on the farm by the same name], he began to burn candles and incense, presenting the image with a demand against the woman who had robbed the clothing and the money. When he was burning the candles, he sprinkled two-eighths [of a liter] of alcohol. The candles went out, but then he lit them again. In twenty days he went to the hill where the girl's father [the other *brujo*] always performed his *costumbres*. Quiché did the same things, asking the god of the sacred world for quick justice for the person. In twenty days he did another ritual. In all he did three well-executed *costumbres*. In a dream he was advised that the *costumbres* were received and that he should wait for justice.

Thus he remained for eleven months, only waiting for the law of compensation. Nothing happened until the twelfth of the month, when the woman (the daughter of the *brujo*) was happy on a Sunday and went to the market of San Antonio Suchitepéquez and returned content in the afternoon of the same day. She came in a car of the *patrón* [landlord] of the *finca,* and she brought a lot of things. In the night the woman was hit with great bouts of vomiting and diarrhea. At five in the morning she was carried to the hospital of Mazatenango, but the doctors could do nothing for her. Then the family took her out of the hospital, and on the road between Mazatenango and San Antonio she died. Not until she arrived on the farm did the neighbors realize the daughter of the *brujo* had died.

But the *brujo* was aware of all that had happened. Then he began to perform *costumbres* in many hills and in the church so that the judge of the world would serve his justice. Félix told me, "In the night of Holy Wednesday, he didn't sleep at all. He felt bothered in his body, and he began to sweat profusely. He got out of bed to open the door, when inside the house he saw a really big serpent. It gave him a big chill in all his body, an immense scare, but he had to be stronger. He went to get a thick wire, ran it through the mouth of the snake, killed it with a machete, carried it in a sack, and burned it at the foot of a big tree. He told me that when he went to burn the snake he had to use an old tire and four gallons of gas. He said that during the night he worked a lot because from the hut to the place where he burned the snake was about two kilometers.

In the same night in a dream he was told he had to leave the *finca* because later something bad might happen to him or his woman. Thus it was when the shaman, Félix, left the *finca* La Memoria.

I chatted with the shaman, Félix Quiché, more than four hours. He told me things like how to perform a *secreto* [sacred or magical act] for a person who steals coffee, just to kiss the footprints of the feet of the thief where he stepped when he stole it. If the owner of the stolen object kisses the footprints of the thief, it's sure that within a short time the thief will fall sick. Also, he said that when a thief arrives to steal corn or coffee, just collect a little water in a gourd. Place the gourd under the *gotero* [the edge of the roof from which the rain- and dew drops fall] for nine days. Put the gourd away during the day and leave it out at night so that dew drops fall into it. Do this for the next nine days, putting it away at night and taking it out in the sun by day. After having performed these *secretos,* carry the water and pour a little on each tree where the robbery was committed. It's certain that the thief will fall sick but with an illness difficult to cure. This *secreto* is a way to punish the thieves.

He told me that presently he is curing a sick person named José Choapac who is a thief for whom some owners [of goods he had stolen] had performed *secretos* in order to punish him. José Choapac went to shamans in Santiago Atitlán and other pueblos, but they had not been able to cure him because he needed the same *secreto*. It is simple and easy.

I asked him how to do it. He told me that the sick person is carried to the same place, is hit twelve strokes with a whip, and has a little dirt rubbed over the affected part. With this the sick person is healed. For these things one doesn't need a shaman.

I asked if José Choapac is going to recover from his illness. He told me, "Yes, but we are going to wait a little while for him to suffer a little so that he won't continue stealing coffee from the people because many know that José Choapac is a thief."

I asked, "Who has performed the *secreto* to make him sick?"

"A *Martinero* [a man of San Martín] has done a bad *secreto* for the thief, but indeed one can fix it."

"Are you going to charge for the cure?"

"No, because I don't want to be responsible for what José had stolen, just a favor to cure him."

Always, they had told me that Félix Quiché was a shaman and *brujo,* but I hadn't had the opportunity to talk to him until now, this month of January when we went to look at a piece of land in Patzunoj that my grandfather Ignacio Bizarro Ramos had left me in the year 1950. Félix told me that he has an interest in buying a little [of my] land, and I told him with much pleasure that the land is good for cultivating coffee. It is six kilometers from town. It is feared that it is a place where the subversives always pass, and they say that the people have seen them. For that reason, I am afraid to cultivate this land.

On this day Félix had brought bread and coffee, which we ate on the mountain. We did not return until three in the afternoon.

Considering everything that he has told me, it seems that Félix is more *brujo* than shaman. This señor lives in the barrio San Josito. All that I have written on these pages is true. And José Choapac was healed in a few weeks of a serious infection that broke out on his butt (anus) and on his testicles. Poor José suffered a lot, but they say it was because of theft.

The Birth of My First Grandchild
13 February 1988

When I was sleeping peacefully, my son José came to wake me. He was desperate for me to accompany him to San Martín to call the midwife because his [common-law] wife, María, was in labor. I had to go while my wife went to advise the parents of our daughter-in-law. Between three and four in the morning, we went to San Martín.

The midwife came with us on foot. She told us she wanted a car, but we didn't have one. On the road there was a lot of wind. When we arrived home, María's parents were already waiting for us.

By the grace of God, the baby was born. Everyone was happy because the truth is that it was another human being that was given life. Afterward, the midwife returned to San Martín.

I chatted with the father of our daughter-in-law while my wife prepared breakfast. Since it is the custom of us Indians to have a little party when a grandchild is born, we drank some *tragos*, although it was true that it was early in the morning. We did it to show respect. But since the parents of our daughter-in-law, María, have money, they bought other drinks (*aguardiente* [firewater, sugarcane rum] and beers). Also, other kin and a friend from San Martín arrived who gave us a lot of food and tortillas, which we ate for lunch. We continued drinking but in moderation; that is, we didn't lose consciousness because we didn't want to lose the esteem of the children. Moreover, my wife didn't want me to drink.

She didn't drink, but I did, out of respect for the parents of my daughter-in-law. Thus we were all day. Since they had more money than I, they drank more than I, and they became more intoxicated.

Only a few days had passed since María had given birth to her baby when she developed a problem—she didn't have any milk. By good fortune, however, my wife still had milk because our own baby was still breast-feeding. So she got up during the nights and gave her breast to her grandson.

We prayed, asking God to let the milk drop for our daughter-in-law. They put her in the *temascal* [sweat house] because the women said that her body had no warmth. They treated her with a sweat bath about five or six times. Also, we looked for avocado leaves, cedar leaves, fig leaves, and the leaves of a local herb known as Santo Domingo. My wife cooked these leaves [together until they were warm], and with these they rubbed María's shoulders and breasts. Milk came down, but little.

María's mother became preoccupied with her daughter. She had to go to San Martín to look for a woman who could prepare remedies. Then this woman from San Martín was curing her but with the condition that the señora would have to be at rest and not touch water, that is, wash clothes, dishes, and so on, that she would not work. We had to do what the woman told us, but it was my wife who did most of the work for her. In addition to cooking and other housework, she took care of María's baby, because María was resting.

Was this the only remedy?

The truth is that the woman gave her something in a small bottle to take orally, but she didn't want to tell us what it was. She was afraid that if we found out the name we would tell other curers and they would be able to cure persons with her medication.

Is she a curandera *(curer)?*

She isn't a real *curandera* because she doesn't cure other things. She only treats women who have problems with their milk, [but] you might call her a *curandera*.

We did everything that the woman told us to do, and then the milk came down. But when the mother of the baby finally had milk, another problem emerged—the baby began to cry day and night. They took it to the doctors in San Martín, and José bought the medicine that they prescribed, but there was no relief.

Then they took the baby to a doctor in Sololá. They spent Q400 on all the medical expenses. This money was provided by José's father-in-law as a gift, but it was wasted because nothing worked; the baby continued the same.

My wife had a similar experience with Samuel Jesús when he was a baby. He was cured by a shaman, and my wife called the same shaman [for our grandchild]. My wife said, "Do us the favor of curing the baby because it has been sick now for weeks."

"Fine," said the shaman. But these things were not done in my presence. They were done in the other house. I hardly have faith in shamans, but neither do I despise them for what they do. Those present when the shaman was doing his job were José, his wife, and my wife. I just said, "That's fine. Do what you can."

The shaman placed his transparent stones and jades on a table. Without doubt certain things appeared within the stones to [help him] divine, and he told María, "The sickness of the baby isn't an illness; instead it's a bad deed, a bewitching made by a *muchacho* [boy, young man] of this same town because this *muchacho* wanted you for his woman, but you didn't want to talk to him." And then he said, "When you married José, the *muchacho* became angry and began to burn candles to bewitch you. The sorcery wasn't for the baby. Instead he had done it directly for you. But because you had a little stronger blood than your baby, it was your baby who suffered the consequences."

They said the shaman asked María, "Do you remember that previously a man spoke to you three or four times? The man wanted you to be his woman, but you didn't respond to him. Mainly it was the bad treatment that you gave the man, and this caused the bad deed. Tell me if what I'm saying isn't true."

Then María acknowledged that it was true. She said that a man by the name of Manuel had spoken to her three times, but she said she didn't want to be his woman, and she had to tell him, "No, I don't want to get together with you." That's when the man became angry with María. Who knows what bad deed he did to her.

But the *zajorín* [shaman] told her, "You see, it's true, what I'm telling you. I don't lie. Well, what the man has done is that he has burned many candles against you, but now we will do a *costumbre* so that the baby will live."

"Will the baby live?" my wife asked him.

"Yes, he will live, but two or three *costumbres* must be done every ten days so that the baby will improve."

"Good," she said.

In that same afternoon he performed a little *costumbre* to cure the little grandchild inside the house. He did it again ten days later. [Altogether] he did it four times. And the baby, little by little, began to improve. That's when the shaman won, because he had spoken the truth, that a man had tried to court María before she joined with José.

When they registered the birth of the baby, my son and my daughter-in-law surprised me, because they hadn't told me what they were going to name him. When José returned from the civil registry, he showed me the birth certificate, and the baby was christened Ignacio Darío Bizarro Ramos. It is the custom among us Indians always to give the first child who is born the name of the grandfather or grandmother.

If it is a costumbre, *why were you surprised?*

Imagine, there are two grandfathers. I am grandfather through the father, and the father of María is grandfather through the mother. That is why I was mistaken, because I thought they were going to give him the name of the father of María. For me it was a surprise because who knew which grandfather they would choose, or if they would give him a name different from ours.

Then the costumbre *is to choose from the two grandfathers?*

Yes, the parents of the baby decide which grandfather's name they will use. The man tells her, "We will use the name of your father."

And the woman tells him, "Better we will use the name of your father."

Well, they have to discuss it a lot. As a grandfather, it's rare that they tell you, "Look, we will give your name to him." They let the two grandfathers know when they tell one of them, "I already put the name [in the registry]."

But José doesn't have the name of your father?

The reason is that my real father did not rear me. I was adopted. It's true that one of the younger children has the name of my father, but not the firstborn.

But you don't have the name of your grandfather.

Well, I have the name of my [maternal] grandfather, Ignacio Bizarro Ramos. Before I was born, my real father went to the barracks [army], and when I was born there was no one who would accept the certificate of birth or the registry. Then my real mother said to her father, "Please go write his name for me in the registry." And that's how it was that I was named Ignacio Bizarro. Legally, I should have been named Ignacio Ujpán Bizarro.

Well, look, I was a little sad about José's son when they gave him my name. It's the custom, but there is one thing. If the baby boy or girl dies, the parents soon reproach the grandparent, saying, "Ah, you didn't love your grandchild, whom we gave your name. Then you are a *brujo* or a *characotel* [a *nagual*, or spirit, that turns into an animal form at night to bother people; the *characotel* has hypnotic power to make someone ill], because you don't love your grandchild. You are an evil person."

Unfortunately, the baby did get sick when it was only a few days old. I was sad because I said, "The baby is going to die, and they gave him my name." But, by the grace of God, the baby lived.[14]

What are your feelings about being a grandfather?

In a large family, the children are not all the same. Each one has its own way of thinking and develops differently. Now my son José has his own wife. Like me, he is a father. He's a father and I'm a grandfather. José is a calm *muchacho,* but he always works. Sometimes I get a little angry at him, because I want what's good for him—to be a working man, a man who knows how to take care of his family.

Because I'm a father, I discipline my children when they don't obey, because I want them to be better off than I am, because in reality I work a lot in the fields, planting corn and beans. I suffer a lot, eating cold tortillas and drinking water from the river, because no one helped me from the time I was a child. I don't want the same things for my children. I want them to improve a little in their occupations. I don't want them to waste time, because the truth is that I don't want them to suffer. If a man suffers from his work, something is lacking. If a man only plans to waste time by resting, things go bad for him.

With José, I always correct him, even though he's the father of a family. I still have influence over him; I want him to be responsible and intelligent, so that he can solve his own problems.

I tell my children, "Look, kids, work, don't waste time. Now, I'm here for you. I can help you with food, with firewood, with anything. But a time will come when I will die; then you will be the ones to suffer." This is my advice, but because the head of a youngster is not the head of an adult, sometimes he or she becomes sidetracked.

I always try, however, to get the kids back on track. Sometimes I share [my thoughts] with them. I gather them together. I make it a diversion, a game, so that they will not get angry with me once and for all, so that they will accept what I have to say a little better.

Well, as I said, right, time changes everything. Do you remember one year when we were conversing here, when we were living here in the bungalows, I wasn't a grandfather? But with time many things happen. Imagine, now I'm a grandfather, and, well, there is nothing more than to thank God for all the years that He has given me, right. I can't say I don't accept being a grandfather, because that's how my children want it. I have to accept it because it's also an experience in a life—how to get to be a father and how to get to be a grandfather.

Being a father is different from being a grandfather because among us Tzutuhiles, when a person is a grandfather, he has to think a lot about what he does. He has to think a lot about what he's saying, because [otherwise] the people soon say, "Look, this man doesn't have any respect. He says bad things; he mistreats. And he is a grandfather." Then his grandchildren lose respect for him. Now, thanks to God, I'm already a grandfather. Now I have to take more care in what I say and do, being careful not to mistreat and to judge people. I have a lot of experience in my race and culture, but I need to take care of my own problems and mind my own business. Now I have to be more careful because I want to maintain the respect of the people. Also, I need to be careful to be humble, calm, and tranquil. As a grandfather, I need to think more about how I behave.

The Hardest Thing in My Life Happens
January to 7 March 1988

In the life of a man many things happen, good and bad, especially when one has many children. At times I have written about other people, about whatever things have happened to them. But now I'm experiencing difficult times with my own children. I can't hide what is happening to my own family. Although a parent plans well for his children, that is to say, to educate them a little for when they are adults, often the children are the ones who don't think well for themselves. When their children have something of an education, that is when the parents are not preoccupied with them. Well, in this world everything happens.

In 1987 my daughter María was in her fourth year studying for the teaching profession in the Instituto Nacional para Señoritas de Occidente (INSO) [Teachers' Training Institute for Señoritas of the West]. She had asked us to let her go to school, but my wife didn't want her to go and said, "There's no reason for María to study because she is short-tempered. Each time that I give her a chore, she sasses me." But María insisted, telling us that she wanted to study to become a teacher, and finally, [as I have said earlier in *Ignacio*] she convinced me. All the year of 1987 she was studying. It's true that in the Instituto she failed a math course [getting a score of 68, when 70 was needed to pass]. She told us that she had to make it up this year. There were new directives of the Ministry of Education, stating that those who had failed a course would be able to make it up if they petitioned to take the examinations. Since the Instituto is a national one, the teachers are strict.

When María, José, and I arrived at Quezaltenango to enroll María in the INSO, there had been certain problems between the students and the teachers. The subdirector told us, "You can't enroll in the fifth year if you have failed a course. It's the order of the ministry that you have to repeat the year. It's not my order. It's the minister's order that, for the moment, the young women who haven't finished a course can't enroll. There is only enrollment for those who completed all their courses." And that's how it was with everyone. For that reason, many of the students left to look for private *colegios* [secondary schools].[15]

Thus it was with us. We considered returning to Sololá for a *colegio* but thought it better to enroll her in Quezaltenango in the Colegio Liceo Quezalteco. When we arrived at this institute, the director told us, "No, here it can't be like that. Moreover, the *muchacha* [girl, young woman] is only behind in one course. We will accept her here with the condition that she pay Q35 for registration of the fourth year so that she can be tested for the course in March. And for the moment she can enroll herself for the fifth year and begin her studies. She will begin the fifth year, and they will give her a class for [some] hours to make up the course she failed."

Well, we said yes, and we paid the registration fees for both the fourth and the fifth years. They also told us that we had to make new uniforms of a standard color. José convinced me to at once buy the cloth for the uniforms and the *útiles* [school supplies] so that we would not have to come again, without knowing what was going to happen later. The director told me that my daughter should show up on 1

February to [get ready] to begin classes.

Thus it was in the month of January [1988], waiting for the month of February when classes would begin in the *colegio* for María and in the *instituto básico* [secondary school, similar to junior high] for my other children. My wife and I made the uniforms required by the *colegio*, and everything was ready. The departure was to be 1 February.

Then the thirty-first of January, we told her that she would go to Quezaltenango in the morning on the boat. But when day broke, I realized that María hadn't gone. She got up late, and I asked, "Why didn't you go?"

"Ah, no, maybe I'll go tomorrow."

"Who knows? You're going then?"

"I'm going."

"Good."

Then on this Monday, 1 February, I told José, "Look, tomorrow go with her. Leave her at the institute because it seems that she doesn't want to go to Quezaltenango. What's more, we already have the papers here. We've already paid for the registration."

"Very well, Papá," José replied.

On 2 February, Tuesday, I got up earlier because I had to go plant onions. I got up and woke him up. "José," I told him, "get up! It's already late. Get up! Tell María to get ready now! The launch will soon come. The hour has come. You have to go take her to Xela."

"Look," José told me, "I want to get up, but if she doesn't want to get up, how can I do it? I can't force her if she doesn't want to go."

Then I asked María, "Well, what's the matter with you? Why don't you want to get up?"

"Look, Papá, I'd better go tomorrow," she told me.

"But today is the second," I told her. "Today, you had to present yourself at the institute."

"No, better tomorrow I will leave," she responded.

Well, then I started to work with the *muchachos,* Ramón, Ignacito [diminutive of Ignacio], and José, planting onions. During the day I told the *muchachos,* "Please, do me a favor. Tell María to go study. I don't want her to waste her classes, because weeks will be lost. Later there will be problems."

"Very well," the *muchachos* told me, without knowing what she was thinking.

She started washing her clothing. Then I said, "Tomorrow she is leaving. Without doubt, tomorrow she is leaving for school because she is washing all her clothes."

By the evening, about eight at night, I went to pay for eleven thousand onion seedlings that I bought from Teodoro Temó to plant in a *tablón* [raised plot]. I had arranged with José that he would take his sister to the *colegio* while Ramón and I would go to plant the onions.

When I arrived home, my wife told me, "Look, María already has left with a man."

"With what man?"

"With José Mario Ramos García."

"Ay, pity, really?"

"Yes."

"Why didn't you hit her?"

"No," she told me. "I can't do anything. She secretly left the house, and the hombre had been waiting in the street. The two went to the house of the hombre."

Well, sincerely, I went loco because I didn't know she would behave like that. Then I said, "What happened? I'll bring action against her in court." [But] no, I reconsidered and thought it better just to leave her clothes at the police station. "Fine," I said, "let her go with the man."

My wife and I were upset because for a whim the money that we paid for her schooling was lost, not just because we are poor but because we have other children who need our financial help. Well, we knew that she had a boyfriend who talked to her and wanted her, but we had told her that it's better for her to marry when she finished her studies so that she would be able to survive in the future. But all was useless. Sincerely, I am telling the truth, it made me really angry. I thought of taking a whip to my daughter and the man, but as I knew they had already gone, I did nothing.

Since it made me mad, I grabbed all her clothing and went to leave it at the municipal commissary for her to pick up there. The commissary told me to have more patience, that they were going to take the clothing to her.

When I returned from the commissary, I didn't eat. There were only problems at home. This was a hard blow to the family, but as I was weak I couldn't bear it. I had to drink some *tragos* to calm my nerves, and only then was I able to sleep.

The following day, Wednesday, 3 February, I didn't get up feeling peaceful because of all that had happened. I was sitting on the porch of the house when José Mario's father arrived to tell me María was in their house and that he apologized for all that had happened. He told me that they were ready to perform the *costumbres* and have a quick marriage.

"We will have a marriage because we are Protestants, and we want your daughter to marry my son at once," he said.

"Look, Don José," I replied, since his name is also José, "I'm María's father, not María. Better you ask her because she is the one who went with the man. She is the one who is to marry him. If she wants to marry him, she can do it. It's up to her. I'm not the one to make her marry the man immediately. Now, if you oblige your son to get married, well, that's up to you, but I can't because I don't have the heart to make anyone get married. I'm not waiting for the [traditional marriage] *costumbres* so that you bring me meat and other things, and, moreover, so be it that my daughter has done what she has. Don't talk to me of marriage because I don't want to oblige anyone to have a marriage contract. They can decide when they are going to get married, or perhaps that they aren't going to wed. We parents can't make our children marry. They can decide for themselves."

He told me, "I'm a member of the Central American Church, and the church demands that the children of the evangelicals marry immediately so as not to live in sin."

I said, "You can't arrange anything with me. It's better that you arrange a wedding with your son, because he is the one who is going to get married, not I."

"But look, it's a matter of respect for us Protestants. There's always a marriage."

"If you are Protestant," I told him, "and have respect, why did your son come to steal the *muchacha?* Don't talk to me about religion. Better that we leave things as they are. I don't authorize the union because I don't want to obligate María. Afterward there will be only problems. If the man is no good, [it will be] a predicament for María. And if María is no good for the man, it will be difficult for both of them. Better we leave it [be]."

He told me, "I'm ready to repay you for the educational expenses you spent on María in 1987."

I replied, "I'm not negotiating about a person; it's better not to talk to me about expenses that are already wasted."

That's the way it was with the father of José Mario Ramos García. I didn't authorize the marriage because I don't think it's right for a parent to obligate his daughter to get married. But I remained upset, serious, and pondering.

Then I asked my wife, "Why did María run off like that? Didn't you ask her? Could she be pregnant?"

"Well, she has told me no," my wife said. "She has told me no. Who knows what happened?"

Well, she didn't go to Quezaltenango to go to the *colegio* because without doubt she was already pregnant. That's why she went with the man. Without doubt, they have been living like that for some time; only we had not found out.

A little later I was regretful for having had the attitude to leave María's clothes at the commissary, but at the moment when these things happened, I don't know what I felt inside. More than anything else, I felt revenge. Little by little, however, some friends supported me by telling me to be more patient because many fathers of families have had this happen to them. This is what gave me more encouragement to endure this disaster in my family.

My daughter thought that her parents were angry. María and José Mario went to Guatemala City on 7 February. They planned to get a job without telling me or the *muchacho*'s father.

The *muchacho*, because he had been out of the army only for a short time, went to present his papers at the national police. They told him to have a little more patience, that within a few months he would get a job as a policeman. [This was a lie.]

Well, for María, a job did materialize, but if a woman already knows she is pregnant, why does she have to look for work? She talked to Señor Juan Roberto Romero Morales, who taught me how to bake bread. She knew that he is my friend, had his address, and went there.

Don Juan asked her, "Look, are you the daughter of Ignacio?"

"Yes," she said, and she explained what had happened to them and said that they wanted to marry.

"Ah, well, you're getting married. If Ignacio had sent you here, I could help you. You could work in the house, attend the bakery, and continue your studies. But if you're already coming with a husband, no thank you, because work for a man I don't have. Or I could have, but then I don't know what you would do in the house, because Ignacio is a man that I do respect. But here, I don't want you telling me stories, for naught."

Then María and José thought that living in the capital city was the same as living in their hometown. In the first place, they didn't have enough money to wait for a job to come open. Thus it was, and they lasted only three or four days in Guatemala City and returned home to the house of José Mario's father.

For a short time, they lived with José Mario's parents. I don't know for sure what the problem was, but on the night of 7 March, José Mario and María arrived to ask my wife to ask me to allow them to spend a few days in the house.

"Well, José Mario," I said, "imagine, you have to forgive me, but I will not receive you in my house."

"Why?"

"For all the damage that you have done to me. I am ashamed of all that. For me what you did is an embarrassment. I can't receive you in my house, and I don't have another house for you to live in," I told him. "I don't have [one], and I don't have *pisto* (money) to build you a house."

"Look," he told me, "better we leave and endure, even in a corridor of a house."

I still told him, "Look, why do you want to be with me? I am not a calm man. I am more *bravo* [irritable, bossy, rude] than your father. Your father is an hombre who doesn't scold, but I am *bravo*, because I don't want my children to be lazy."

"No," he told me, "I know your demeanor. I can live here with you. I will live with you here in the house. I will work, and we will see if María can continue studying."

Well, I didn't tell them to go again because there was nowhere else for them to go. Since they had already left his father's place, no one else would let them in.

"Okay, you can live here," I told him.

He didn't want to study, but since he already had a commitment with the woman, I told him, "Well, here, half the day you are going to work. From seven to eleven o'clock you will work, and at one o'clock you will go to the institute, because María has lost her studies and you will be the same. The two of you [losing your studies] would be foolish. Better, if she has lost, maybe you will win. Continue studying your [*instituto*] *básico* [courses]."

"That's fine," he said.

He went to enroll in the *instituto básico,* but it was an order of mine that he should continue studying at least the third year of *básico.* And that's what he did.

One suffers with one's children. A parent sometimes asks, "Why do I have so many kids?" But what more can he do when his children are growing up. And the bigger they are, the bigger their problems.

The Problem of Catholic Factionalism
3 August 1987 to 20 March 1988

Only eighty-five families remained in favor of what Padre José is teaching. They always agreed with the father to correct their faults, and they didn't want to be against him when the big group began an all-out fight to discharge him. The small group remained quiet. Their desire was to celebrate prayer in their houses, to visit families according to what the Bible says, and to attend mass on Sundays in San Martín. The small group was in favor of the priest and the bishop. But this small group was oppressed by the big group, which threatened six families of the small group with death.

There was a lot of criticism by the large group, which went to many places in the country asking that the church disown the priest, José McCall. But everything was difficult for them. Then they went to Tiquisate to talk with the political priest and Guatemalan Andrés Girón de León, so that he would come to San José to officiate mass, now that they don't want the mass of José McCall or Father Gino Barillas Tecún. They want a priest who complies more with their wishes, that is, one whom they can direct and who won't give orders in the church. But according to the canonical laws, the priest has the right to be in control of the church. Only the bishop is the legal jefe of his diocese; that is, each bishop has as his responsibility two or three departments according to the number of Catholics. In the diocese of Sololá, the bishop has under his hand forty-eight priests for three departments, which are Suchitepéquez (Mazatenango), Chimaltenango, and Sololá. Monseñor Benando Gálvez Chamorro is unable to order priests to celebrate mass outside his three departments.

Thus the bishop of Escuintla is not able to order the priest Andrés Girón de León to come to officiate mass in San José either. But since Father Girón de León is a priest who also likes politics, his ambition is to become a candidate for the president of the republic. Father Girón de León is famous for being the leader of the campesinos of the south coast and of the western part of the country. His fight is the expropriation of the private *fincas* to give them to the campesinos. This fight he began in May 1986 when he organized a march from Santa Lucía Cotzumalguapa to the central park of the capital city of Guatemala to demand that the government expropriate the farms for the campesinos. In this march there were more than five thousand campesinos. Thus it was when Father Girón de León became famous. He was heard on television and seen in the press.[16] Also, in the large group in conflict with the church, there are five political parties seeking to fulfill their own ambitions; that is to say, the directors of the Partido Movimiento de Liberación Nacional, the Unión del Centro Nacional [UCN, Union of the National Center], the Democracia Cristiana [Guatemalteca, DCG, Guatemalan Christian Democracy (Christian Democrats)], the Partido Revolucionario [Guatemalteco, PRG, Guatemalan Revolutionary Party], and the Partido Socialista Democrático [PSD, Social Democratic Party].

The small group [in San José] doesn't have a political party. They are just Catholics who profess their Christian faith.

To look for a solution to the problem, the director of the socialist party [PSD] went to Tiquisate to ask Father Girón de León to help in the fight for the poor but with the condition that he had to come to celebrate mass in the church of San José. They expounded the theme that they are the true religious persons and that Padre José McCall doesn't want to celebrate mass. "We are abandoned," they said.

When Father Girón de León heard these things, he thought they were true and said, "Whatever it costs me, I'm going to celebrate a holy mass in San José," without his knowing or recognizing the caprice of these men.

On Monday, 3 August 1987, Father Andrés Girón de León was to arrive at ten o'clock in the morning. Because of a delay on the road, he didn't come until two o'clock in the afternoon. The big group was now murmuring against Father Girón de León, and they wanted to hit some of the members of the small group, saying that some of the group had given Father Girón de León an excuse not to come. But the truth was that they were delayed because of [trouble with] their vehicle.

When Father Girón de León finally arrived, they received him jubilantly and forgot about the murmuring. I considered them hypocrites and liars. What was indeed strange for us was to see a priest who went around with armed guards.

Father Girón de León came to town and entered the Catholic church with two well-armed national policemen. The father walked with a pistol on his waist, so he was thought to be a violent priest, because the person who walks around wearing arms (a pistol) has something that is going to serve to kill. To speak more clearly, if a campesino goes to the *campo* where he works, he carries his hoe, his pickax, and his machete because these are the things that are going to serve for his work. Now, for one who is dedicated to the service of God, he should go around with sacred things like the Holy Bible and other books to evangelize the people. We have seen bishops and priests who always wear around their neck the image of crucified Jesús but never wear a pistol on their waist, as Father Andrés Girón de León is doing. Many of the big group kept silent, demonstrating their disapproval when they saw the weapons.

In his preaching, Father Girón de León said that he is on the side of the poor, to help them and to do something for the good of the church. He said it was possible for him to be the padre of the church of San José and not to be afraid of foreign priests who are oppressing the Indian people. Finally, he said that on 24 August he would have to come again to celebrate a mass in honor of San Bartolomé Apóstol.

Monseñor Benando Gálvez Chamorro and the two priests, José and Gino, saw that the large group didn't want Father Gino to arrive to celebrate mass in the church. And as the small group is obedient and respectful of the authority of the church, it was thus when Monseñor Gálvez ordered that a *galera* [a large shed that has benches and an altar in front] be constructed so that Father Gino could come to give mass to those who wanted to attend without worry.

Then they began to construct the shed on 27 July in the *sitio* of Andrés Ramos Toc. Andrés is very religious and has a big *sitio,* and he said to construct the shed there. They did the construction collectively; some gave money, others gave *lámina* [pieces of sheet metal for roofing], others gave wood, some gave timber, and the masons among them gave their labor, as did others who did not give materials. In all it took nineteen days to construct the shed, or chapel [oratory], which was dedicated on 15 August. On the morning of this same day a mass was celebrated by the new father, Gino Barillas Tecún. It was pleasant for the small group, but the big group threatened to burn the oratory before its inauguration.

On this day there were no benches. The people of San Martín, San Jorge, San Benito, and Tzancuil sat on the floor to hear the sermon. Later benches arrived donated by persons who didn't want to give their names for fear that something bad might happen to them. I didn't go to work with them, but I sent some *muchachos* to help them, although I did go on the day of the dedication. I also went with them at night to see and hear what was happening each day between these two groups. The small group wanted me, but the big group marked me as an enemy of the people for not being with them. But the truth is that I don't want to mistreat anyone or be against the religious people because I'm neither religious nor secular, just a campesino who wants to observe and distinguish the good from the bad, or, better said, an observer of what is happening.

The construction of the shed, or oratory, cost Q3,300, without taking into account the labor. The chapel isn't elaborate, just ordinary. Monseñor Gálvez ordered that mass be celebrated each Saturday afternoon and Holy Rosary every day in the afternoon. And so it was done.

On 8 November fifty-four *Joseños* went on foot from San José to Sololá and from Sololá took a bus to [Zone 1 in] Guatemala City. Among them were men, women, and children, and they went to the Metropolitan Cathedral [a large cathedral in the plaza next to the national palace]. At four in the afternoon Radio Fabulosa and Radio Nuevo Mundo said that the fifty-four Indian *Joseños* arrived to occupy the Metropolitan Cathedral to pressure the archbishop of Guatemala, Próspero Penados del Barrio, to take steps to remove Father José McCall. The *Joseños* said that they were demonstrating because they don't want him anymore, that they are tired, and that they never have found a solution to the problems they are suffering. At night it was on television on Channel 3, "Aquí El Mundo," and on Channels 7 and 11. We were able to see it, but the two priests, José McCall and Gino Barillas Tecún, were insulted.

They pressured Archbishop Próspero Penados del Barrio a lot. They told him they would not leave the cathedral if he would not find a solution to the problem that they had been suffering. The archbishop told them that they weren't going to gain anything by taking over the cathedral, just a disobedience to God. And he told them to vacate the cathedral because mass was going to be celebrated, and if not, well, the authorities would have to intervene. The archbishop also said that he would ask Monseñor Gálvez to talk to him tomorrow, the ninth.

Thus it was when the fifty-four *Joseños* vacated the Metropolitan Cathedral. These things were seen on television. They [the news media] insulted Monseñor Gálvez and the two priests, José and Gino, claiming [that they were] thieves and pillagers of the church. But the truth is that nothing was lost in the church.

On 9 November 1987 many *Joseños* left for a meeting in Sololá with those who were coming from Guatemala in an attempt to get Monseñor Gálvez to assign a priest directly to San José. They did not want a priest based in San Martín to serve them. On this day hundreds of *Joseños* went, and the bishop of Sololá, Monseñor Benando Gálvez Chamorro, attended to them.

On television and in the press, the bishop and two *Joseños* agreed that the people would have to receive the priest, Gino Barillas, who would be in charge of officiating mass in the church in San José. The *Joseños* said that they would receive Father Gino Barillas Tecún with much pleasure but with the condition that he would not reside in San Martín so that he would not be manipulated by Father José McCall. The bishop said that it was well that the father had to travel from Panajachel to San José to do the mass, while the *Joseños* construct a house for the father in which to live.

These things were not worth it, because Bishop Gálvez already had offered and ordered that Father Gino be in charge of the church in San José. It was a pity that the ringleaders of these problems had not made it clear to the rest of the people, to the point of saying that they had won a fight because finally they had been given a priest [of their own] for the town of San José. But this was false. They made a lot of trips and spent a lot of money to come to the same conclusion.

On this morning when they arrived at the pier, they lit many *bombas* [bombs, fireworks shot from mortars] and firecrackers. They lit about a thousand quetzales [worth] as a show of joy that they had been able to ignore the father based in San Martín. Monseñor Gálvez had told them that Padre Gino would take possession to officiate the mass as the person in charge of the church no later than 15 November, and he said it would never be like a parish, that the parish would continue being in San Martín.

On 25 November 1987 Monseñor Benando Gálvez, Padre José McCall, and Padre Gino Tecún arrived at the new chapel. Together with the small group they entrusted themselves to God for the unification of the [big and small] church because already months had passed since the division between those who say they are [true] Catholics and the small group. After the prayer by means of a processional hymn, they arrived again at the church. The opposing group was very angry, because they saw that the padre whom they hated the most also had come. In the mass, the bishop said not to have any more division within the Catholic Church and to reconcile with Father José for all that the people of San José had made public in the press and on radio and television—a calumny before the whole world. They said that the father had to pardon all the calumnies and injuries caused to his person and that this was a temptation that the devil had prepared. In this mass not a single *Joseño* spoke; they just listened to the sermons and advice of the bishop and Father Gino. Father José didn't say a single word.

Thus it was when the two groups united, but as usual the big group was contemptuous. They didn't want to see the small group inside the church because they had been unable to remove Father José. Thus the small group arrived at the church fearful, because the big group considered them enemies.

At seven at night when the small group began to pray the Holy Rosary inside the church, four of the ringleaders of the big group belonging to the revolutionary party turned out the lights that illuminated the interior of the church. The people praying were in total darkness.

Father Gino arrived every Sunday very early by launch to give mass from 22 November, but a little later he got tired of rising early in the morning. He remained sleeping in the parish of San Martín. That is when the Catholics became angry again because they didn't want the father to sleep in San Martín. But he did this because San José is a poor town and there was no place for him to sleep here.

Then the murmuring began. The father told them to change their attitude for a better spiritual life, but my people didn't want to obey the priest; they always wanted to give the orders inside the church, and they didn't respect the orders of the priest. Finally, the padre said good-bye to San José and left for San Juan Comalapa.

The last mass was celebrated on 31 January 1988. Then the Catholics headed anew to the bishop to ask for another priest. Monseñor Gálvez conceded and authorized Father Samuel Cristóbal to officiate the mass in the church. Father Cristóbal took possession on 7 February 1988; that is, he celebrated the first mass on this date, and then he said good-bye on 20 March. He only celebrated seven masses. He said in his sermons that he didn't want to put up with being among people who didn't want to change for the better. He said that they should stop murmuring, have no more drunken parties, indulge no more in adultery, do no more stealing, try not to abort, and say yes to life.

This Sunday, 20 March, the *principales* Juan Mendoza and Juan Pantzay told Father Samuel Cristóbal that they were elders of the town and that they were not dominated by a priest and that they were the ones who maintain order in the town and in the church. Then Father Samuel Cristóbal said, "We are through with performing the mass. The *principales* can do it themselves."

And that's the way it went from November until March. There have been two priests. They don't want to put up with working with the Indian people. It's difficult for my Tzutuhil people to change, because they have been doing their *costumbres* since childhood.

For this Holy Week, the Catholic Actionists marched again to ask the bishop for a priest to officiate the mass for this best week, but it wasn't possible. The bishop said he was going to do whatever possible to look for a padre for San José. But they say that none of the priests wants to be in San José, only because they learned about the false accusations against Father José [aired] on television. They say that we, the Tzutuhiles, are bad, but the truth is that not all of us are.

Holy Week
1 to 3 April 1988

During Holy Week I was baking bread, but as I have said, here in Guatemala the prices of ingredients for bread have gone up. What we use to make sweet bread, or, say, bread of lard [made with cottonseed oil], costs Q47 a *quintal* [100 pounds]. Now, to make good-quality bread, it costs Q57 a *quintal*; a twenty-five-pound box of lard costs Q33, a *quintal* of sugar costs Q40. Thus to do a big job takes money. But this morning I didn't have the money. I had to go to my friend Roberto to ask whether he would lend me Q100 for a week. He did.

The bread that we made we sold in Santiago Atitlán and also in my town. By the grace of God, during the week, we earned Q150, but it required my working at night with my children. Saturday we added up the expenses for the material, and indeed we earned Q150. In the morning I went to return the Q100 to Roberto.

In the afternoon of this same day my friend Félix Quiché arrived to offer me three hundred cut stones for Q35 each hundred. I had to buy them because we needed them to finish a wall.

The old folks say a refrain, *El que escucha consejo de un viejo llegará a ser un viejo* [He who listens to the advice of an old person will become an old person]. It happened this Holy Thursday, 1 April 1988, with Señor Abraham Temó Pantzay, who is addicted to alcohol. He never had any peace because he was held prisoner by alcohol and tobacco.

They say that Holy Wednesday he was drinking a lot. Then Holy Thursday dawned. He said that he was going to take honey from the bees on Gramal Hill and that it would be better for his children to go with him because he had seen a lot of honey inside a tree.

"Very well," said his woman, and she gave him his breakfast. Then they began to arrange his things to be carried—a hatchet, three-gallon tin cans, and large, plastic vats in which to put the honey. The man told his woman that he would return in the afternoon, and they would go to sell the honey. But before leaving, they say his mother told him not to go because it was a sacred day and he shouldn't work. His mother told him, "Remember that our forefathers never worked on these days."

The hombre, however, did not pay any attention to his mother and had to fulfill his wishes. With him went his two sons, Arno and Gabino. They took another companion with them on the road, without knowing what was going to happen.

Happily they climbed the summit until arriving at the place where the bees were located. Abraham lit a cigar and began to smoke while he was resting. Then they prepared to fell the big tree, but when the bees sensed Abraham was cutting the tree, they swarmed out, persecuting the man and his sons.

The bees were dangerous, and they came out in droves and began to sting them. Without doubt because of the great pain of the stings,

Abraham and one of his sons fell into a barranca that was three hundred meters deep. The other son and the *muchacho* who fell ran to the other side, and nothing happened to them. But poor Abraham was stretched out dead over the rocks. What was most strange was that his son Arno fell the same distance but only was bruised. He didn't die. The news about Abraham was heard Holy Thursday at noon.

This resulted in a serious problem, because it was necessary for the justice of the peace to retrieve the cadaver. But the [new] regional justice of the peace has his office in Panajachel, and the dead man's family wasn't able to pay for the cost of the launch that would take the justice to San José and would return with Abraham's remains to the hospital in Sololá for the legal examination [autopsy]. This family didn't even have money to buy food for themselves, much less pay for a lot of mortuary expenses.

Thus the mother of the deceased asked the mayor and the secretary to do them the favor of retrieving the body without the presence of the justice of the peace. It's certain that the law doesn't permit the mayor to retrieve the body because it wasn't in his jurisdiction. But the mayor and the secretary decided in favor of the family. Together with many residents they went to where they found the body, carried it to the town, left it in its house, but didn't send it to the hospital, because the truth is that it wasn't convenient for them. In the death certificate they said he died of a sickness in his house. There was no mention that he died from falling into a barranca because the law prohibited them from doing what they had done. That is to say, the mayor and the secretary had compassion for the mother and the wife of the fallen Abraham.

Abraham Temó Pantzay was buried on Holy Saturday [3 April]. It was the mayor and the secretary who did the family a big favor. But a few days later the mayor and the secretary were denounced before the justice of the peace in Panajachel for acting outside the law. Then the justice of the peace sent the case before the justice of the [court of] first instance in Sololá to investigate and proceed against the mayor for overstepping his office.

At that time the mayor was Benjamín Peña Cholotío. First he was called before the justice of the peace of Panajachel to declare whether it was true that he had ordered the burial of Señor Abraham Temó Pantzay who had been killed by falling into a barranca on Holy Thursday in the place of Gramal. They say that the mayor denied it, because if he had admitted it, at the same moment he would have been imprisoned. Then the justice of the peace was upset because he didn't have a reason to imprison him. Within a few days he was called to the court of first instance to declare whether it was certain that he and the secretary had ordered the burial of Abraham Temó Pantzay. The mayor saw that the situation was grave, and he had to tell the kin that if the justice interrogated them, [they should] say that Abraham had died from a sickness and not from falling into a barranca. The poor mayor and his secretary fought to dispel these accusations. When everything was calmed, the justice of the peace and the justice of the [court of] first instance told the mayor that he had been denounced by Juan Mendoza Ovalle, but this was at the end. The truth is that they struggled a lot to dismiss the charge that Señor Juan Mendoza had made. Also, the kin were frightened because, according to the justice, the kin and residents present or participating in the burial of the body would all be imprisoned.

The truth is that Señor Juan Mendoza doesn't get along well with the mayor because of politics and religion. Benjamín didn't get involved in the problems of the church, and for that reason, Señor Juan is looking for a way to put him in prison, which is a promise that he had made before a majority of the townspeople.

It's true that the mayor had committed a crime, but also a majority of the people had witnessed that the deceased had not been killed by someone, that he had died only because he had fallen into a barranca. The residents pleaded with the mayor to bury him as if he had died of an illness to avoid the expenses of sending the body to Sololá for an autopsy. Later this cost the mayor and secretary many days. And they truly were afraid.

An Unusual Case in Santiago Atitlán, Holy Friday
2 April 1988

This case was reported in *El Gráfico* and on Radio Nuevo Mundo and Radio Fabulosa. And also the news ran through the towns of San Martín, San José, San Jorge, San Benito, and without doubt in many other towns of Guatemala.

The news says that a señora and her son, Jaime Quinto, were sleeping happily in their humble little house after celebrating Holy Thursday, that is to say, after they had returned from the [town] procession. When the señora woke up, she heard something walking on the roof of the house. The woman was frightened and then woke up her son, and he put on his clothing and went outside with a machete in his hand. When he was looking over the house, they say that a dog was walking over the *lámina,* and the dog wanted to get down. But the *muchacho* was watching to see where it would get down and what it would do when it got off the roof. Finally, the dog jumped from the roof to the ground, and that is when the *muchacho* hit it with a machete until it was dead. But the news says that is when the *muchacho* saw that the dog changed into a woman, but the hands remained like the hands of a dog. The boy went to get his mother to come out and see this strange thing. It was thus when the neighbors began to wake up, and then they went to advise the authorities. The news says that the cadaver they buried had the body of a woman but the hands of a mutt.

The poor *muchacho* [who killed the dog-woman] went to jail. What is not known is whether he still is in prison or whether they set him free. This is why it is said among the Tzutuhil people there always are persons who sink to doing wicked deeds. The old folks tell us that there are *characoteles,* but we thought that it was just a story. Now in these times we are observing that the old folks are telling the truth. And it is certain that there are female [and male] *characoteles.*

A New Weaving Project
18 to 25 May 1988
My main work is in the fields. Today we were working in Xebitz. While Ramoncito [diminutive for Ramón] and José Mario were cleaning the field to plant corn, Susana Julia and I were planting forty-three sprigs of coffee. This was just an experiment to see whether coffee would grow in this hot place. When we finished planting the coffee sprigs, I began working with Ramón and José Mario. We ate a lunch of cold tortillas in the field, as we campesinos are accustomed to doing. Our lives are hard. Once in a while our wives give us good food to take to the fields, but more often our lunch is cold tortillas with salt and water. And this is how it was on this day. Because it was hot, we drank a lot of water from the river. There are many stones in this place, and the sun burns hot.

Thus were the days, Thursday, 19 May, Friday, 20 May, and Saturday, 21 May. José and Ignacito didn't go to work with us because they were at home sick with a fever and aches in their muscles. Last week,

Ramón had suffered the same thing, but this week he was able to work with us in the fields.

Also, my daughter was sick with a high temperature and a lot of coughing. She just drank water with *manzanilla* [*Matricaria chamomilla,* chamomile]. It wasn't possible to pay a doctor or buy medicine.

But we aren't the only ones. From the beginning of this month, many children and adults have been sick. But little by little this situation is being alleviated.

In San Martín many children and adults died. It seems that it is an epidemic. In the first days, it begins with a headache and a high temperature, and blood comes out of the nose, and they die. In San Jorge a lot of people have died because of the same illness.

On this day, 24 May 1988, I feel sad. We don't have any money. It's certain that I have crops in the field, but until the harvest, I am unable to earn money. This money, however, serves for the year. For that reason, my heart is sad. Also, it's that my two sons have the occupation of making *cortes* with the looms, but in this month, there are hardly any sales. The same is happening with the bakery. There isn't any business. The majority of the people are suffering the same thing. The people are not buying either clothing or bread because the coffee harvest turned out to be bad. Well, we have corn, but there are people suffering even more than we—what they make daily they have to spend to buy corn.

My wife saw that I am sad because of my children's work. I don't want them to waste time and to continue working in the fields. The truth is that I don't want them to suffer as I have suffered. Then my wife chatted with the women who are working on a project, Artesanía, of typical weavings. She told the jefes that we have two sons who are able to make *jaspes* [tie-dyed figures or designs in thread or yarn]. She says that the jefes told her, "We want an example of their work. We need persons who can do the work here in San José. It will make it easier."

Then my wife arrived to tell me what they had said. But I hardly have money to buy the material. We have some material, but it is for making *cortes*. Then I asked José and Ramón if they wanted to work on this project. They told me to get the money to buy the material needed for this project and they would work.

Thanks to God that when I had received checks from my friend

6 ● JOSEÑO

Jaime Sexton I had put a little money in savings in the Banco Agrícola Mercantil in Panajachel. Each time I find myself without money I go back to the bank to withdraw part of my small savings. At this point, I only had Q274.80 in the account. At noon, I left to go to withdraw Q120 from the bank, and then I went to Paxtocá to the house of Juan Domingo Toc. I decided to stay there because it was already too late to return home. I slept on the floor and got up early the next morning, 25 May.

From Paxtocá I went on foot to Salvajá. There I bought the dye, thread, *guindana* [rolls of special cotton thread] to tie the *jaspes,* and a pair of gloves to dye the thread.[17]

Then I went to Quezaltenango to get María's bed where she had been living when she was a student. The owner had sent me two telegrams and even a letter telling me to come get her things.

When I arrived at Quezaltenango, I was overcome with sadness. Tears fell from my eyes because I had never thought I would be coming to get her things before she had finished her degree. I had thought that some day she would be a teacher and would be able to help herself. But it wasn't so.

Incredible But True
Month of June 1988

In earlier times my pueblo was quiet, because there weren't many people living in the town. One time during Christmas, my aunt and her husband [Agustín] began to drink a lot of *aguardiente.* The twenty-sixth dawned, and they continued drinking all day. In the night some friends arrived to sip liquor with them, but since they had finished off the *guaro* (liquor), about 10:00 P.M., my aunt's husband made me go out to fetch *aguardiente* in a cantina, which formerly was the only cantina in my town. It then was the cantina of Don Pablo Ixtamer, near the cemetery. I didn't want to go, but if I disobeyed Agustín he would hit me. To speak more clearly, he always would make me go to buy *aguardiente* in the late hours of the night, and when there wasn't any to buy in San José, he would send me to San Martín. The truth is that I would feel a great fear when I traveled through the streets because I had to walk in the darkness without a flashlight or candle.

Thus it was that night. Fearfully, I left the house. The streets were all empty; no one was out walking. They gave me the money for six *octavos* [eighths of a liter], when in 1957 to 1958 an *octavo* of *aguardiente*

7. *A white roll of* guindana *with tied and dyed thread on a table.*

was worth about twenty-eight centavos. I passed the first block and took the street to the cemetery that led to the cantina, where I heard a big wind that was banging the gate of the cemetery. The wind was too strong, shaking the branches of the trees and [making] a big whirlwind in the street. I heard the whirlwind come toward me, and it scared me a lot. It's true that the night wasn't too dark because the stars were clear and the moon was out, but since it was nighttime, it certainly scared me. The air was only in one place, shaking the trees with force, and there was a great whirlwind of dust in the road, near the gate to the cemetery. I was waiting for the strong wind to subside. I stopped about ten minutes in the crossing near the house of Ignacio Bizarro Ramos, but I wasn't able to reach the cantina because it's near the cemetery. I heard a strong gust of air pound on the door and sweep away the stuff in the street where I was standing. I ran some steps and hid at the door of Ignacio's house to see what the strong wind was doing. I saw well that the wind, in the form of a hurricane, carried an hombre about a meter off the ground. It was a ghost, or spirit, who was wearing typical[-style] trousers. In the opening of his jacket, I could see well his shirt and scarf on his right shoulder. I also could see clearly that he was wearing a Texan sombrero [expensive felt hat]. What I could not see was his face. All of it [the image] was the color purple, like a ghost. It came about seven to ten steps from where I was standing. I was terrified, thinking many things at this moment. Finally, I remained calm and surprised at what I was seeing. One more thing—when it came near me I thought it might have been a drunk swept away by the strong wind. Not so. What is certain is that it was a spirit. I watched the ghost for a *cuadra* and a half until it reached the municipal hall, where it let out a cry like a drunk person. This scared me even more. But as I lost sight of the wind and the ghost in the distance, I regained my composure and went on to the cantina.

Don Pablo was sleeping. He got up and opened the door, and I ran inside, frightened. I told him what had happened to me and that I had seen the form of a man swept away by the force of the wind. Don Pablo was surprised and told me to be careful when walking at night and to carry a cross of *ocote* [pine with resin] in my hand so that evil spirits will not bother me. I didn't want to leave the cantina because I was so afraid. Don Pablo told me, "Go without fear. I'm going to illuminate this block with my flashlight." Only then did I leave the cantina.

When I left the block where the cemetery is, I ran down the street until I reached our house. Upon entering, I told my aunt's husband what had happened to me, but he acted as if it had been nothing.

Dawn came the following day, and I was thinking something bad would happen in the pueblo or to me. I was young, but I set to meditating. By the grace of God, by midday my fear went away.

In the afternoon of this day, I went to the soccer field to play soccer with other *muchachos*. We stopped playing at 6:00 P.M. While we were returning on the road, the death knell sounded in the church. When we asked the people, "Who died?" they told us that Señor Benjamín Cholotío had fallen. But this was strange because this man had not been sick. I had seen him myself the twenty-fifth of December, Christmas Day.

It's positive that this señor always dressed in typical clothing, wearing typical trousers, a shirt of *jaspes,* and always a jacket, and always carrying his *sute* [head cloth] on his shoulder. Without doubt the ghost that I saw during the night of the twenty-sixth that was swept away by the wind was the spirit of the fallen Benjamín Cholotío.

The family of Benjamín Cholotío said that their father had not been sick. It was a sudden death. Benjamín's woman, Carolina Jiménez, said that the death of her husband was because of the Ronda del Mundo [Round of the World, or Earth]. They say that the Ronda del Mundo passes at six in the morning, twelve noon, six in the afternoon, and twelve midnight. A dangerous wind passes that is called Pastor del Mundo [Pastor of the World], or Ronda del Mundo. It looks only for bad and disobedient persons, especially adulterers. The old people of the town said and reassured me that Benjamín Cholotío was killed by the Ronda del Mundo. His woman said the same thing, because on this day, 26 December, Benjamín left the house early to go to the house of a lover named Rosa García. His wife said that every time he left home, he headed to the house of his landlady (mistress) and that he had been living this way for a number of years until finally he lost his life because of the bad way he was living. They said that Benjamín had a lot of women. The truth is that he was not religious, neither attending mass nor the evangelical sects.

What is the Ronda del Mundo?

It is a wind that passes four times a day—6:00 A.M., 12:00 noon, 6:00 P.M., 12:00 midnight. If a person is walking down the street, he or she has to move aside because he or she will die. The wind is to clean the world of sins of men and women. A person should not have two to three women because it is easy to fall to the Ronda del Mundo. Another name for this is the Mala Hora del Mundo [Bad Hour of the World]. This seems to be not a god but a force, or power.

When a Catholic dies, it is the custom to carry his body to the [Catholic] church for a last good-bye. From there they carry the deceased to the cemetery to bury him. And if the person was an evangelical, they carry him to the [Protestant] church. But this time when Don Benjamín Cholotío died, the religious people didn't allow his body to enter the [Catholic] church. His body stayed at rest only in front of the church near the door, but not inside, and he was carried to the cemetery. This happened because he didn't depend on a religion.

Benjamín's woman said that before he died he arrived home and suddenly vomited blood. His body swelled up, and they couldn't take off his clothes. They had to cut them off with scissors. When he died, they placed him in his coffin and nailed it shut, but the body continued swelling until it burst. So as not to lose the coffin, they had to tie it with lassos. For us youngsters it wasn't strange because we didn't know anything, but for the adults it was [a cause for] gossip. They said that it was a death as a punishment for his sins, that is, it happened because of the Ronda del Mundo.

They say that when a person commits adultery in the mountains, at the moment he is having sex, the Pastor, or Ronda del Mundo, hits his back like a bullet, carried by the strong wind. The shot destroys his intestines, kidneys, and liver, and for that reason, he vomits a lot of blood. There is a cure, however. The man must confess to his woman what has happened. This was a real deed, not just a story, and the people still remember it.

What happens to the woman?

They say that if the man is clever he can hear the strong wind coming and change positions, and the woman will receive the shot in the back. Otherwise the woman is protected because she is shielded by the man.

I'm going to write about another similar case that happened in the month of June of this year of 1988, a serious act that happened to Juan Gordillo Solís. His wife, Elisa Elena Ramos y Ramos, didn't know he had another woman by the name of Catarina. They say that Juan left early in the morning, telling his wife he was going to graze his horse in Chojox. And Catarina did the same—leaving in the morning, saying that she was going to go sell things in the villages. They met in a place in the mountains and gave each other pleasure. But they already had been doing these things for some time. When he returned from Chojox, he went to work at the church, but at midday he arrived home to eat lunch, and suddenly his stomach and face swelled; and then the rest of his body swelled. He stopped eating lunch because of the swelling and felt as if his stomach was being destroyed. He hurried to the hospital of Sololá on 9 June, but the doctors could not diagnose what illness he had. From there, he went to Quezaltenango. But also the doctors of Quezaltenango could not determine the sickness, and he returned to San José. His wife asked him if he had committed a sin with a woman, and he told her no. He didn't want to say yes. They called a shaman [Octavio Toc] to divine the cause of Juan's suffering. The shaman said that it was a serious illness and that within a few days he would die because the sickness had to do with the Ronda del Mundo. And the shaman told him to confess to his wife that he had committed adultery with another woman. But Juan didn't want to say it because without doubt he was afraid of his wife. The shaman only said that it was the Ronda del Mundo and that sometimes men could last one day and that sometimes they could bear it up to twenty days, but no more. They vomit blood, their body swells up, and they die for sure.

When Juan felt gravely ill, he called his woman and asked her to pardon him and said it was true that he had committed a sin in the mountains in a place called Chojox and that it would be better if they cured him because the medicine of the doctors had not helped. Each day his body swelled more. He said he had committed adultery in the mountains with Catarina Pérez. His wife was frightened because she had believed that her husband was an honorable man.

It was at night. At dawn Juan's mother went to the house of Catarina Pérez to call her. Catarina came to Juan's house, and when she arrived the two of them confessed before Juan's wife the sin that they had committed.

It was arranged that they were going to cure him. Then Juan's wife went again to the shaman to tell him that the two had indeed confessed and that it was true what he had told them. Then the shaman told everything to Juan's señora—the *secreto* to cure her husband. This is what the shaman said:

> Go tell Catarina that she and you will leave early in the morn-
> ing to go to the place where she and Juan sinned. Tell her to
> carry a machete and to show you the place where her body
> (anus) was when they were having sex. With the machete
> excavate a *cuarta* [portion of dirt] eight inches deep. Grab a
> handful of soil and wrap it in a blouse. Leave as an enchant-
> ment two candles around the surface of the hole where you
> took out the dirt. Then return together. When you arrive
> where the sick person is, put the dirt inside a jug and pour
> water in it. Then give it to the sick person to drink. After
> drinking [the dirty water], tell Catarina to take off the sash
> of her *corte* and put it around the neck of the sick person.
> Put the blouse in which you bring the dirt on his head. This
> is the remedy. It is going to cure Juan, but Catarina has to sleep
> three nights on the floor near the bed of the sick person.

"Fine," said Elisa, and she did everything that the shaman said. During an early morning, the two women went to the place where the sinful act had taken place and scratched out the dirt. Catarina did what the shaman ordered. But there is one thing more. They say that when the adulterous woman was scratching the dirt, Juan's wife was planning to run her through with a knife on the sly because this damned woman had made her children suffer. But she changed her mind and remained calm. She decided it was better to cure her husband.

By everyone doing what the shaman said, Juan was able to recover his health. This case was new but true, and it was talked about in the whole town, because Catarina is very religious and enjoyed privileges in the Catholic church. For that reason, there was criticism. To insure that what the people were saying was true, one afternoon I sent my wife to Elisa's house to give her some bread, and she said that Elisa told her the same things that I have written here. Elisa is kin to my wife.

Father José Is Transferred to Panajachel
1 June 1988

On this date the reverend, Father José McCall, was transferred to Panajachel by the order of the bishop, Benando Gálvez. José was to be the vicar-general of the bishop, the one who goes to the pueblos to represent the bishop.

In this fiesta there was much solemnity. The father was given farewells by many religious groups of San Martín, San Benito, San Jorge, and the *caseríos* [hamlets] Jumay and Chabaj, and the small group of San José. There was a lot of sadness among the Catholic people, more for those who had much appreciation of him and listened to his preaching. Truly he wanted good things for us Indians, but we didn't want or appreciate what he wanted.

On this same date came the substitute for Father José, Father Ciro Pantzay, an Indian of Sololá, who stayed. His reception was solemn with the same persons who supported Father José.

Frankly, I didn't see these things, but my wife did because she went to the good-bye mass. When Father José got into the launch, hundreds of people—men, women, and children—were crying. Then they walked to the shore of the lake to say good-bye.

But also, many *Joseños* were happy when they heard that Father José had left because they had been fighting with him for more than a year, saying that they didn't want him anymore because he is an enemy of the town who by force wants to end the traditional *costumbres* of the *Sanjoseños* [people of San José]. It's true that those who remained sad were the ones from Jumay and Chabaj because they are poor and the only person who was concerned about them was Father José. He gave clothing to the men and the children, and he helped the women with food. And always he was saying to the men not to drink *aguardiente* and to think a little better for their children and their wives. Then the people of Jumay, Chabaj, and Rexabaj experienced a little change [because of Father José's influence], as did the people of Tzancuil.

Criticism of the Government among the People
15 to 17 June 1988

For us, it was a day of rest because it rained all day. We hardly worked. Always it is difficult for us to get firewood, and it's worse when it rains.

On this day they told all the students of the *instituto básico* that they have to march on 22 June, since it was the town's fiesta day. My youngsters asked me if I could buy them shirts and trousers so that they could participate in the parade. As a father I had to say yes. They were happy, and on the same afternoon they went to San Martín to arrange to have a seamstress make their pants and shirts. They now are working [and earning money], but they never just go alone to buy something. It's the custom in our house to discuss everything we do; that is, the children always discuss purchases with my wife and me.

There was a lot of criticism against the government from 14 to 17 June of this year of 1988. The press and the radio stations of the country said that the government of President Marco Vinicio Cerezo Arévalo continues to exploit the poor people, especially the people in the rural areas. Without consulting the people, by order of the Ministry of Economics, they raised the price of sugar. A *quintal* of sugar officially costs Q38, and a pound costs 40 centavos. In the towns it costs Q40 a *quintal* because they include the cost of transport. But in the *fincas* and the *aldeas* where there are no roads, it is 50 centavos a pound because of the extra transportation costs. Before this date sugar cost Q28 a *quintal*, 32 centavos a pound.

In San Martín there is a rich person by the name of Luciano Puzul Soto who had hundreds of pounds of sugar. When he heard that they had raised the price, he didn't want to sell any for the cheaper price of Q28. He sold it but at the new price. He says that he is a Christian, an evangelical pastor who sets a good example. But he is the one who exploits the indigenous people. Always this man has the idea to hoard things and take advantage of the situation when the government raises prices. He has something like a supermarket, four trucks, and a new car. I write these things because always the rich are those who take advantage of such situations. When the poor person is exploited each day, the rich person has a smiling face because it is more money for him.

A Child Is Run Over by a Truck during a Marriage Party
1 July 1988

On this day everything at first was happy at the marriage party in the house of the daughter of my uncle Bonifacio Soto. All of Bonifacio's kin were at this fiesta. The children were playing happily. Because of negligence, a grandson of Bonifacio was killed by a truck. This accident happened close to my house. I didn't see it because my sons and I were walking to work.

The child who died carried the name of his grandfather, Bonifacio. It was the second case for the justice of the peace in this municipality.

When we returned from work, they told us what had happened. The body of Bonifacio's grandson was carried to the hospital in Sololá for the examinations according to the law. It wasn't returned until nighttime. The parents were conscientious and didn't want to prosecute the driver who was responsible for the accident. He was just responsible for the expenses, and he was freed the next day.

José Mario, My Son-in-Law, Deserts María
2 July 1988

Last night all of us were cleaning and bunching onions to sell in the market. These were the same onions that we had planted when María left with the man. They had already ripened. On this day, 2 July, at 5:00 A.M., my wife and I were planning to go to sell them.

Since José Mario [the common-law husband of María] had already moved in with us, he said, "Look, where will you sell them?"

"In Santiago Atitlán," I told him, "or maybe Santa Ana."

"Ah, better in Santa Ana. I'll go sell them. Let me," he said.

"That's good, magnificent," I told him.

Then we fixed the onions.

"Put the bundle in a pickup, because there are pickups that go to Santa Ana to sell [things]," I said.

"No, better, I'll carry it *cargado* [on his back, to save money]. This cargo doesn't weigh anything."

"It's a lot for you," I told him. "Better put it in a pickup; it only costs one quetzal. Fifty centavos for the load, one quetzal for you. It would be Q1.50."

"Fine," he told me.

Then he began to place the onions in the net, preparing his cargo. After readying the cargo, he took off, leaving the bundle of onions in the corridor of the house all day. He didn't come back.

I asked my daughter if the two of them had had some problem. María told me that she didn't know where he had gone. In the afternoon of the same day they told us that José Mario was at his parents' house.

Then, so that his father would know that the two didn't have a single problem, I sent my wife to call the parents of José Mario. They said that his father had walked to San Benito la Laguna to preach. Thus it remained. Neither the parents nor the son arrived.

I didn't want to say bad things against José Mario. It might be that he would return. But I didn't have a word to justify, or to say, how or why he left without even saying good-bye. I won't say that it was because of too much work, because I also have children studying in the institute, and they work the same hours. My thoughts about the man are that he doesn't want to work. Instead he wants to stroll in the streets. It didn't suit him when I told him to work, because since he left my house he has only been loafing. Then [one day] I told him, "Thanks for leaving, because you don't want to work."

Thus it was. We really don't know why he left his woman. My wife and I thought the reason that José had left was that he had seen that María was pregnant or that perhaps he didn't want to work with us. But the truth is that no one knows what the reason was. The one who suffered a lot of scolding by her mother was my daughter because she had brought this man into our house. It's all the same to me because I don't have any interest in a son-in-law. Always I am accustomed to my work.

A Problem with My Son José That I Won't Forget
6 July 1988

This was a memorable day when I had a problem with my son José. But he was not to blame. For some days I had been angry for all that his wife, María, was doing, acting badly with us. On this day José answered me a little badly, and the truth is that I got angry and I told him, "Get out of my house! You can live where they will give you whatever you want! I don't want you to be with me because you will do the same thing your sister is doing. You can live very well away from my house by yourself. I don't want to support more people here because you are here with me and they are here with me. I don't want you to kill me with worry. Better for you to go get your own house. I know that I still have small children and that God and the law oblige me to support them, but you are already big. You can live by yourself."

He answered me with humility, "Papá, forgive me if I have offended you. With much pleasure I will leave the house. I know I can rent a house where we can live. Remember what you are doing to me. Never have I thought of leaving you. I thought I would continue living here and helping you with your jobs, but, if you wish, that's fine, I will obey you."

At the moment he told me these words, more refreshing, more serene, answering me with good words, I reflected a lot and told him, "No, M'hijo [Mi hijo, my son], better you don't go. You can live apart from me. You can live in the house where you are living, and your kitchen can be there where we are making bread."

"Really," he told me, "that's good. I respect you as my father. I'm not bad. I respect you very much. I know it's not that I have committed some big fault. Rather, it's because María has made you mad because she is behaving badly. My wife is behaving badly with you, and for that you will dispense with me. I don't think it's fair. Calm yourself."

"It's all right," I told him. On this same afternoon I reconciled with my son, because the truth is that his fault was not serious. I was the one who felt angry.

Later I thought that my son José is a reserved and obedient boy. Because of this problem, I didn't sleep the whole night long.

I thought that my son would be offended, but he wasn't, because he went with me to work in the village of Tzarayá. In a large family there are always many things happening. But what I think is that it's better to be calm and patient in order to come to a better understanding and do good things. In this fault that I had, I needed to meditate and ask for God's help.

Alcohol and Violence among Us Indians
11 July 1988

This has been the saddest day because of the suffering caused by alcohol. Among us Indians, there is this habit of alcoholism, which causes many to wind up in jail or dead. I believe the reason stems from the lack of education, that is, having no schooling or guidance.

A sad event happened in the vicinity of the Cakchiquel town of San Benito la Laguna. I heard the news that at 11:00 P.M. yesterday, four hombres were sipping clandestine firewater in a house. It's not known why these men began to argue. It's only known that one of them was killed with a knife. But they say he suffered a horrible death. The two were captured by the municipal guard, but the other got into a canoe to cross the lake because he works in Sololá. He never appeared again, however. Most people believe that he drowned, because his kin looked everywhere and they could not find him. The other two men were shipped to the prison in Sololá by the order of the regional justice of the peace. This was the first case that the [regional] judge heard in San Benito la Laguna. The name of the deceased is José Tambriz, son of Abraham Tambriz.

A few days later Abraham Tambriz went to Zone 14 of the military located in Sololá. He asked for the execution of the two assassins by a firing squad, but they told him that civil law and military law are separate [that the military had no jurisdiction in civilian cases]. This unfortunate man wasn't able to do anything [about the death of his son by appealing to the military].

My Son José Obtains a Job Preparing Thread
for the Weaving Cooperative
16 to 23 July 1988

I'm not wasting time but working very hard. I'm longing for a change at the end of this year. Finances are tighter because I'm not borrowing money to get by. I don't want any more debts. This year I have not asked for a loan for the value of the coffee harvest in advance, as in previous years. For that reason, we are struggling. We are doing our best with our work in the fields. It's true that in these times we are eating poorly, almost in full crisis. Only my wife is making a little money on her weaving project, but when we don't have money to buy thread for the project, she earns very little.

What is helping us in these days is that we have plenty of corn. When we have a great need, we sell it. But we don't want to sell any more because then we will be without corn, and we consume it in great quantities since our basic food is the tortilla.

I was pleading and praying to God that I need a job for my sons so that they can help us a little. God listened to me. When José sent the samples of his work to Artesanía, since God is so great and so blessed, the women realized that his work was better than what was coming from Salcajá. Then the women told the board of directors, "It's better to buy *jaspes* here with José because we are seeing that they are coming out better than the ones you are bringing from Salcajá." That is when the directors called José to tell him to make more *jaspes*.

We discussed with the directors what we would do. They told him to deliver twenty pounds of *jaspes* a week, but we told them that twenty pounds for José alone takes too much time to warp, tie, and dye. I told them that my two small sons will work with José because I need work for them. They are studying half a day and are working half a day in the fields.

It's true that I feel sorry for my sons because my work in the fields is hard. They are small and suffer. Thanks to God, on this day we agreed that all three would make the twenty pounds weekly.

We didn't have the money to buy twenty pounds of thread, so first we bought ten pounds. We warped, dyed, and sold the ten pounds. And with that money, we bought ten pounds more so that within the week, we could sell the twenty pounds of *jaspes*.

The sixteenth of July is the day that the boys delivered to the cooperative the first ten pounds of *jaspes*. On that day, we earned the first fifty quetzales. With that same money, I had to buy fertilizer because I needed it a lot for my crops, since I hadn't taken out a loan. Thus I was more in need of money in this month of July, because this is the month, along with August and September, that a man has to invest a lot in his fields, mainly buying fertilizer, to be able to harvest in November and December.

On this day when my sons delivered the first ten pounds of *jaspes*, I gave infinite thanks to God that the Lord has helped me a lot in this way, because principally it's a job, even though it's not for a long time, but it's worth more and it took us out [of dire straits] in a hurry because our money was almost spent. The truth is that Ramón and Ignacito

8. *Military base, Zone 14, on the road between Los Encuentros and Sololá.*

work for the project, but the only one with the commitment is José. I can't tie and dye. His brothers deliver to him, and he delivers the *jaspes* to the project. He is the one who receives the money. Then he gives my two young sons' share to me. The agreement is that each ten pounds of *jaspes* is worth Q80, but the expenses in material for the ten pounds is Q30. Since the agreement is for twenty pounds, the cost of the material is Q60. Thus, they—that is to say, José and his two brothers—earn Q100 for the value of their work. Thus José makes Q50 a week, and Ramón and Ignacito make Q50. Also, María helps her brothers.

The person who reads these pages may not believe it, but truly I felt that this blessing came from heaven. I bowed my head, giving thanks to God almighty for his ability. I said, "Honor and Glory to you, My Lord, you have heard the prayer of this humble sinner." I wanted to cry from happiness.

My wife also received her pay of Q36, which served us for kitchen expenses. Can you imagine, we didn't buy clothes, shoes, or other things.

Wednesday, 20 July, was the second time that my sons delivered the *jaspes*. We bought another *quintal* of fertilizer for the milpa.

On 21 July my *muchachos* remained working at home. Uncle José and I went to clean the milpa and to spread fertilizer. The twenty-second of July was the same, happily working in the fields.

Saturday, 23 July 1988, I didn't leave to work in the fields. I was working winding thread to help my wife and sons, encouraging them more. It's true that making *jaspes* is tiring, but I believe all work is difficult because in the beginning God said to man, "Eat bread earned by the sweat of your brow until you return to the ground from where you came, because you are of dirt and into dirt you shall be transformed."

Violence in Santiago Atitlán
24 to 26 July 1988

For a short time the situation of the *Atitecos* was calm, but soon it turned to violence again. On 24 July, a day before the titular fiesta, it was heard on the radio that on this day an hombre who was a military commissioner was shot in that town. The countrymen said that this man who was killed was a man of money. It had only been a month since he had finished building a house. It isn't known who killed him.

The same thing was heard on 25 and 26 July. That is to say, on the main day and on the second day of the fiesta, three persons were killed with firearms. The news says that one of them was an ex-soldier, but the only thing that is known is that no one is in jail because of these crimes. These four who lost their lives in these three days were pure Tzutuhiles.

The Mayor, Benjamín Peña Cholotío, Is Threatened with Death
7 August 1988

Benjamín Peña Cholotío is a member of Alcoholics Anonymous. The Partido [Democrático] de Cooperación Nacional [PDCN, Democratic Party of National Cooperation] selected him as their candidate for mayor. In his political campaign he was the most controversial person (enemy) of Juan Mendoza. During the two and one-half years, there was never peace [between them]. Juan said that Benjamín was a novice who was ignorant of the law and who couldn't administer justice as well as he could. But let's put to one side what Juan said. It's better to talk about what the administration of Benjamín Peña Cholotío actually did. Benjamín's administration included an evangelical, Alejo Rafael Bizarro P, as syndic; an evangelical, José Sandoval Coché, as first councilman; and a Catholic, Julián Chorol Ajpop, as second councilman.

This ex-administration did good things and showed respect for the *principales* and for the students of the *instituto básico*. They got along well with the teachers. We never saw one of them drunk. Every time that a resident came to ask for something, they always stood on their feet [in respect], serving everyone in the same way. They constructed a *circular* [an enclosure with a three-meter-high, stone-hewn fence] for the public cemetery. They did the stone paving of the road that goes to the lake. They also struggled to purchase two *cuerdas* of land in the *aldea* of Patzilín for the construction of schools. In Patzilín they bought property and established a soccer field that the poor villagers had been requesting for many years, which former mayors and their councils had ignored. In the pueblo they enlarged a school and constructed a new building that also serves for instruction. In addition, this administration accomplished works in the *aldeas* of Pachichaj and Tzarayá.

Formerly, when the young people wanted to play basketball in front of the Catholic church, they first had to obtain the permission of the president of Catholic Action. If the youngsters did not have his permission, they were escorted out of the *atrio* [atrium, courtyard] of the church. Benjamín's council constructed a basketball court in front of the old municipal hall. When they began to construct the basketball court, Juan Mendoza persuaded a group to protest against the said construction. They wanted to stop the work because the merchants stay in this *sitio* during each fiesta of San Juan Bautista. They said if the council didn't stop the work, then they would gather all the residents of the town to pull down the basket.

The municipality also contributed to the work of the students of the *instituto básico* by carrying sand and working as masons. Also the children from Castellanización [preceding first grade] to the sixth grade contributed by carrying sand. Indeed, there are teachers who donated their work on this project.

When the students heard the news that these men impeded the construction, they felt upset. But they continued working until they finished it. I was encouraging the students of the *instituto básico* and the teachers, and they encouraged the council. The basketball court was finished in December of the past year, 1987.

A little problem of the health of the boys and the children emerged, however. When the basketball court was finished, it was pleasant for the young people, but every afternoon until midnight they played, and many of them became sick from too much exercise.

That was the way Benjamín's administration was. Their enemies viewed them unfavorably because they had been able to accomplish things that their adversaries had not. Benjamín Peña was criticized by the big group [Catholic faction], saying that he was a thief and enemy of the town because he was not helping to throw out Padre José. But the truth is that Benjamín had never been a catechist or a religious person. Only at times did he go to mass.

Benjamín handed over the mayorship on 15 July of this year, 1988, to Juan Mendoza, but they [Juan and Benjamín] had a lot of problems. Juan Mendoza had sworn that when he obtained the mayorship, for sure Benjamín and his companions were going to be put in jail while he conducted an investigation about the money that Benjamín had stolen from the municipal treasury.

Then the people thought that what Juan had said was true. The people were alarmed to see whether Benjamín and his companions would go to jail. Juan took over the mayor's office in a big fury. He didn't want to receive amicably the documents of all the works of the previous administration, saying that these documents have been altered to hide embezzlement of money.

First he wanted to question them like prisoners, carrying out interrogations to see if they had taken money from the treasury. He told us, "We don't want to talk. The documents speak for themselves."

They said, "If we have taken money from the treasury, well, with much pleasure put us in jail."

Since Juan thought he was clever, he began to check the documents of the works that they had done. But all the documents turned out to be in good order. Then the new mayor was mocked because of all that he had said.

To the former administration, it was a mockery, because after the examined documents turned out to be in good order, they felt that they were vindicated. And they began to mistreat the new *alcalde*. They threw in his face all that he had done when he was mayor for the first and second time and what his father had done when he was mayor. Benjamín and his [former] council almost came to blows with Mendoza and his new, larger council [the new council had three syndics instead of one]. Little by little, however, the former council calmed down because the documents were in good order and for them there was no threat of spending time in prison.

Juanito Mendoza's enemies took him to be a liar because he was not able to prove his accusations against the former municipal corporation. Juan had said that when Benjamín and his companions were in jail, he would call the marimba players for a fiesta as a celebration for all of his sympathizers, but he was not able to put them in jail. Out of pure shame he didn't put up a marimba, nor did he have a fiesta. Those who had a fiesta were the former administration, that is, Benjamín and his companions, and they invited their friends. They also invited me, but I didn't go for lack of time.

On 7 August 1988, Benjamín Peña Cholotío came to visit me. He began to tell me what he had suffered when he was in the municipal tribunal. I asked him about the more serious cases.

He told me that during the time, that is, the two years that he was justice of the peace, the most common crimes among the *Joseños* were adultery and robbery. He told me that he sentenced many *Joseños* for these two infractions. The third problem was the drunks. I asked him if these cases were just in the town, and he told me no that they were also in the *aldeas*.

I asked him, "What were your thoughts about what happened in the Catholic Church in the last year?" I knew that he also was maltreated by the religious persons.

Benjamín told me he had to tell me about a case caused by the religious people that happened before he left the mayorship. Thus I was benefiting this night that he came to my house. Then Benjamín began to relate these things. He said that during this period, when the problems between the two factions of Catholics were severe, he suffered a lot because he also was threatened with death. He was sent anonymous letters that said within a short time he was going be killed. He received four letters that threatened him with death. Another letter arrived that told him to join the big group so that he would not suffer the consequences. But Benjamín acted as if nothing had happened.

He told me that when he suffered the most was when *desconocidos* [unknowns] came to take him from his house in the night. He was sleeping when he heard someone knocking. He got up and opened the door.

"Put your clothes on," they told him. "We're going to a meeting."

"Where's the meeting?" he asked.

"Come, don't talk anymore," they replied.

He couldn't deny them because it was dark and they were heavily armed. Benjamín said he didn't tell his wife so as not to alarm her and his children.

They took him to a place that is called Patzunoj, which is not far away, about an hour and fifteen minutes on a path up the mountain. They were walking with him in front and the men behind.

When they arrived on this mountain, they asked him, "Are you the municipal *alcalde?*"

"Yes, I am."

More than anything else, he was scared because it was at night and on the mountain. They ordered him, "Say truthfully, how many guerrillas there are in the town of San José."

"No one in the town is a guerrilla," he answered. "There aren't any. I only know that there are workingmen who struggle to earn the bread to sustain their families, but guerrillas there are none."

"No, don't be afraid here. Here you are with the army. We will take care of you; we will protect you, but you have to give us a list of how many bad people there are in your town, including the ones we already know."

"Again I say that there are none in my town, no guerrillas or vagabonds; rather, there are only men who work in the fields and who work for others, but they work honestly. There are no guerrillas."

"Well, we want to know," the jefes said, "how your town is, because we have received a list with names of people who they say are guerrillas, but the truth is we don't know. That's why we sent for you. How is the situation in your town? Some religious people handed us a list of people that they say are guerrillas."

"I don't know if there are guerrillas in the town. Look, for over a year the town has had problems with [the Catholic] religion. The town is divided into two groups. There is a large group that calls itself religious, and there is a small group that is truly Catholic. What happened is that the large group wanted the small group to join with them to go against the priest and the bishop. The large group didn't like that the small group separated from them. That's [what's] the matter."

"In which group are you?"

"As the mayor of a town, I don't have a group. I have to be with everyone."

"Don't be a liar. We know that you are on the side of Padre José's group. Also, the religious people accuse you, but we don't want justice for revenge. We want to verify whether there are guerrillas in the towns."

"There are no guerrillas."

"Truly?"

"Yes, truly," said Benjamín.

"Well, if it's like that, we want to be sure because right now we have six names of people of your town, but the army doesn't want to be unjust; rather, we want to carry out justice, but [we want to] be certain that they are guerrillas," they told Benjamín. "Do you know these men?"

"Yes," he told them, "I know them, but I know them as workingmen, not guerrillas." But Benjamín also was thinking about his own life, whether he would return alive or dead.

"This is the only reason we sent for you. Now you can go back," they told him.

And he returned by the same path accompanied by the same men to the edge of town.

In this talk they told him not to tell anyone in the town what had happened in the night. He said that these things happened in the year of 1988.

Then where did the soldiers go?

They returned to the mountain.

In the direction of Santa Ana or San Martín?

Between San Martín and Santiago Atitlán.

Then they were from Santiago Atitlán, the detachment there.

Without doubt, without doubt they were from Santiago Atitlán, because Benjamín says they had a list. What I don't know is the names of the people on the list. I asked Benjamín, but he didn't want to tell me.

"No," he told me, "because you know the names."

I have little doubt that they included me on the list because in reality they also have ostracized me a lot because of religion. But this was a foolish case in which they involved me since I haven't been religious, only a friend. What happened is that I didn't get involved with the large group and in anger they singled me out as a comrade of the small group.

But nothing happened to any of the six men on the list.

Look, by the grace of God, that's what Benjamín told me. "It's better to have an independent *alcalde,*" he told me. "If I were bad, I would have said, 'Ah, this [person] is a guerrilla,' and there would have been a big kidnapping in the town."

But Benjamín told them that the people on the list weren't guerrillas. The truth is that there are no guerrillas in San José. But the tongues of people say everything. And it is somewhat dangerous when the mouths say false things.

I asked Benjamín, "Why didn't you prosecute the thieves that broke into your house in the month of May? Moreover, you know who they are."

He told me, "No, Ignacio, I didn't want to prosecute anyone because it costs a lot to pursue a suit. It takes time and money." He also told me that earlier the thieves had sent him letters asking for Q5,000 and telling him to bring this amount to the soccer field at midnight on a Sunday without a date, but it had to be on a Sunday. This was confusing and unusual to tell him this without a date. It could have been just to scare or harass him. Benjamín, however, didn't give them the money, and for that reason, they broke into his house.

María Has a Baby
27 to 29 August 1988

In the life of a man, many things happen, especially when there are many children. The children are not the same; there are conscientious children, some disobedient, and others sly. But, as the father of a family, a man has to have much patience with all his children. [At times] a father gets angry, annoyed, or embarrassed, but that's the way it goes.

The problem with my eldest daughter is that she got together with a foolish, lazy man. And to worsen the situation, he left her and went to the house of his parents on 2 July.

While María was pregnant, things were a little drastic. Her mother gave her a lot of work as punishment. "You have to do this; you have to do that," her mother would say.

"But Mamá," María would respond, "I'm already tired."

"I don't know," her mother would say. "This is our work here. Your father and I thought you would study so that you would not suffer like us, but since this is what you want, do this weaving. Make these tortillas. Go wash the clothes."

On 27 August 1988, I had to go out at five o'clock in the morning to finish a job in the field in Pajocá. But, before going out, I decided it would be better to have some coffee.

"Will you make coffee?" I asked my wife.

"All right," she told me.

Then María told her mother, "Look, I'm in pain."

My wife then told me, "Look, María is in labor, and she doesn't have a spouse. Her [common-law] husband has gone."

Then I had to go to San Martín myself to fetch the midwife while my wife stayed with María. The midwife left for San José while I stayed and bought some vegetables.

At eight o'clock in the morning, a baby girl was born in the house. I must say without hiding anything that on this day, I became angry. I felt like hitting my daughter. The reason for my anger is that the expenses have accumulated for me, and having a baby always requires more money and care. And to add more pain in my heart, her husband was taking the luxury to walk about in the streets like an innocent. I don't feel good about the problems he has caused in my home. Sometimes I wanted to forget, but one can't, since the words of a saying are true: *Se perdona pero no se olvida* [One forgives but doesn't forget].

In the afternoon I called José Mario. A problem here [in San José] is that men don't want to take care of the birth certificate of their children. Of all the problems we had with the birth, not one of his kin knew—not his father, his mother, or him.

When he arrived, I told him, "Look, today a baby was born. I only would like to know if you will take care of the birth certificate, or, if not, as grandfather, I will have to do it. But first I'm asking you. If you will, that will be fine, but I tell you, if you take care of it, we will not ask you for child support. You won't give [anything] because we know you are poor; you don't have any work. No, God help us and God help María, because she's the one who did these things."

"No," he told me, "I will get the birth certificate."

"And what name will you put down for her?"

"Look, I would like to put down the name of your wife, Josefa," he responded.

"Well, let's go ask her, see what she says," I replied.

I asked my wife. "Well," she said, "it's an infant that was born. We can't despise it. It's all right."

That's how they gave María's infant the name Rose Josefa Ramos Bizarro. By late afternoon of this day, I had some drinks, but I didn't feel drunk when I went to sleep.

My Sons Go to the Great Ruins of Tikal
10 to 11 September 1988

From Monday until today, Saturday, 10 September, my three sons José, Ramón, and Ignacito worked hard from morning to night tying *jaspes*. Ramón, Ignacito, and the rest of the students of the *instituto básico* have planned to take a trip to become acquainted with the ruins of Tikal in Flores, Petén, [and to go to] Puerto Barrios and other places. Ramón and Ignacito asked me for the money that they need to cover the [travel] expenses and other things. But sincerely I didn't have any money. They could, however, sell *jaspes*. Then they, during the week, earned Q100. It's true that they didn't attend classes, but it was because of real necessity.

By the night of this day, my wife was working to prepare food for our two sons to take with them since there is no more money to buy any food. At the same time, I had to make a little bread for them because I thought that Q100 was not enough. At one o'clock in the morning, Sunday, 11 September, the students from the *instituto básico* left toward the north of the country in the bus of Benito Xicay of San Martín la Laguna. The trip cost Q900.

On this day, 11 September, I was harvesting beans in the *sitio*, but I felt sick from so much work and need. I must sell the beans to buy food to cook.

Attempted Assassination of Father Girón
Monday to Friday, 12 to 15 September 1988

I awoke with a high fever; my wife sent for a practical nurse. He took my temperature, gave me an injection, and told me that I had to have another shot tomorrow.

On this day a bulletin on Radio Fabulosa was heard throughout all the country, and it appeared in the newspaper. It reported, "Attempt against the life of the Catholic priest, Andrés Girón, when he left the church of La Democracia, department of Escuintla, after officiating mass. He left the church, then got in his automobile. In one of the streets, he was attacked by some armed men, but they were not identified. In that same place, one of the policemen who was serving as a bodyguard lost his life." Also, it said that an altar boy was wounded.

9. Temple 1 of the North Acropolis at Tikal in the department of Petén, Guatemala.

But the priest was safe and sound.

Days later, the priest declared in the newspaper and on radio and television that the government was responsible for the attempt against his life and that the government was responsible for the death of the policeman and the wounds of the altar boy. He said that the government didn't want him to be on the side of the poor, and for that reason, it was trying to kill him. Father Girón didn't blame the other organizations, and he said that the day the government killed him, it would be held responsible.

One day later the president of the republic, Marco Vinicio Cerezo Arévalo, declared in a press conference, "It is not the government or the army that has made an attempt against the life of the priest, Andrés Girón. The government of the Christian Democrats is not pursuing anyone; its ideology is only for the development and progress of Guatemala." The same leader said, "Without doubt it was the guerrillas who wanted to kill Father Girón because he previously was associated with the subversive groups and he now has abandoned them. The government declares that the accusations of Father Andrés Girón are false."

Of the two versions, neither is certain. The truth is that the assassins were probably the politicians. Better said, they perhaps were the political leaders, because it is well known that Andrés Girón is more politician than priest. He is a candidate for the presidency of the republic backed by the party Movimiento de Acción Solidaria (MAS) [Movement of Solidarity Action]. Many people support him, and most of them are indigenous campesinos of the coast and of the highlands. He has won their confidence, offering them land; that is to say, he has promised to divide the farms that are not cultivated by the proprietors. Who knows if he will do it; maybe he is just trying to gain the support of the poor people. The attempt against the life of Father Andrés Girón happened Sunday night, 11 September, because the news was heard on the twelfth, Monday.

At dawn on 15 September, the students of the primary school arrived bearing the torch, the symbolic fire from the city of Tapachula, Mexico. By the grace of God, all went well.

Following them arrived the students of the *instituto básico* from the ancient city of the Maya—Tikal, Petén. Also, they all arrived without incident.

I had a temperature, but I had to go to meet my sons in front of the municipal hall to show my support and to acknowledge the effort of the young people.

Mosquitos Make Me Sick
16 to 22 September 1988

My uncle José and I went to clear land to plant chickpeas in Xebitz. But we thought we would finish before midday, and because of that we didn't take lunch. It was impossible to finish the work before noon, however, and we had to keep working to complete it. The work made us hungry and thirsty. I had finished the water that I had taken from the house. Because I was so thirsty, I had to drink water from the river, and many mosquitoes bit me. When I arrived home, I no longer wanted to have lunch, but by now it was about three o'clock in the afternoon. All night I had a high fever and a chill. I was the same all day until the afternoon, when they sent to call Don Clemente to give me an injection. Not until then, by the night, did I feel some relief.

I didn't go to work until the twentieth. I also worked on the twenty-first and the twenty-second. Thursday, the *muchachos*, my sons, were working with me planting chickpeas in Xebitz.

Baking and the Inauguration of GUATEL: A Good Story in My Town
6 October 1988

I also have another job as a baker, but it's much harder because one works close to the fire while baking the bread. I don't like this work much, but I have to do it out of necessity. On this day my wife and I decided to go to Santiago Atitlán to sell bread. It was the first time for us, but previously my sons had sold bread in that town. Then, on this day, we made bread for the market of Santiago Atitlán, that is to say, for the following day.

Today the new office of GUATEL [Empresa Guatemalteca de Telecomunicaciones (Guatemalan Telecommunications Company)] was inaugurated; it's an interesting service for the town and its villages: the installation of only one telephone for the whole town, which is registered as a community telephone. This was one more work of the government of the Guatemalan Christian Democrats.

The cooperatives, other organized groups, and representatives of the national army and central government all participated in this inauguration. The ceremony was enlivened by the marimba orchestra Alma Joseña [Soul of San José]. The telephone booth was installed in the house of Andrés Bizarro, and a son of his was put in charge of the telephone and assisting the people to make calls. One only pays Qo.50 for the *citación* [summons, or call].[18] The *alcalde,* Juan Mendoza, requested that the telephone be installed in the municipal hall, but it was impossible because the jefes said that GUATEL is a private, not a state, organization. For that reason, they left the phone in a private house.

What are your thoughts about there being a telephone in San José?

Thanks to the understanding of the authorities, GUATEL is a company. The president of the republic says that he gives money to GUATEL to support the employees in each town to run the communications center. They call it a subsidy. In this year, 1988, Benjamín Peña, when he was the mayor, authorized the site. They said, "If it's GUATEL, thanks to God we are going to put the site here." Then they designated the site for the booth, and this service is fine. Not all are in agreement with the president of the republic, but the majority of them don't understand that he is doing a little better. He can't please everyone. Some argue that he's not doing well, but the truth is that there is a majority who are in favor of GUATEL. The government said that it was for emergencies: for calling firemen, for calling a doctor at a hospital, for finding out how a sick person is, for calling to find out how a family is, and for better communication in general. Then I can't say that this thing for us poor people won't be of service. I can communicate with a doctor in Solalá or a doctor here by only knowing the phone number. Then this is a positive change for Guatemala. It will serve our children very much and us perhaps less, because the youngsters are the future of my beloved town of San José.

And is there one telephone for the whole town?

Yes, there is only one community phone. But they say they are giving the opportunity to those who want to have their own telephone in their own house. One has to request a phone. When there are ten people who want to have a telephone, they request phones, and they give the authorization for ten telephones. And later if there is another ten, then little by little they escalate until having a larger number of phones in a town. But for the moment in San José they need ten people who want to have telephones put in their homes.

And for the first time I talked to you on the phone.

Yes. It's the first time that I talked to you on the telephone. I had already talked on a telephone, but from Guatemala [City] and other places and here in Solalá and Panajachel. But the first time I had the opportunity to talk on the telephone in my town was when we communicated. And I expect that from San José I will be able to communicate one day with you when you are in the United States.

A Strange Dream While Working with Sexton in Panajachel
6 October 1988

The first night in Panajachel when I was sleeping suddenly a dream ended when I heard gunshots. I didn't know if it was at the beach or in the street. Later, I continued sleeping. Another time when a dream ended I looked at my watch. It was one o'clock in the morning. I had a dream, but it was difficult to understand the meaning of this dream.

I dreamed that I found myself in Santiago Atitlán, only walking, looking at many people in the market and in the main street of the town. I went up the street that passes in front of the Catholic church. I saw that behind the Catholic church there were many men, and I stayed watching. A woman told me, "Take this machine." The machine was like a telephone, or like a small tape recorder. In the dream I told the woman, "Señora, what good is this machine to me? I'm not from here."

She told me, "It will allow you to see all that is going to happen here at this time and in the future." Later the woman left, and I remained alone. I saw in the dream when other men arrived, running to tell them [the men standing] that they were going to hide. "Get ready, because now the truck is coming, bringing a *cuadrilla* [crew]."

"Very well," said those who were going to hide. They began to prepare themselves, talking among themselves, saying, "Now, we really are going to tie them up with lassos and kill them in the evening."

I saw when the truck arrived at the town and the workers began to take down their suitcases and leave for their houses, but on the road they were captured by the men who were hiding. Those who were hiding were indigenous people. The campesinos also were people of the town, but the ones who were hiding tied the campesinos by their feet and hands, tossed them behind the church alive, and left them there. They said that at night they would be executed. When the people in the market and the streets realized what was happening, they took off, running to hide. They abandoned their sales, women and children crying. Only the bad men remained, saying the same words at night, "We're going to kill them. They are the guerrillas that have caused much harm in the town. Those men leave, saying they are going to the coast to work, but it is a lie. They go to the mountains in order to practice guerrilla warfare, and they come to kill our people."

When I heard and saw these things in the dream, it scared me very much. I thought about running, but I said to myself, "If I run, they will think that I am a guerrilla, so I will stay and watch what is happening." In the dream two old men approached me. Later I asked them why they were tying up their own people. They answered, "Be quiet, you don't need to know anything about this. The guerrillas don't come from other towns; they are the same citizens of this town. They have sown the violence; they have killed good men, sons of this town, and because of this we are going to kill them. Only this will stop the violence." The same men told me, "It is certain that the militants had killed many of our Indian people, but those responsible are these men, and because of this there is no other solution. We have to kill them." And at last they told me, "You must go, because if you stay something will happen to you." All these things they told me in the Tzutuhil language.

In the dream I felt a lot of fear and I said, "Why am I here? In my town I did not see or hear things like these I am seeing [here]." In the dream I was aware that I went down the street that goes to the beach where one catches a launch. At this same moment the dream ended, and I awoke. I meditated a lot, asking God not to let these things happen and to help me make sense of this dream.

I think the dream is a warning not to continue selling bread in the town, because it is certain that in Santiago Atitlán there are people who buy a lot of bread. There is a man who lives close to the soccer field. He told me that he needed a lot of bread every two days. Well, my wife and I only went four times to sell him bread because it is a little distant and because I was a little afraid to go there. One time I asked him, "Why do you sell so much bread when your house is not a store?" He answered, "I sell bread to some men who always come here. I don't know if they are from the town. What interests me is the money." Then I decided not to deliver the bread to him anymore. I thought to myself, without telling my wife, that this man may be selling bread to bad men. Perhaps he isn't selling bread to bad men, but we quit selling bread in Santiago Atitlán, because something bad could happen.

Problems in the Evangelical Galilea Church
7 July to 15 October 1988

Everywhere problems are near. [Earlier] on 7 July, a problem emerged in the Evangelical Galilea Church. The pastor of this church did what the Bible says, to preach conformance with the scriptures. But it happens that in this church there is a family of just women. They say that they go to Santiago Atitlán to perform *costumbres* with Maximón.[19] Since the rules of the church prohibit these kinds of ceremonies, the pastor reprimanded the women so they would not continue in [what he called] these false adorations.[20]

The women were unhappy when they were criticized for performing these *costumbres*. They felt offended. They looked for a way to pester the pastor. Then they went to Guatemala [City] to the mission to tell the jefe that the pastor is acting very much outside of what the evangelical mission requires and that he only jokes [flirts] with the women. Without conducting an investigation, the jefe in Guatemala ordered him to move out of the *sitio* of the church and told him that now he was not part of the mission.

10. *Maximón in Santiago Atitlán.*

On this same day they closed the church. There are only ten families who are members of this church, but when the jefe ordered the closure of the church, these believers were left with nothing. They had been the ones who struggled to construct this building, giving money, material, and time. They say that the deed to the *sitio* where the church was built, however, was in the United States, by the order of the missionaries.

The pastor, who was disenfranchised by the mission, rented a house where he went to live with his family. Of the ten families, eight of them asked the pastor to celebrate the sect in a house of one of their companions. He agreed.

Then they began to celebrate the sect in the house of the evangelical Diego Ixtamer Sumoza. There they remained from July to 15 October, when they rented a house for the service of God.

The same pastor contacted the mission Iglesia de Dios "Las Cumbres," which is based in the United States. Now they are obtaining a *sitio* to build another church. Probably there will be another denomination in my town.

Another pastor, sent by the same mission, came to the Galilea Church.

There are only two families attending, however, and it is a heavy burden for them because they are supporting the pastor and his family.

My Ex-Son-In-Law, José Mario, Takes Up with My Half Sister
15 November 1988

I didn't believe it when they told me that José Mario was sleeping with Marta Juana Ujpán Sánchez, my [half] sister. I said, perhaps the people were telling me in order to cause gossip in my family. The day came, however, when Marta Juana's mother arrived to tell us that José Mario and Marta Juana have been sleeping together for months. The truth is that I felt ashamed, and I told the woman that José Mario isn't my son-in-law, besides now he isn't living with my daughter. It bothered me because the man is my former son-in-law and the woman is my half sister. She is my half sister through my father; she leads a wayward life. She married a man in San Martín, and they had three children. She is about thirty-eight years old, and her eldest daughter [by the *Martinero*] is eighteen years old. But Juana left her spouse for an ex-military commissioner from San Martín by the name of Lucas Chac Bolaños. She had a child by him, but when he went to prison, she went back to her first husband, only to leave him again later.[21]

On 15 November José Mario arrived at about 4:00 P.M. to visit my daughter, but since she knew he had another woman, María didn't want to talk to him. Then José Mario talked to me, saying that he wanted to return again to live with my daughter in our house. Then, God forgive me, I became angry and I told him frankly that now I didn't want to see him in my house anymore. "You are a shameless man," I told him. "This is the last time [I want to see you], and if you come back again, I'm going to kick you out of the house. If my daughter wants to talk to you, then you can talk in the street but not in my house. If María wants to join with you again, you can go at once to live wherever you wish but not in my house."

Those things I told him because what this man was doing hurt me. He treated us as if we were his playthings, so I told him those things in order for him to learn that I am an authority figure. When I was saying these things he didn't respond anymore; he only said that he didn't have anything to do with Marta Juana, that it was only people's lies. And he left.

Three days later it was clear that what Marta Juana's mother had said—that José Mario and Marta Juana were sleeping together—was true. She began to live with José Mario in his parents' house. His parents said that she was the woman of their son, but José Mario said that she was only a servant.

They lived in his parents' house for only one month. His parents kicked them out too because neither the man nor the woman wanted to work. They wanted his parents to give them their daily sustenance, but all was to the contrary.

Later they moved into the house of Marta Juana's mother. In a few weeks she also booted them out of their house for the same reason. Later they stayed at the house of Damián Juárez Sánchez, the woman's brother. They were only there for a few days, when Damián told them to leave. The same Damián told me that he had to remove [them] from his house because José Mario didn't want to work and Damián didn't have the means to give them meals.

Now José Mario and Marta Juana live two or three days in San José and another two or three days in Panajachel. This is what has happened with the one who was my son-in-law. God [knows what's best] for him, and God [knows what's best] for us.

Violence Continues in My Beloved Guatemala: The Case of the Massacre of the Village of El Aguacate
29 November 1988

In my beloved Guatemala the violence continues. The spokesperson of the army and of the government announced by radio, television, and the press that Guatemala is living in an era of democracy and it is respecting the lives of the Guatemalans. But this is only talk. Each day the violence is taking more lives, more families mourning, more children crying, hoping for when their fathers will arrive, more wives weeping in solitude, thinking of that humble husband who left to work in the fields or to carry out the orders of the civil defense patrol and did not return again to his family. Of course it makes us sad, but what are we going to do?

[This is] the case of the massacre of the village El Aguacate in the municipality of San Andrés Itzapa of the department of Chimaltenango. There are two versions. Of the two, who knows which is true? One version says that the twenty-two countrymen were kidnapped from their houses at dawn Sunday by heavily armed men who executed them on the mountain. Later the cadavers were put in a ditch, like a common grave. They were not found until Monday, 28 November. They were identified as countrymen of the town of Aguacate.

The other version says that only the military commissioner was kidnapped by the extremist guerrillas. Later the rest of the campesinos were obligated to form a civil defense committee to rescue the commissioner, but all was in vain, even losing their lives.

Also, they say that the patrols left to look for the kidnapped commissioner at the same time that the military was on the same mountain. They said that it was a confusion, the military thought that the countrymen were the guerrillas and they had opened fire on them, and the campesinos did nothing because they were unarmed. They only carried machetes, and, because of this, all of them died. But it seems that there is some doubt, because Meléndez de la Riva, the human rights lawyer, does not have concrete data on this bloody act. The truth is only the devils themselves know who committed the crime.[22]

Honoring the Gods of Corn
16 November to First Days of December 1988

From 16 to 30 November Ramoncito, Ignacito, and I were baking bread almost day and night. We sold more here in my town, but also we sold some in Santiago Atitlán. The truth is that we didn't earn much, but since it is a consumable, it is sellable. Also, times are a little better because it is the beginning [of the season] of the coffee harvest.

In the first days of the month of December we were harvesting milpa in Xebitz. By the great will of God, He gave me a regular harvest, not less or more. I was doing the harvesting, and some *mozos* were carrying the sacks on their backs with a porter's strap. But they got tired, because it takes a lot of energy since the place is steep, with many rocks. As I finished carrying the corn, I was content because it is my work as a campesino. As always, it has been the custom of my parents and grandparents, may they rest in peace, after recovering the harvest, to perform a small *costumbre* to the gods of corn, Toj and Ka'nel.[23]

When we finished gathering the corn, we had a small fiesta. I lit my candles and sprinkled the corn with incense as a sign of good life to the god of corn so that we will have a rest. I drank some *tragos*, and my family and I ate together. After eating, I slept because I felt really tired.

11. *A campesino working in his terraced onion fields on the shore of Lake Atitlán.*

Death Comes without Warning

25 to 26 December 1988

We human beings don't know where or when we are going to die. Man may be full of envy, pride, and egotism, but death humbles everyone.

When many were celebrating Christmas in their homes, enjoying rich tamales of the Good Night, a family member named Antonio Bizarro Vásquez died. He was an intelligent man, but he was dominated by alcohol.

When he was young, he dedicated himself to music. He was the best trumpet player from this area, but he abandoned music and left for the barracks for military service in the army. Many say that he was one of the best sergeants of the second artillery and was jefe of a 105mm[-round] tank of the Guardia de Honor barracks.

When he left the army, he took up music again. He was the first saxophonist, playing with marimbas and prestigious orchestras. Because of alcohol, however, he gave up music and devoted himself to agriculture, mainly growing onions and coffee.

At that time Antonio was famous. It seems that he was the "don" of agriculture; whatever he sowed turned out well. When he began to develop the art of planting coffee, Antonio was sought out by *Martineros* and *Joseños* to plant their coffee because it is certain that he had a good touch. To this day, there are no better coffee plants than the ones he planted. But also the treachery of alcoholism was growing, and much later he couldn't stop his addiction to *aguardiente*. He was in jail many times because of drunkenness, but, because his father [Juan Bizarro Gómez] had money, he paid his son's fines.

Ultimately, Antonio became an incurable alcoholic. Many times he came for an "adjustment" for a *trago*. In other words, if he had eighty centavos and needed twenty more to buy a *trago*, I gave it to him when I had the money. He pleaded, "Ignacio, help me; I am dying of a hang-over. You also are a man, and you have your children. I hope that you all don't suffer from this sickness. I don't know what [sin] I'm paying for; perhaps my parents did something bad when they were young."[24]

These were Antonio's words, and he cried a lot. I would ask him, "How many days have you been drinking, Antonio?" At first he would tell me sixty days. Then, as he drank more, he would say ninety days. In the end, I would give in to giving him money for the *trago*. People say that it is bad to give money to a drunk, but to my conscience, I was not the one who had given him the drinks. He only asked me for money to ease his illness.

Death came to Tono at 11:00 A.M. They say that he entered Alejandra Cholotío's house, drunk. He asked her to give him a tamale to eat. The woman gave him a chair so that he could sit down to be served a ta-male. But, before eating the tamale, Antonio bowed his head and fell dead with the tamale in his hand. He died less than a *cuadra* from his house. Alarmed, Alejandra ran out of her house to notify the family, but they didn't report the death immediately. What they did was to carry him in their arms to his house and place him on his bed. An hour later they said that Tono had died in his house. They did this to avoid the investigations of the justice of the peace. In the evening of this day, many, but many, people arrived at the house!

The twenty-sixth was the burial of this relative and friend. His body was put in a family *panteón* [aboveground tomb]. Many relatives and friends were drinking and talking about he who was Tonito.

María Asks for Forgiveness

5 January 1989

At night when I was tired and reading a book, my daughter María approached me, saying, "Papá, forgive me for all that I have committed. I will never do it again. I need to continue my studies. Tomorrow I want to get money to go to Quezaltenango to see if they will allow me to continue studying in the college, Liceo Quezalteco."

I told her, "You are forgiven, but I alone cannot make it right. Ask for forgiveness from your mother and apologize to your brothers and sisters." At this same moment she received a pardon from her mother. But, also, I called to my children so that they would be witnesses to the promise that María made that she would not do it again. Our meeting was at 9:00 P.M. We agreed that my wife would look after feeding and taking care of the baby girl; that is to say, my wife and I are going to feed our granddaughter while María continues her studies.

I told María if she gets involved with another man while studying, she will be disowned by the family. She can marry only after she has a degree, so that she can better herself. I told her we didn't have money to be throwing away, and, besides, we also have small children who need food.

After the meeting, my wife and I were a little content but, at the same time, sad because it is a big responsibility to feed a baby of five months. But, as parents, we have to be tolerant and forgive the faults of our children. On this night I drank, getting a little drunk.

María Leaves for Quezaltenango and José Mario's Mother Comes for a Visit

6 to 8 January 1989

On 6 January María went to Quezaltenango. I had planned to go with her, but because the night before I had drunk a little too much, I didn't go. Instead, Erasmo Ignacio went with her. I gave her Q100 to cover her expenses at college.

They returned the same day. She told me that there weren't any problems. She was accepted by the director and was told to return again for registration.

On Saturday, 7 January, at night, the mother of José Mario, Señora Caria, came to visit the baby. The woman was crying a lot. She told us that there is no peace in her house. The one who provokes problems is her son. Each time that José Mario comes to see her he says that she should give him his inheritance, and because of this, there is a problem.

On Sunday, 8 January, a big problem erupted in the house of José Mario's parents. José Mario's woman wants his parents to give them a house, but the parents only have one house. José Mario hit his mother. Then Señora Caria abandoned the house to live in the house of another son. On the night of this day, the señora arrived at our house to ask us to sue José Mario, but I told her no, because I didn't want to get involved with other people's problems.

A Confrontation between Soldiers of the Army and Guerrillas
16 January 1989

In Santiago Atitlán there is no peace. It is a town where always, day after day, violence continues. On this day there was a big confrontation between soldiers of the army and the guerrillas. They say that the guerrillas first began to harass some elements of the army by throwing bombs and shooting rifles in the place that they call Cristalina, close to the road that goes to Cerro de Oro. The bullets from both groups were flying over the lake. They say that a launch was hit by the bullets, but the engine did not die. What wasn't known was who had died in the conflict. What was only known was that there was fear in all the town. They prohibited the departure of the launches for Panajachel and San Martín. They say that men and women from the towns San Martín and San José were sad and didn't know where to hide. Not until three in the afternoon did they give orders to the conductors of the launches to continue on their destination.

On this day my son José was in Santiago Atitlán to pay a bill at an agency. He was hiding in the business office, El Hogar Moderno. He says that he stayed there for more than two hours, until the shooting abated. They told him that he should stay another day in order not to suffer serious consequences on the journey. But he didn't want to remain there because he worried that we would look for him, and it would be better for him to come home. Luckily nothing happened to him.

Two Strange and Confusing Dreams
Saturday to Sunday, 21 to 22 January 1989

A dream I had was a little strange and confusing. I was in Quezaltenango running. Suddenly my wife appeared, running with me. In the dream my wife went to see a fiesta, and I stayed inside a house to wait for her.

When she returned, we were in Santa Rosa la Laguna, observing the fiesta, seeing a man making many crystal vases to give to the people with which to drink *tragos*. Suddenly I realized that we were passing under the frame of a rustic house without a roof and a woman greeted me, saying, "Ignacio, how long has it been since you visited me? My husband and I always remember when you were a [labor] contractor and we were working on the coast with you."

Also, the husband spoke to me, "Ignacio, I want to talk to you, but it's a shame I feel much pain in my body. Besides I am deaf; I can't hear." In the dream I only looked and I didn't want to answer, because the truth was that I didn't know those two old people.

In the dream I felt myself walking alone, a little forward. Suddenly I arrived at the bank of a small river that was at the edge of a narrow road, but it seemed to me as if I were in San José. On the road I found myself with the grandfather of my father-in-law. It has been years since he died. His name was Jaime Ramos Pérez. And he asked me, "Ignacio, how are you? I feel sorry for you. When I was with you all, you were an obedient man and worker. You worked with me and I always paid you. Look, now I cannot do anything. I can't walk because of the pain in my legs, and I am blind." And he said, "Please take me inside. I want to be in my house in order to visit my grandchildren and lie down a little."

I told him, "Very well," and I grabbed his hand. We entered the homesite and went into the house, and the old man lay down on his bed of *tapesco* [cane bedframe]. But inside the house there was a fire, and over that fire was a clay dish with some roasted chickens in it. The old man told me those roasted chickens are going to serve for a fiesta that they are going to celebrate in this house. Then my sister-in-law's little girl and my little girl appeared and fell into the fire. I screamed to save the two children from the fire, but at that moment the dream ended. I asked Ramón what time it was, and he told me it was four o'clock in the morning. At the same time, I told my family what I had dreamed.

Early Sunday morning, 22 January, I dreamed that I found my grandmother Isabel Soto in front of the Catholic church. In front of her flowed a muddy river. She got close to me, and I asked her what she was doing there. She told me, "I'm getting a little water to drink; I'm thirsty."

"Don't drink that water," I told her. "It's dirty. In the house, there's clean water." Without answering me, she drank that water. This was my dream, and I woke up and looked at my watch. It was five o'clock in the morning.

The truth is I don't know if those two dreams mean anything. Perhaps they are just a weakness of the brain. Things stay encumbered in our minds, and they come back like an echo. When I was young, I had worked with the deceased Jaime Ramos. When he was old he became blind, and he couldn't walk alone. The truth is that I respected him a lot, and he treated me like a son.

A Treatment for the Baby: Breast Milk Flowing
23 to 25 January 1989

On this day, together with my two sons Ramón and Ignacito, I was reconstructing the *temascal,* which will serve us a lot. The reason is that my daughter María is going to go back to school, but her baby is going to stay with us. Since it is small, it needs its mother's breast. We decided that we are going to treat my wife in the *temascal* so that her breast milk will flow again, so that the baby will not suffer much. We are buying her canned milk, but it isn't sufficient. Always she needs breast milk.

In the night we finished repairing the *temascal.* My wife went looking for fig leaves and other [avocado, cedar, herbal] leaves.

Later she picked the leaves [from the branches] and entered the *temascal* when it was ready. In the *temascal* she rubbed her shoulders and breasts in the water and the cooked leaves, which were warm. When she left the *temascal,* she drank a warm beer. Later she embraced the baby, laid down, and gave it the breast to make her milk descend. This was the first treatment. The truth is, however, she will have to do many treatments until the milk flows.[25]

The wet leaves were put on Anica's [Josefa's nickname] shoulders. The treatment worked, making more milk flow from her breasts, but María's infant didn't nurse much from Anica, only sometimes at night. It seemed that the infant preferred canned milk (NAN powdered milk) [because it might have tasted sweeter].

On this day, 25 January 1989, the baby Rose Josefa now didn't suck her mother's breast. On this day my wife began the work of caring for and feeding the baby. This is hard work for us, but with the help of God, all is possible.

The Murder of Juan Sisay, a Pure Tzutuhil
21 April 1989

Juan Sisay [his real name] was a pure Tzutuhil whose art and culture elevated the name of Guatemala, to say nothing of his natal land, Santiago Atitlán. Sisay was a man famous in art but simple in his way of speaking with strangers (foreigners) who came to visit him, always with his traditional *Atitecan* dress [typical clothing of Santiago Atitlán]. He devoted himself to the spirit of painting. Juan Sisay, a great asset to the Tzutuhil Maya race, knew many parts of the world, and many people of the world knew him, since he was among the best indigenous artists of our race.

I met Juan Sisay in 1961 when I was discharged from the military at the Manuel Lisandro Barillas base in Retalhuleu. Sisay visited with General Miguel Ydígoras Fuentes when he was president of the republic. In that same year [1960] he received the Order of the Quetzal for being the best Indian painter.

Juan Sisay was born 1 January 1921, a child of Juan Mendoza and Micaela Sisay [their real names]. Due to the poverty of his family, he never had the opportunity to attend school. He was dedicated to the business of carrying his *cacaste* [wooden frame, usually with four legs and shelves sustained by a tumpline, that traveling salesmen use to carry goods on their backs] from Atitlán to the coast to earn a living for his family.

God gave him the gift and love of the art of painting in 1947, when he was twenty-six years old, so he didn't draw his first pictures until he was an adult. He was sixty-eight when he died in 1989.[26] In 1969 he visited Pope Paul VI in the city of the Vatican, Rome. As a prize, he received a gold medal. Juan Sisay always served as a faithful devotee in the Catholic church. Because he was well respected in his dear town, in 1989 he became president of Catholic Action.

Earlier Juan Sisay said that he had received threats from an extremist [right-wing] group. The parish priest of San Lucas and the archbishop of Guatemala, Penados del Barrio, were told of the threat. It is said that the archbishop told Juan Sisay it would be better for him to take refuge in the archbishop's residence. But Sisay did not want to take refuge or go into exile. Always with spirit and love for his natal town, he said, "I am an honorable man and have done nothing wrong."

The prominent Tzutuhil painted many interesting things. No one can deny that his ability came from his intelligence. Few of us have such an ability.

When Friday, 21 April 1989, arrived, the people of Santiago Atitlán did not realize it would be a gloomy afternoon—they lost one of their sons of incalculable worth. Neither Juan nor his family could imagine what was going to happen.

Juan Sisay made his way to the Catholic church, always like an authentic Tzutuhil, wearing his expensive typical dress, tying his head, with a red *sute,* as is the custom. Once the meeting with the directors of Catholic Action had ended, everyone headed home. Sisay also left the church and made his way to his house, which was some three *cuadras* away. President Juan was almost home when he was shot down by some men who had followed him on the path. No one knows who they were; it is said that they disappeared in the crowd of people.

On the following day, news spread of his death in all of the towns of the lake. In our Tzutuhil tongue people now refer to Juan Sisay as X'camisax Taá Xwaan, which means "they killed Señor Juan." Others say X'camisax Maxaan, which in the Castilian language means "they killed Don Juan."

Truly this was a great pain for the town of Atitlán and for the neighboring towns, because it is said that it was a loss of great worth. He is the only artist who elevated the name of Sololá, as he was an important figure in the history of Guatemala. They say he is the most famous native painter in the department of Sololá and in the country of Guatemala, land of eternal spring.

[I say] "Juan Sisay, you have died because of a minority [your enemies], but you will live in the hearts of the majority, who loved you dearly. Taá Xwaan, now you are prostrated at the foot of God, asking peace for your town and for us, your brothers. [We've had] enough violence.

"Juan, ask the Supreme Being for a benediction for those who cut down your life, so that they will understand that all of us are brothers [and won't continue the violence]. Now your new home is in paradise, where you will live eternally, praising the All Powerful."[27]

They Capture Two Desperadoes and My Wife's Home Remedy Cures María's Baby
25 March to 6 May 1989

This happened at night in the village of Patzilín of this municipality

12. *Men of Santiago Atitlán wearing their red* sutes *during a procession.*

[San José], when they happily were celebrating the fiesta of San José on 19 March, as usual. But Holy Week itself is a time of reflection; therefore, they don't celebrate it until after Holy Week. Then in the village they were enjoying the celebration when suddenly three men arrived.

It is said that one was from Santa Ana and another from Santa Elena. It isn't known where the third one was from, because in truth they only captured two of them. The one from Santa Ana is called Regino Sicay, and the one from Santa Elena is said to be a specialist from the military zone of Santa Cruz del Quiché. Over drinks, they said that they were seeking to kill the truck driver and his assistant who work for the transport line named Clarenita. However, the volunteer civil defense patrols found out that the three men were searching for the driver and his assistant. Then they [the patrolmen] called more people to help them find and capture the desperadoes.

They succeeded in capturing two of them, tied them up, and took from one a .38-caliber pistol. But the third one fled. It is said that the patrollers severely tortured the two during the rest of the night. Meanwhile, the assistants of the commissioned soldiers phoned the military zone of Sololá, asking them to send a patrol to investigate the desperadoes.

Well, the patrol came [across the lake] by launch and walked to the town to fetch the suspects. But it is said that when the military patrol arrived at the village, the man from Santa Elena was identified as a specialist from the military zone of Quiché and the one from Santa Ana as a military reservist from Sololá. Sunday afternoon, the twenty-sixth, the military patrol and the two men left by launch. The next day the two men were set free without an investigation. José Heroldo told me that he was notified because he was the chief of the volunteer civil defense patrols and that the two weren't suspects, only drunks, and that they didn't intend to kill anyone. This time, the ones who were viewed unfavorably by the military were the patrollers.

Sunday dawned with María's baby girl very ill with a fever and bad cough. All night my wife and I were caring for her. By the morning of this day, they took her to Don Juan Ixtamer in San Martín to give her an injection. It wasn't until after midday that she got better.

On 6 May the baby fell sick again with diarrhea and fever. We took her to the doctor, but she didn't get better. My wife prepared a home remedy. She pounded *apazote* [herb used in cooking to flavor food such as beans and in medicine], and then she fried the *apazote* with oil. After frying the *apazote,* she put it hot on the baby's stomach and then covered it with a cloth. She soaked more *apazote* in hot water [making a drink like an herbal tea] and gave the baby a spoonful for the next three days. By the grace of God, the baby was cured. My wife has experience because we have many children. When it isn't possible to cure with medicine, at times home remedies are better.

An Attempted Presidential Coup
9 to 10 May 1989

At dawn the broadcasting stations of all the country were happily airing their regular programs when suddenly they were interrupted by the official radio TGW, the Voice of Guatemala [La Voz de Guatemala Radio Nacional (Government)]. At 5:00 A.M. the spokesman said that all the broadcasting stations and television channels were paying attention to what was happening in the capital city.

Well, all the private radio stations and television channels obeyed the TGW's order to play only pure marimba music but without knowing what the situation was until 7:00 A.M. when they made an announcement on radio and television that there had been an attempted coup by a group of soldiers who wanted to overthrow President Marco Vinicio

Cerezo Arévalo. The news was divulged by governmental groups, and it is said that the national radio station, TGW, was the first thing commandeered by the protagonists. Also, they targeted the director-general of the national police, and they surrounded the house of the minister of national defense, Héctor Alejandro Gramajo Morales. Then Guatemalan Air Force planes began flying overhead, but there hadn't been a military confrontation.

Upon discovering the attempted revolt, artillery troops loyal to the government were sent to secure the White House [president's house] and the house of the defense minister. It is said that all was now calm, that the attempted coup was repressed.

The president of the republic and the minister of national defense, accompanied by the other ministers, declared in a press release that the attempted overthrow was by four military officials of the national army and that for some time they have been causing damage in the ranks, that they were treacherous people, and that they were already looked down on in the military ranks. For these reasons, the president and the defense minister wanted to calm the spirit of the Guatemalans so they won't overthrow the Democracia Cristiana government that is in the process of development. The minister of defense said that everything is under control, that the national situation is quite normal, that all the Guatemalans are peaceful, that the protagonists gained nothing, and that there was an order for their arrest to face judgment for the crimes they committed against the country's constitution.

One hour after the declarations from the government, the politician, Dr. Mario Castejón, declared that he supported the attempted coup because of Mario Vinicio Cerezo Arévalo's irresponsibility in governing and because of his disrespect for the armed institutions of Guatemala and, [what's] worse, the people in general. For these reasons, Castejón and elements of the army wanted to remove him from power. They think the señor president of the republic and his ministers should not just snicker or burst into laughter when others offer suggestions. "Vinicio Cerezo, as the father of the nation, should teach more respect," he said.

Another version that aired on radio and television was that the planes that flew over the capital city of Guatemala at dawn did so because the soldiers were celebrating the anniversary of the failed coup of 10 May 1988.

A Visit by an Anthropology Student
27 July 1989
At noon on this day, 27 July, when I was reading a book, an anthropology student came to visit me. She told me her name, and I told her mine. Then she asked me if I was the one who works with Dr. James Sexton, and I told her yes. I asked her what she was doing in the town, and she told me that she wanted to know the history of the town and to write something. She told me that her stay in San José was for two months and three weeks and she would return to Texas, U.S.A. This was all there was to the conversation.

But my observations are that the anthropologist was asking many people for the names of the bones of the human skeleton in Tzutuhil, translated into Spanish, then into English. She also obtained part of the history of the women of the project, the artisans of San José. But I saw a problem because her communication was with young people who now have mixed Tzutuhil with Spanish. Because of this, I think that she obtained information that is not true. He who was her companion is José Mario Ramos García, my former son-in-law.

Later José Mario began to say that he is keeping a diary to write a book with the anthropologist. José Mario, showing off with two or three notebooks in his hand, was walking in the streets and sitting on the shore of the lake, saying that now he will have a book. But who knows? There is a saying, *Perro que ladra no muerde* [The dog that barks never bites]. Another that says, *Boca cerrada no entra mosca* [A closed mouth doesn't let in a fly]. I say these things because this man is arrogant and excessive, but it is yet to be seen whether he will [write a book], because to do a literary work demands time and much patience. Also, help from God is needed.

Guerrillas Enter San Lucas Tolimán
29 July 1989
The guerrillas entered the town of San Lucas Tolimán; what is not known is whether they knew that in the town there was a military detachment. They say that more than two hundred guerrillas arrived, among them well-armed men, women, and children. In the military detachment there were only two platoons of soldiers. The abusive insurgents interrupted the peace of the residents. They entered by the road that leads from Santiago Atitlán to San Lucas, and when they

arrived by the cemetery they split into two groups. Then they attacked the military detachment where there was truly an armed confrontation in the center of the settlement. At least ten guerrillas died. Only one was captured, but he was wounded. Later he was taken away in a helicopter. Also, a soldier of the national army was wounded but not fatally.

They say that the dead guerrillas were taken away by their companions and that after the confrontation a foreign commander died. The insurgents that were carrying the dead two kilometers from the settlement encountered Father Tomás accompanied by a nun. They were coming from Santiago Atitlán to celebrate the mass of the anniversary of the death of Father Francisco (Aplas) [Stanley Rother]. Father Tomás was robbed of his car. The padre and the nun had to walk on foot, faint with fear. The father's car carried the dead guerrillas to an unknown place, where they were buried. The car appeared three days later in the same place where they took it from the priest. All these things are true.

Reflections about My Life on My Birthday and Political Fraud
13 to 16 August 1989

[On my birthday] I'm giving infinite thanks to God for permitting me one more year of life. It is certain that my life is difficult; I work hard in the fields and other places. I'm a man with many children; my responsibility becomes larger every day. The children get bigger every day, and they ask me for more food, clothing, and room. How can I not say that they need more education? It's true that I never had the opportunity to study for a career, but this is because my parents didn't take responsibility for educating me. They abandoned me when I was a baby. I'm the one who received this moral blow, and because of this, I don't want my children to suffer the same things. As long as God gives me life I will always think of my children. At times during the night I wake up while dreaming, and I begin to think about what I can do for my children and how I can earn more money to pay for food and studies for them. I bow my head and get down on my knees, asking direction from God. Often in my work in the fields I give thanks for my crops, understanding that His power governs my family. I ask God: "Father of all science and wisdom, bless and illuminate my friend James Sexton with the pages we are working on." And up to now God has helped me much and has heard my prayers, blessed and glorified God, Father of our Señor Jesucristo.

I'm going to write a little about the politics of the Democracia Cristiana Guatemalteca. For the first time in Guatemala a vote took place in all the *municipios* [municipalities, districts, towns] in the country to choose the party's presidential candidate. This took place on 13 August 1989.[28]

The candidates were Dr. René de León Schlotter and *profesor* [teacher] Alfonso Cabresa Hidalgo. In this political campaign there was much squandering of money on the part of the candidates. It was calculated that in all the country there are 140,000 members [in the party Democracia Cristiana]. But the people were stirred up the day of the voting. Alfonso Cabrera said that René does not have the capacity to govern the country. René de León said that Alfonso Cabrera Hidalgo is not a true democrat, only an opportunist. The people called the two *lobos de la misma loma* [wolves from the same hill]. Many of the people affiliated did not cast their vote for either one. The vote was carried out in the respective districts of each town.

In my town Alfonso Cabrera's group was stronger, because this group had a lot of money. René de León Schlotter's group was weaker. Well, Señora Raquel Blandon de Cerezo, wife of the actual president of the republic, was also a candidate [for the nomination], but those sympathizing with Doña Raquel were few.

There was no uproar on 14 August. Not until the fifteenth did great criticism break out on the part of Señor René de León and his sympathizers, saying that there had been fraud in the vote, primarily on behalf of *profesor* Alfonso Cabrera, who had manipulated the census of the members of the Democracia Cristiana. This criticism appeared in the press and on radio and television. René de León demonstrated his disagreement with the vote and asked that it be annulled.

The fraud was seen clearly enough, because the names of many of those who were in favor of René did not appear in the census of the membership and so they could not cast their votes. This was clearly the case with the *licenciado* minister of education, Señor Ricardo Gómez Gálvez, who was aspiring to the vice presidency with Schlotter, but his name did not appear on the census and thus he did not cast a ballot. This happened with the highest and lowest officials. It is clear that in Guatemala it was a dirty and revolting primary election because there was fraud even in the same party, and what's to stop them from doing it in the other parties and in the general elections of 1991?

This example demonstrates that in Guatemala there is always fraud. It seems certain to me that the party Democracia Cristiana will be the losing party in the 1991 elections. With luck it will come in in third place.

Inflation and Hard Times in Guatemala
Month of October 1989

The country of Guatemala is feeling whipped every day by inflation and speculation. Beginning in the month of October, there was total discontent among the people who live in Guatemala, in the cities and in the provinces. The prices of things are as high as the clouds: a pound of corn costs 45 centavos in the towns and in the cities, but in the rural areas it costs up to 60 centavos. Sugar is between 45 and 50 centavos a pound. A *quintal* of flour for ordinary bread costs 60 quetzales; flour for french bread costs 70 quetzales a *quintal,* which is a much greater penalty for the poor people. The daily wage of the campesino is no more than 5 quetzales. A father who has six children can earn only enough for daily corn. His family has to eat tortillas and salt three times a day. There is no way to buy basic foods, much less sugar and coffee. This year (1989) in Guatemala there are more malnourished children because of lack of food. This is not the fault of the parents but the fault of the government, witnessed by the whole world, because these things are happening in Guatemala.

Also, on 1 October, the *patrullaje* [news patrol; periodic news for the day] of the Radio Fabuloso said that the señor president, the *licenciado* Marco Vinicio Cerezo Arévalo, announced by radio and television that Guatemala had recovered from a total economic crisis; all the Guatemalans live better than before. But this is all false, more lies.

It is certain that there are little groups that are not affected by the crisis, like the señor president, his ministers, deputies, high political directors of the governing party, and the big employers that the same government authorized to raise prices. They earn millions of quetzales, and because of this, the president says that they have ended the crisis.

But if people of developed countries come and witness the situation in which we Guatemalans live, they may tell the world that we are being cleaned out by the government. Each day we are poorer; who knows how much poorer we are going to get.

In this month of October my family and I began a poorer life also.

At times we drink coffee with sugar and other times without it. It is like this also with food; we cannot eat well because prices are so high. The money already is not worth anything. What is certain is that we are living with the help of God. What helped us in this month of October was that I received a check from the University of Arizona [Press] as a percentage of the sales of the two books, *Campesino* and *Son of Tecún Umán*.

All Saints' Day and All Souls' Day
1 to 2 November 1989

It is the day that all the saints are commemorated. Many people do not work on this day. But my family and I worked. Thanks to God, we had a pretty good harvest of pole beans. In the morning we ate breakfast and then I carried a load of beans to sell in San Martín, returning at noon. In the afternoon we did other work in the house.

In the afternoon my señora cooked corn and lake shrimp. It is the custom in all the indigenous towns to cook ears of corn, sweet potatoes, pumpkins, *güisquiles* [climbing plant whose fruit is the size of an orange; an edible fruit with a spiny outer membrane], and other things and leave them in a basket to offer to the spirits of the deceased relatives. And this is what we did.

During the night, we went to the cemetery to visit the graves of my grandmother and other deceased relatives. There we lit candles and burned incense and prayed to God to remember our relatives who had been alive like us. We are alive now, but one day we will be resting in this holy place.

At 10:00 P.M. we arrived home. Then we covered the inside of our house with pine needles, and we prayed again. We finished the vigil at 3:00 A.M., and then we slept. We did this vigil to ask protection of God and to remember our [deceased] parents and relatives, not because I am a *zajorín*. We did this because this is what our hearts told us to do. When dawn broke on 2 November, the religious ones went early to the cemetery to offer prayers to the dead ones.

Some things are good. Few priests perform mass in the open air. At 10:00 A.M. the priest arrived at the public cemetery to officiate a holy mass to God in honor of the good spirits. The truth is that it was indeed delightful to feel the presence of God in the cemetery full of people. Thanks go to the good understanding of the Cakchiquel father, Ciro

Pantzay, who volunteered to celebrate the mass in the cemetery. This sacrifice was over at noon.

Lack of Respect for Human Rights in Guatemala
2 to 7 November 1989
In Guatemala there is much lack of respect for human rights. They speak of democracy, but these are words, not deeds. They only say this in order that the citizens of other countries hear that in Guatemala they live in full democracy. Democracy, however, is respecting the laws and the physical integration of the citizens, but in these times there is much violence [and many] abductions, assassinations, and violations. The relatives of those who have been massacred appeal to the government to shed light on this situation, but the government acts as if nothing has been heard.

An unpleasant event of this day, 2 November, was the kidnapping of the North American nun by the name of Diana Ortiz [her actual name], twenty years old, who was working in the diocese of Huehuetenango. On the order of her bishop, she was making her way to the city of Antigua, Guatemala, to attend a conference in the Belen Church of that city when she was abducted by armed men who, under the threat of death, forced her into a car.

She appeared the third day in a travel agency. Twenty-two hours after the kidnapping, the nun, Diana Ortiz, confirmed that she had been kidnapped but refused to say what had happened to her in front of the national press. The following day, 4 November, this religious person returned to the United States of North America.

Over the Radio Fabulosa, 7 November, it was made known to all the people of Guatemala that the religious sister declared in the United States that she had been kidnapped, taken by a policeman, locked in a house, tortured and raped, and even burned with the butts of cigarettes.

After the liberation of Diana Ortiz the authorities of the country did nothing to identify who these bad Guatemalans were. And that's the way it was. Nothing happened.

Talk about Establishing a Private Primary School
3 to 22 November 1989
On Friday, 3 November, I went to the post office in Panajachel to register two manila envelopes containing daily episodes [of my life] and

three folktales, with the destination of the United States, for Dr. James D. Sexton.

On Saturday, 4 November, as is the custom, craftswomen of San José met to listen to the good advice of the administrative council. After the conversation, the president of the artisans told the women that the foundation of a new private school, with the help of the Christian International Mission, is possible.[29] The president said that it's not certain yet but that the mission may sponsor one hundred boys and that each member may enroll a favorite son.

In the afternoon my wife told me that she was inclined to enroll Samuel Jesús in the *colegio* [private primary school]. I told my wife that it would be better to put him in the national school because I don't have much time to donate to help establish the new primary school.

When I answered her in this manner, she became annoyed and sad. "Ignacio," she said, "I know that you are an intelligent man. Why don't you want to work to help in the founding of the school that is going to do much for the future of our town?" And she told me, "I am an illiterate woman, but this was because of my parents [who didn't send me to school]. Nevertheless, I want our children to learn more, and they will learn more in a *colegio* than in the national school."

Truly I understood that in this matter it was wrong to contest my wife. Then I reflected and I told her very well. I know that she very much wants the new *colegio*.

On 18 November 1989 establishing a new private evangelical *colegio* was discussed again. On this day some men came from Panajachel to write down the names of the one hundred children to be sponsored, each with a grant of three quetzales monthly. On this same day they took photos of the children to send to the United States, because this country is going to send the money to pay the teachers and to cover the expense of school materials and other things.

Sincerely, I did not much believe this would happen until today when they took the pictures. Then I thought, yes, it is certain. My wife took Samuel Jesús to be photographed.

Also, they wrote down the names of us parents. They gave Samuel Jesús the number 86. Then I decided to find out where the idea of a new school originated; that is to say, I planned to help in the meeting in order to write a little about what happens.

On 18 November, after taking the photos, it was decided to rent a place where sheds could be built where the children will have classes. Then the parents convinced Señor Aldelfo Ujpán García, and his wife, Virginia Meranda Ujpán, to lease them a place in the center of town. The land where the parents want to build the large sheds has been planted with coffee trees, but Don Aldelfo and Doña Virginia agreed that the coffee field could be cleared. The craftswomen were happy because they had secured a place to build the school.

On 20 November, at 3:00 P.M., as planned, all the parents gathered to clear the field. But when the parents presented themselves to begin working, Aldelfo and Virginia hid. They had changed their minds.

The parents were upset because it costs a lot to lease such a place. But thanks go to the understanding of the ex-mayor, Benjamín Peña Cholotío, who agreed to rent two *cuerdas* of space and who permitted the clearing of a coffee field. Then the parents cleared this coffee field on 22 November. Much coffee was lost that still was not ripe.

After cleaning the site, they then began to excavate dirt in order to make adobes. Each parent was to make twenty-five adobes to build four houses that will serve as lecture halls where the children will receive instruction. Everyone could not work at the same time, however, so some groups worked in the morning and other groups worked in the afternoon until the adobes were finished.

The Case of the Rich
10 December 1989

[I'm going to write about] what is happening with the coffee lands in this town. There are many *beneficios* [plants] where they process the *café pergamino* [second-class coffee; hulled once, pulped but unshelled, or with the parchment still intact]. But also there are thieves who like to steal the coffee.

One of the owners of a *beneficio* is named Ignacio Hernández Toc, an assistant of the military commissioners who has weapons in his possession that the patrolmen of the civil defense patrol previously used. Now these weapons are being used to guard his *beneficios*.

It happens that Ignacio Hernández Toc hired a caretaker for the *beneficio* and gave him a weapon, with instructions to shoot any thief who came at night. The guard received the order and the weapon. Since it is known that the guards have weapons, it was believed that the thieves would not dare enter.

Then it is said that the owner, Ignacio Hernández Toc, wanted to test whether the guard was complying with his orders to take care of the *beneficio*. This Señor Hernández sent his son Ramón, together with others, to pester the guard, throwing stones over the house and acting as if they wanted to enter in order to steal [something]. Then the guard, Gregorio Juan Puzul, grabbed the weapon and wanted to shoot, but he pondered much about what to do. He hung the weapon in its place, left in the darkness, and grabbed a rock. He threw it in the dark and accurately hit the owner's child in the head. Ramón fell to the ground shouting. When the guard shined light on the person with a lantern, he recognized that it was the child of his boss.

Ramón's companions ran to the house to advise his father. The father ran with a thousand demons and beat the guard; after beating him he locked him up in a house, took the keys, and did not free him until the next day.

On this same night Ignacio Hernández Toc carried his son to the hospital in Sololá, but in Sololá the doctors said to him that they would have to send him to Guatemala [City] to the Roosevelt Hospital. The condition of the boy was serious, and they had to send him to a private hospital. The cost of the medicine alone was more than Q2,000.

Thus are the rich. This boss had ordered the guard to shoot with the weapon at any thief that came close, but when the guard threw a little stone at the boss's son and hit him on the head, he became angry and began to beat up the guard. He forgot that he himself had given the order. Or perhaps he values more the life of his son, and the life of the other human being is not of equal worth.

Tragedy on the Lake
1 to 4 January 1990
Todos sabemos donde nacemos pero no sabemos donde vamos a morir y ninguno puede saber lo que va a suceder [We all know where we were born, but no one knows were we are going to die, and no one can know what is going to happen]. Many come from different places to spend the day, 1 January, on the beaches of the Chuitinamits of Lake Atitlán.[30] On this day some students from Santa Bárbara came. What is not known is whether it was because of foul play or drinking that a student, who would have finished his studies this year to become a teacher of education, drowned. The drowned one was a native of the

canton of Patzilín of Santa Ana la Laguna.

Like the hounds who become happy when an animal dies, there are the corrupt who make death a business. The regional judge [who is the justice of the peace for San Martín, San José, San Jorge, and San Benito] was not in his office because it was the new year. The accident was in the jurisdiction of San Jorge la Laguna, but the location where it happened was ignored because it was the mayor of San José, Juan Mendoza Ovalle, and the assistant of the regional justice of the peace [Mendoza's cohort] who retrieved the corpse. They negotiated the body of the young student for a sum of money. They did not follow the law and report the death and send the body to Sololá for a medical autopsy. Instead, the family paid them to take the body directly to the village of Santa Ana. In this case, there were witnesses present who saw that for the mayor and the official, it was a good business.

The lake continues to gather victims. On Wednesday afternoon, 3 January 1990, there were three North Americans who struggled [to fulfill their mission] in the Mormon Church. In order to celebrate rites in the town of San Jorge la Laguna, they hired a launch from Señor Roberto Sánchez of Panajachel. It is said that the three foreigners boarded the boat, but when they were passing in front of Santa Rosa, the Xocomil [strong wind] caught them. The pilot lost control, and the launch broke up and sank in the lake. Only one of the three Americans was able to save himself; the boatman also died.

The American who was able to save himself without doubt could swim well. He gave notice [of the accident] in Santa Rosa. Then they mobilized themselves to notify the navy and the authorities in Panajachel in order to rescue them [the others], but all was impossible. The navy personnel worked almost all night. Not until dawn of Thursday, the fourth, was the small launch found in the depths of the lake. The civil and military authorities struggled to recover the three corpses, but it was not possible.

Days dragged on in the search of the three disappeared ones. It is said that some scientists came to find out in a study why the bodies weren't found. They concluded that the drowned ones fell in a strong, deep current that dragged them into the crater of the volcano.[31]

This event caused much sadness among Indians and Ladinos, because they [the Mormons and the boatman] lost their lives to announce the message of Jesús, fulfilling what is written in the Bible, where Jesús ordered his apostles with these words, "Go then to the people of all nations and make them my disciples; baptize them in the name of the Father, [and] of the Son, and of the Holy Ghost (San Mateo 28:19–20)."

A Historic Day in My Dear San José
26 November to 17 January 1990
Not until this day, 26 November 1989, did we meet the persons who fought to bring the project of a new *colegio*. All of us parents gathered together to give a good welcome to Señor Jacobo Morales, general director of the project, and the preacher, Don Juan Ramos, accompanied by the illustrious *Joseño*, Geraldo Vásquez Oliva, graduate of pedagogy.

Jacobo Morales spoke first, giving thanks to the goodwill of the parents who are working for the construction of the places where the new *colegio* will be established. Then Don Juan Ramos spoke about things for the good of the indigenous people.

And finally Geraldo Vásquez O. spoke, relating how this project began and how it arrived at San José. He said that Jacobo Morales had gone to Los Angeles and San Diego, California, in the United States of North America. It was there where he fought hard to obtain a project for Guatemala. After a lot of struggling, he succeeded in opening channels with the International Christian Mission, which helped him to do something for the foundation of a private evangelical *colegio;* but the conditions were that the school had to be in one of the three departments of Quiché, Chimaltenango, or Sololá.

When Señor Jacobo Morales returned from the United States, he was thinking a lot about where the program he now had secured could be introduced. He knew *profesor* Vásquez well, and they had talked about what town would be given this opportunity. Geraldo said that they first went to Santa Cruz del Quiché, but they noticed that there were many *colegios* in this northern region. Then they went to Chimaltenango, but he said that in Chimaltenango there were more *colegios* than in El Quiché.

They thought about making this offer in Santiago Atitlán or in San Lucas Tolimán, but also there are many *colegios* in these towns. They returned to Panajachel because *profesor* Geraldo lives in Panajachel. There, he consulted with Don Jacobo to discuss where this *colegio* would be located. Then *profesor* Vásquez agreed on his natal town of

San José and decided to see whether the *Joseños* wanted this opportunity. So he told Jacobo they would go to San José.

When they arrived at the town, they could not find anyone with whom to discuss the offer of building a new school. Then a teacher and his brother named Enrique agreed that Enrique would talk to the Artisans of San José. These women who were organized in the work of making and selling typical clothing were interested, and Enrique told his brother in Panajachel. And this is how the project originated.

A few days after construction of the school began, the parents of the families elected a committee to manage the work. We husbands of the women of the Artisans of San José committed ourselves to work harder because only one month remained before the beginning of classes.

The committee bought the sheet metal that was used for the roof. The committee decided that each family with a child in the *colegio* would pay tuition of Q3 per month (Q36 per year) as a commitment that their children were in school. (Not all would be paid for by the mission.) With this money they bought the wood and the roof. Bricklayers were not paid; it was purely a contribution of the parents of the families.

Since we were doing the construction, the technical director, Geraldo Vásquez O., initiated the steps to get the minister of health to approve the founding of the said *colegio*. The regional supervisor, *profesor* Xico Santos, offered to help us. He gave his approval that the premises were suitable for a *colegio*.

The inspector of health, however, obligated us to fulfill all the requirements of the health law. The premises were ready, but furniture for the children was needed. Still they confirmed that 16 January would be the inauguration of the new evangelical school that had been named La Esperanza by the committee.

By late December the committee still did not have money to buy benches and desks for the children. We met again to see what could be done because the children could not sit on the ground. We decided to organize ourselves in groups of five people to buy boards and to build the benches and desks. Thus each group bought boards and did what was needed.

On 15 January, one day before the inauguration, almost all of us worked on the site of the *colegio*, making the benches and desks. We obtained a handsaw, a hammer, and nails, and each group began to make one bench and one desk. Since we were not carpenters, the results were not as good as those made by professionals. They came out regular, as is said "más o menos" [more or less; not good or bad but average].

On the afternoon of this day, we met again to prepare some decorations for the following day. The committee and the women of the project also made coffee to serve after the inauguration. During the night of this day, a small program was prepared for the designated day.

Invitations were sent to all the teachers of the National School of Rodolfo Juan García, to the Catholic Church, to the two cooperatives, the evangelical churches, to the highest local authority, the municipal corporation, and especially to the señor departmental supervisor of public and private primary schools.

Days earlier, the parents had registered the children in the *colegio* and paid for the scholastic materials. We had been told that the International Christian Mission would provide the scholastic materials, but, instead, the technical director requested money for the materials in advance. It was expensive, because those with children in the first grade paid Q37 while those with children in *párvulos* [pre-primary school, similar to kindergarten] paid Q25. To me it seemed that this was just a business for the director. I did not want to pay this amount, and I thought it would be better to buy the notebooks and other materials for Samuel Jesús in the stores.[32]

On Tuesday, 16 January 1990, it was a historical and important day for my dear San José. The inaugural program was at two o'clock in the afternoon. We husbands of the women who work in the project happily set up the benches in the patio of the new *colegio* where we had invited guests, including the local and nonlocal authorities. Meanwhile, the wives prepared the coffee and straightened things up.

The hour of inauguration was delayed because the launch carrying Jacobo Morales, his wife, and *profesor* Geraldo Vásquez O. was late. The people were becoming a little alarmed because they continued to wait for the formal program to begin.

At 3:30 P.M. the señores arrived, and the inauguration took place. First the evangelical pastor, Jacobo Morales, explained to those present the history of how the founding of the school came about. His wife also spoke, recognizing the value of the *Joseña* women, who with their own efforts were participating in the development of the community. Then a representative of the cooperative La Voz que Clama en el Desierto

[The Voice That Cries out in the Desert] spoke, giving thanks to the goodwill of the parents who in one way or another did what was necessary to make this establishment a reality. Xico Santos, the regional supervisor, read the text of the founding *acta* [document, or record of all the steps to establish the school], stating that the evangelical primary school La Esperanza was inaugurated. Next, the parents of the students asked me to say some words of appreciation about the effort of Jacobo Morales, Geraldo Vásquez Oliva, Xico Santos, the people present, and the parents who contributed their work. Finally, Señor Samuel Ujpán Pérez, the president of the Artisans of San José, brought closure to the program with his words of farewell. After the inaugural program was over, everyone was invited to have coffee and bread.

It surprised us that no one from the municipal corporation was present. Neither the mayor, Juan Mendoza, nor any of the councilmen was present because these things were unimportant to them. Most of the townspeople, however, condemned the irresponsibility of the corporation. When it comes to promoting education in the pueblo, they are almost dead.

Classes began on Wednesday, 17 January. Of the hundred parents who enrolled their children, ten withdrew. But when the people realized that the school had become a reality, they enrolled 125 children. The parents of the extra 25 students were told they had to pay a fee of five quetzales monthly.[33]

A few weeks after the school's opening, the health inspector obligated us to make a cement floor and to plaster [the walls], saying that if his order is not carried out the school will be closed. Again we parents met. The committee decided that it would buy cement and that each parent would bring sand. This we did on a Saturday and Sunday. We covered the rustic floor with cement, but we only covered the walls with lime because we did not have the time or money to do otherwise.

The twenty-five parents who enrolled their children late volunteered to dig a pit that served for the sanitary services. The señor inspector was severe with us, but indeed we struggled to go forward with the job, to enhance the name of San José.

The truth is that there were days that I myself could not work on the construction on the school because I had a lot of work to do in the *campo*. But on those days I sent *mozos* to work in my place.

Twice Becoming Godparents

Sunday, 4 February, to Sunday, 18 February 1990

My *compadre* [male friend; ritual coparent] Juan Sisay Ujpán came to my house to ask me and my wife to be the godparents of his daughter, Josefa Nicolasa Sisay Yojcom, who would receive the baptismal water next 11 February.

My wife and I agreed to be the godparents. My *compadre* told us that we will have to attend three days in the parochial *salón* [assembly room] in order to receive prebaptismal sermons, as always is the custom of the Catholic Church.

Then the prebaptismal sermons were on Monday, the fifth, and they were finished on Thursday, the eighth. Sunday we attended mass, and at this same time we were the godparents of Juana Imelda. This rite was solemn because forty-five children were baptized. All the godparents are religious; perhaps for them my participation was rare.

After the mass the parents of the baby took us to their house for a dinner and a little beer, but not much. The *compadres* wanted us to drink more, but I said no to them because it saddens me to drink a lot since that's how one loses control. After we left this house, we arrived home happy with our children. As always giving thanks to God.

On Friday, 16 February, Señor Ernesto Ujpán Oliva came and asked us to be the godparents of his baby named Huberto Mariano Ujpán Pérez, who was to be baptized in the church of San Lucas Tolimán on Sunday, 18 February. Then I discussed with my wife whether we would have time to go to San Lucas. We decided to accept in order to stay on good terms with the señor. Then we told him yes, that we will go on Sunday.

Sunday arrived, and we got up early and went to the beach to take the launch to Santiago Atitlán. From Santiago Atitlán we went by bus to San Lucas Tolimán. Ernesto went with his señora and his mother-in-law. They went to eat breakfast at one *comedor* [small restaurant, diner], and we went to eat breakfast at another. Afterward we made our way to the Catholic church to write down the name of the baby. At 9:00 A.M. the priest started the mass. The baptism lasted until 11:00 A.M. A photographer took photos of us, but he was paid by the child's parents.

After we left the church, the parents invited us for a lunch at a *comedor*. Before eating lunch, Señor Ernesto and his señora told me that we will have to use different words. As respect for their first son, from now on, we are going to address each other as *compadres* [god-father] and *comadres* [godmothers]. We accepted their wishes because this is what we have done with everyone.

Also, the baptism was solemn because children from different towns arrived. The reason that we went to San Lucas for this baptism was to not lose time for the prebaptismal sermons. In this town the prebaptismal sermon is only one hour, and then there is the baptism [unlike in San José, which takes three days just for the prebaptismal ceremony].

On this trip to San Lucas, Samuel Jesús went happily with us. After all the activities, we bought some fruit for the children who had stayed home. In the afternoon we arrived at the house, peacefully, thanks to God.

A Pregnant Woman Drowns in the Lake
11 March 1990
Sunday, 11 March 1990, we attended a solemn mass where we were the godparents of the baby Clemente Jaime Cholotío Quic, son of Ernesto Cholotío Mendoza and Virginia Quic Bizarro. After the baptism we went to the house of the *compadres* to accompany them for dinner. The baptism ceremony was at five o'clock in the afternoon. We ate dinner at seven o'clock in the evening and enjoyed ourselves with the *compadres*.

My friends from Tzancuil told me about a drowning that happened on Sunday, 11 March 1990. Juan and Arminda were parents of a girl. Because of bad luck, all but one of their children had died.

The woman got pregnant again, but after eight months into the pregnancy, she and her husband became afraid the baby might die when it was born. A well-intending neighbor suggested they go to a *zajorín* to perform *costumbres* to protect the baby during childbirth.

Then Juan and Arminda looked for a good *zajorín* in the village of Tzancuil, but unfortunately they couldn't find one. Another person told them that in the city of Sololá there was a first-class *zajorín*. So they arranged to make a trip to Sololá this Sunday, 11 March. They were happy; they brought gifts for the *zajorín* and everything necessary for a ceremony.

The *zajorín* performed the ceremony and said it was received well [by the gods]. The *zajorín* said that there was no danger, that the woman's pregnancy will go well, that a son will be born, and that for sure he will live.

After having this ceremony, they were happy with all that the *zajorín* had told them, and they had some drinks with him. There is no doubt that they left Sololá quite drunk. At 3:00 P.M. they arrived at Panajachel to take the launch to Tzancuil. The launch that went directly from Panajachel to San Martín arrived. Since Juan and Arminda were drunk, they got on this launch thinking that it would go by Tzancuil and drop them off. When the launch went past Tzancuil, they yelled to the pilot to let them off, but the pilot told them that he would stop for them on the return. The husband fell asleep, but the woman was delirious, and suddenly she fell on her head into the depths of the lake without uttering even one word. The pilot and his helper tried to rescue her, but it was impossible. This woman disappeared once and for all.

The launch *Gorrión del Lago* was detained in Panajachel; he who remained under arrest was the helper. The owner of the business, Haroldo Puzul, had to pay Q1,500 for the bail of the assistant in order for him to have his freedom.

What Goes around Comes around: The Law of Compensation
Events of the Days 29 June 1989 to 26 March 1990

As is the custom on 29 June 1989, the patronal fiesta of San Pedro Apóstol in San Martín la Laguna is celebrated. People from many other neighboring towns arrive to spend a happy day, but at times it ends in tragedy.

On this day the transporters were doing a lot of businesses, especially the enterprises that transport [goods and people] over the lake. In the afternoon of this day the people began to return to their towns by the trucks and also by the launches. The owners of the trucks were already tired, but they had to keep working until 7:00 P.M.

Since there still were people from San Jorge, San Benito, and Santa Rosa [who needed to travel], they went down to the dock to try to ride on a boat. When they arrived onshore, the only launch that was ready to depart was the *Martinita* of Don Juan García Sumoza. The passengers began to board the launch, and when it was full, the pilot steered the boat away from the dock.

Among the passengers were many *bolos (ebrios)* [drunks]. Halfway across the lake, between San Martín and San Benito, one of the drunks needed to urinate. He got up and without a doubt thought he was on land. When he tried to walk, he fell into the depths of the lake. Those who saw him said that the drunk fell shouting, and then these alarmed passengers told the pilot to stop the launch because a person had fallen overboard. But the pilot, the son of the owner of the boat, said that he did not want to change course to rescue a drunk.

The name of the man who fell is Delfino Ixtamer. The owner of the launch, Señor García Sumoza of San Martín, threatened the passengers not to denounce him before the authorities. Then in order to not receive reprisals from the owner, the passengers did nothing. It was as if nothing had happened. The next day news circulated that the previous night a *Beniteño* [person of San Benito] had fallen from a launch and that those who witnessed this deed did not want to press charges before the regional justice of the peace for fear of reprisals.

When the relatives went to ask the owner, he said that he did not know anything about it. He told them that if they continued bothering him, he would accuse them of making calumnies before the tribunals of Sololá. Thus the relatives remained mute.

The relatives went out over the lake to look for the body of Delfino. *Beniteños* in little *cayaques* [canoes] finally found his corpse near the pier of San Jorge la Laguna. It was recovered in the presence of the local justice of the peace. Because of the [poor] state of the body, the judge had the consideration not to send it to Sololá. And the relatives said that he drowned accidentally, covering up what actually had happened.

The owner of the launch was content not having to admit anything, not even spending any money for the life of the drowned one. But he indeed was responsible. As owner of the boat, it is his duty to have competent helpers to handle whatever happens on the launch.

Sometimes the law of compensation is not tardy. Hardly nine months had passed when on Monday, 26 March of this year, Señor Juan García Sumoza went to the capital city of Guatemala in his pickup. He went with his children to trade in his used vehicle for a new one. The children said that the deal already had been made, but before leaving the car dealer, Juan and his son Mauricio went to get something to eat. As they were crossing the street, Juan was hit, thrown in the air, and killed by a car; that is, the owner of the launch *Martinita* died, and his business now is in the hands of his children and his wife.

La Esperanza Primary School
1 to 22 June 1990

We had three meetings with the teachers at La Esperanza Primary School to select a uniform to be worn by the school's students during the parade of the titular fiesta. We decided that we parents would buy the uniforms for our children. For the boys the uniform would be black pants, black shoes or sandals, white shirts, small hats with a red ribbon, and red belts to circle the waist. For the girls it would be black *cortes,* white blouses, brown and black head scarves, and red belts. The dress for the girls was the same as the old costume for the women of the town.

The parade will take place on 22 June, and it will be held during the fiesta in honor of our patron saint, San Juan Bautista. The organized groups of the town decided that the parade will begin on Xechumil Road, which leads to San Martín from San José. Then the parade will cross the principal streets of the town and end up at the soccer field. The participants in this parade will include all the local sporting groups, the national school, the night school for adults, DIGESA [Dirección General de Servicios Agrícola, Office of Agricultural Services], the *instituto básico,* the Comité Nacional de Alfabetización [CONALFA, National Committee of Literacy], and the student group, K'asal Yaa (the Baptist). And why not mention the new La Esperanza Primary School? All of the groups will carry their respective banners.

Preaching Catholic Actionism and the Law of Compensation
10 July 1990
On this day died the wife of Señor Juan Bizarro Gómez, brother of my grandfather Ignacio Bizarro Ramos. The wife of Señor Juan was named Juana Vásquez. Juan Bizarro Gómez and Juana Vásquez were the first persons who struggled to establish Catholic Action. Earlier there were just *católicas antiguas* [folk Catholics], but upon the arrival of the curia at San Martín la Laguna, they began to organize Catholic Action. It was then that Señor Juan and his wife went to other towns, San Jorge, San Benito, Santa Ana, and Santa Bárbara, and the *aldeas* of San José, Patzilín, Pachichaj, and Tzarayá, to teach the people. It is certain they had great success, and they converted many people to Catholic Actionism.

Señor Juan was the first president of Catholic Action in San José la Laguna. But this man zealously attacked the other religions and customs in the town. He viewed the dancers and *zajorines* with great contempt, and he did not want anyone to drink. During the fiestas, he would send catechists to control the members of Catholic Action so that none of them would have a drink. If through thoughtlessness someone had a drink, they were expelled from the church and branded workers of the devil.

Everybody was compelled to marry [in the church and not just live *juntos,* or joined]. Only when they did so was the baptism of their children permitted.

When a member of a family dies, the custom of the people is to take the body of the deceased to the church as a final farewell. Then Señor Juan Bizarro ordered that those who had died without the sacrament of matrimony would not be allowed to be taken inside the church for this final farewell. Like a punishment or mockery, the bodies of those who died without marriage would be put on the patio of the church, so that everyone could see that an unbeliever had died and his or her body would not be permitted to enter the church.

I remember well when the two señores Benjamín Cholotío and Juan Pop died in 1958 without receiving the sacrament of matrimony. Their bodies were placed on the patio of the church, and they were not allowed to be put inside. This was a type of discrimination, so that everyone could see what happened to those who did not get married. Seeing such condemnations, each day more people would convert to Catholic Actionism in order not to fall under the disfavor of its directors.

In 1956 Señor Martín Coj was the tutor of the Dance of the Conquest. To Catholic Actionists, he was an enemy of the church; they would not allow the dance to be performed on the portico of the church, because it was considered an act of the devil. Señor Martín obtained permission from the government in Sololá allowing the dancers to perform in front of the church, since the dance is dedicated to our patron saint. But the president of Catholic Action did not respect this permission from the government. Then the tutor of the dance went to a great deal of trouble to ask permission from the parish priest of San Martín. The parish priest gave his permission to the dancers, but the Catholic Actionists did not respect this permission either. They told the parish priest that the dancers gave a bad image to Catholic Actionism, because all they did was drink *aguardiente.* That was why they did not allow it. But in truth, there was no place else to perform the dance. Once again the dancers went to the priest to ask that he consider permitting them to perform the Dance of the Conquest on the two days of the twenty-third and the twenty-fourth. Then the priest, Catholic Actionists, and the dancers entered into an agreement, that the dancers could perform for those two days in front of the church but without drinking a single drop of liquor. Also, they were told they would be watched by the catechists, and if they caught one dancer drinking *guaro,* they would immediately be removed from the area. The tutor and the dancers had to sign a document of commitment, which obligated them to abstain from alcohol during the fiesta.

The specified day arrived, and the dancers gathered in front of the church under the watchful eye of the catechists so that no one could have a drink. But since the dance was tiring, there was a need for drinks. Then the dancers looked for a way to have something to drink. Indeed, liquor was given to the dancers and the musicians, but it was given to them in coffee. The catechists were watchful, but the dancers were able to drink their liquor tranquilly and nobody found out that the coffee had liquor in it. At that time, I was a dancer; my role was that of Pedro [de] Portocarrero.

I say these things because it is true that at one time the Catholic Actionists behaved harshly toward the folk Catholics. This was all due to Señor Juan Bizarro Gómez, the religious leader who led these attacks against the old customs. I knew Señor Juan, and he used to drink. But when he got the opportunity to become a religious leader, he became the number one enemy against drinking *aguardiente.*

But there is a law of compensation. Señor Juan did everything to the people, scorning those who drank and treating them like demons [and mistreating those who did not marry in the church]. He said many things, believing he was safe from retribution. With the passage of time, however, when he least expected it, he fell into the hands of misfortune.

In addition to his wife, Juana Vásquez, dying on this date [10 July 1990], two years ago his daughter, María Bizarro Vásquez, died. A few months later his nephew died. His two sons [finally] died of the disease of alcoholism after spending most of their lives drinking. On 28 August [1988] his son Huberto Warren Bizarro Vásquez died, and on 25 December 1988 his son Antonio Bizarro Vásquez died [as mentioned in the episode "Death Comes without Warning," above].

As I write these things, I ask God's forgiveness, because, truthfully, I don't want to appear to be judgmental. The fate of Señor Juan might serve, however, as a lesson for us to restrain our tongues and to be merciful. If we are compassionate, God will be compassionate; if we are merciful and patient with the faults of our brothers, God will in turn give us His mercy.

Politicians Begin Their Tricks and Lies
5 to 11 August 1990

In August the politicians began their tricks. They promise to do everything, but when they assume power, they forget all about what they have promised. It is clear what the President Vinicio Cerezo Arévalo said he would do. He said he would better the lives of Guatemalans, improve the cost of living, improve health services by giving half his salary to pay for medicines for the hospitals, restore human rights, and have no more military, etc., etc., etc. But the first thing he did when he assumed the presidency was to raises the prices of goods in order to raise the salaries of the military, his deputies, and himself. It is not known exactly what the president's [monthly] salary is; some say Q5,000, others say Q65,000. There is one version that says his salary is Q90,000. This last version was announced by the *magisterio* [teaching staff or assembly]. But who knows which of these three versions is correct. What is said with certainty is that Señor Vinicio Cerezo Arévalo bought the finest mansion in Central America; the information going around says that the president purchased a beautiful island and a splendid yacht for his comfort.

And Señor Alfonso Cabrera Hidalgo, the presidential candidate of the party Democracia Cristiana, wants the same thing. Señor Cabrera offers many things for the good of the *indígenas* [indigenes, Indians], especially the native women, who are marginalized by the white race. But this is all a lie. The people already know this, and they no longer believe in such lies. According to the newspapers and radio, in many parts of the country the candidate Alfonso Cabrera and the representative of *listado nacional* [a list of congressional deputies not elected by a town but appointed by Congress or the Executive Branch], Father Andrés Girón de León, have received insults and ill treatment. They have even had mud thrown in their faces, especially in the districts of Quiché, Totonicapán, Quezaltenango, and Sololá.

On 5 August 1990 the candidate of the party Democracia Cristiana came to San José la Laguna to try to convince the people. He asked the directors of Catholic Action if the meeting with the people could be held in the parochial *salón,* but this was denied. The meeting was held on the basketball court. To add to his greatness, the candidate called on the four [main] *cofrades* [members of a *cofradía*] and gave each one Q1,000. He thus gave Q1,000 to the *cofradías* of San Juan Bautista, María Concepción, Santo Domingo Guzmán, and San José. This last *cofradía* (San José) is newly activated. For the *cofrades,* this was good business, or perhaps it is better to say this was a beautiful gift to use for drinking. In the afternoon the *cofrades* of Santo Domingo Guzmán started drinking with the money donated by Don Alfonso. Without question, they drank excessively. On the following day, 6 August, a *mayordomo* of the *cofradía* of Santo Domingo was injured. He fell among the rocks and cut his face. He had to stay home for many days.

On 11 August 1990 Jorge Carpio Nicolle came to this town. He is a lawyer and presidential candidate of the party Unión del Centro Nacional. He offered many things, but in truth he did not offer to donate money. He merely offered his plan for governing when he is president, saying there that there would be a change for Guatemala, that he would punish the corrupt officials of the government of the Christian Democrats, that he was very much against the prices we Guatemalans were paying for things, and that the only beneficiaries [of the high prices] were a group of political representatives of the present government. The people paid attention to what he said, but who knows if they will vote for him.

My Son Marries His Woman
Saturday, 25 August 1990

On this date my son José Juan Bizarro Ramos contracted a civil marriage with his woman, María Ramos García. The matrimony was celebrated in our home by the municipal *alcalde.* It took place at five o'clock in the afternoon so that those invited would not lose any time [have to take time away from work].

We invited all my wife's relatives and members of my family so that all of us could witness the marriage. In addition, close friends stopped by. After the ceremony we served coffee and bread.

After everything was all over, the invited guests all went home. We stayed inside the house with my wife's parents in order to give some advice to José and his wife on how to live better lives so that in the future they will have a happy and tranquil family. They may be poor, but they will not be conformists [doing things they shouldn't, such as vices]. This was the advice we gave to them. The father of my wife bought some drinks after the ceremony, and we did drink but not too much because we had other obligations.

A Lot of Problems When You Have a Large Family
30 August to 15 September 1990

[There are] quite a lot of problems when you have a large family. There are many expenses, and one has to have a lot of patience with one's children. As a father, one has to face many obstacles and problems. But every event gives one more experience, and a father with experience must advance little by little in order to achieve something better, not for himself, but for his children.

In my case, I am a patient man who has suffered and worked hard because I have many children, but I am also content with my family. I like to counsel and discipline them. At times I give them [the children] a whipping so that they learn respect, and when they are older, this will be all for their [own] good. We are a poor family; we do not dress well, nor do we wear expensive shoes. We merely possess the necessary clothes. We are honest in our work, and [perhaps] that is why we do not have money.

On 30 August 1990 there was the selection of the Niña de Independencia [Child of Independence]. Among the candidates participating was my daughter Anica Catana. The candidates were presented to the examining panel of judges. The selection was based on presentation and participation.

For me, it was a bit comical, because Anica Catana is a child who doesn't give the appearance of being clever. Nevertheless, she was able to win. This past June, she took over the post of Flor Infantil [Flower Child] for 1989–90.

On this day the examining judges certified that Anica Catana Bizarro Ramos was selected as Niña de Independencia for 1990–91. The teachers [judges] arrived at my house to ask if I was in agreement with them in the matter of preparing the typical costume for the day of the coronation. I told them I was in agreement with them, and that I would do everything possible to prepare the necessary items. After our discussion we drank some soft drinks.

Beginning in the month of September 1990, we have no money in our family. We are a bit dismayed that everything has gone up in price, and our currency, the quetzal, is only worth twenty cents. For people like us, who are poor, it is a calamity, while for the rich, every day is filled with glory, because they are happy with having exploited the poor. Moreover, the rich hardly lose. We poor people are, as usual, the turkeys of the fiesta.

My wife did everything possible to weave the *huipil* [traditional blouse] with all its embroidery. We also made the *corte,* so that all we had to buy was the thread. Thus it cost us little to make the costume.

By 10 September everything was ready. We prepared the *ropa antigua* [traditional costume] for the queen of the Independence Day activities of the school. At 8:00 P.M. the teachers and students along with a school band arrived to get Anica Catana. We had to accompany them. The investiture and coronation were very beautiful and joyful. It made us forget for a moment our problems at home. After all the ceremonies, I returned home with my wife and children.

During the night of 10 September, we hardly slept. My wife and my daughter Susana Julia were preparing take-out food for the two boys, Ramón Antonio and Erasmo Ignacio. They are involved with the boys from the *instituto básico* for an excursion to the north of the country. This trip includes the bringing of the *fuego simbólico antorcha* [symbolic torch] to celebrate the anniversary of our homeland's independence day on 15 September.

The truth is I did not want my boys to go on this journey because I did not have the money to cover the cost of the trip, but I realized that they needed more experience and knowledge. That is why I had to do my best to obtain the money. My brother Gaspar gave me Q100 to help cover the cost of the excursion. The fare for each is Q50, in addition to the other expenses. My wife said they should not go, because she is conscientious about our household expenses, but little by little we convinced her they should go.

The students from the *instituto básico* left on a bus from San Martín at 2:00 A.M. on 11 September. Two of the students were left behind because they missed the bus. They were sleepyheads.

During the morning of 11 September 1990, I felt a sadness for the situation we are experiencing. The quetzal has lost its value, and everything has gone up in price. There is a majority of us *Guatemaltecos* [people of Guatemala], about 70 percent, who are suffering due to this rise in the cost of living. We are suffering these things in my family. But, in truth, there are families who are suffering more than we, such as those who work for others, like the *jornaleros* [day laborers], who earn only Q6 a day. With those Q6 they must buy maize, sugar, beans, and other items. If they have a large family, how much can they buy with Q6? Because of this, I say that we *Guatemaltecos* are in total crisis. My hope is that I will receive a check from the [royalties of the] two books, *Son of Tecún Umán* and *Campesino.*

Wednesday, 12 September 1990. When a man labors, he will receive compensation, even though it may be delayed, and I am reminded of the words of my good friend, Jaime Sexton. I used to ask him questions and tell him that I respect the written word and published books but that I wanted compensation right away. My friend Jaime Sexton would tell me, we need to have more patience. He would always tell me this, and it has truly come to pass.

On this day, I had no money, but it turned out to be a day of relief. At 10:00 A.M. I received a notice from the post office. When I went there the postman gave me a certified letter from the University of Arizona in Tucson. After receiving the letter, I went home, where my two daughters were working. We then opened the letter, which contained a [good] check. I cried for joy, and my two daughters kissed me. I did this because I still owe Q300, need to pay for room and board for María, and owe another debt to the Banco Nacional de Desarrollo Agrícola (BANDESA, National Bank of Agricultural Development). When I informed my wife that I had received a check from the book earnings, she felt as if we had been blessed.

On this same day, I went to Panajachel, to cash the check at a commercial house. If you cash a check at the Banco Agrícola Mercantil, you must wait twenty days to a month to receive the money. Because of this, I went to the house of Señor José María Poco Barreno. After cashing the check [at an exchange rate of $1 equals Q5.5], I went to the market to have breakfast at a *comedor.* I arrived home at 5:00 P.M. and then went to the *caja rural* [rural cash desk; small agency where loans can be paid but not taken out] of the Banco Nacional de Desarrollo Agrícola to pay the interest and part of the debt. In total, I paid Q512.

In the afternoon of this same day, I went to San Martín to pay Q252 for six bags of chickens that I had ordered from the institution of DIGESEPE [Dirección General de Servicios Pecuario (Office of Livestock Services)]. The chickens will be delivered on the nineteenth of this month. It is certain that I do not want to waste this money that I earned from my work with Señor Jaime D. Sexton. That is why I am interested in buying these chickens.

On 13 September 1990 I went to Quezaltenango with my wife and Maruca [nickname for María]. The reason for going was to pay the Q300 still owed for the room and board and tuition for the month of September. But before this we had to go to Paxtocá, Totonicapán, to pay Q50 to my friend Juan Diego Tuc Chac. From there we went to Xela. After we returned from Quezaltenango, we had to go to the city of Salcajá in order to buy thread and *guindana*. In total, I spent about Q600 for these materials. We had to return on the same day in order not to spend any more money. After we had returned from this trip, we gave thanks to God for the benefits we had received.

On 14 September 1990 it rained all day and all night. At 11:00 P.M. the students of the sixth grade of the primary school arrived, bringing the torch from the second capital, Antigua.

The students from the night school for adults went to the city of Quezaltenango to bring the symbolic fire [there was more than one torch]. They arrived at the town about 11:30 P.M. amid pouring rain.

The boys from the 4-S group went to the *cabecera* [departmental capital] of Sololá on this civic-minded night and brought the flame.[34] They arrived at 11:45 P.M.

The boys from the *instituto básico* arrived at midnight, bringing the torch that proceeded from the ruins of Tikal and that passed through Petén and Puerto Barrios. Amid all the rain, we parents came out to receive our sons in front of the Catholic church, to give them encouragement and demonstrate to them the value of the sacrifice they have made for the good of their homeland.

For the first time in the history of the town, the civic night was celebrated in front of the Catholic church. The entire night was festive, and we hardly slept. All the people were harmoniously celebrating a night commemorating the political emancipation of Guatemala.

For the parade of 15 September 1990, everything was joyful, but the group that had the most children was the evangelical primary school, La Esperanza. The parents of all the students contributed Q300 for the expenses. With that money, a marimba band was hired, which served to liven up the parade, adding a touch of splendor to these civic activities.

There are many events in the life of a man, but it is good when he works for a living and does not steal, even if he barely gets by, because stealing is a crime and is punished by the law. In my case, I am a man who works hard, and I am beginning to suffer from arthritis, which is difficult to cure, since in order to do so one must rest. A man like myself, however, cannot afford to rest, because to lose two or three days' work is too much. This is how it is for people like us, the *indígenas*.

Technicians from DIGESEPE Bring Chickens
19 September 1990

On this day the technicians from DIGESEPE came to bring me the six bags of chickens. Each bag contains twelve chickens. In sum, we bought seventy-two, consisting of sixty chickens and twelve roosters when fully grown. According to the instructions, I must buy the proper feed. The food concentrate costs Q53.50 for each *quintal,* and each day they consume nine pounds. This is because the chicks are small; they are only seven weeks old. I want this breeding of chickens to be a job for my two daughters Susana Julia and Anica Catana.

To properly breed these chickens, they must be in a separate place. That is why I had to build a chicken coop. I built it out of adobe and cane. I used some old pieces of *láminas* to make the roof, but I needed two sheets of *láminas* to finish it. I then went to the father of my wife, since he has many secondhand *láminas*. I asked him if he would lend me two sheets, or if not, sell them to me. My wife's father then told me he would not lend or sell me any *láminas*. I asked him again, [telling him] that I only needed them for two weeks until I could buy some *láminas* of my own. He repeated the same thing. This attitude by my father-in-law bothered me greatly. I left his house feeling a bit resentful. My father-in-law has many *láminas*, all old and lying about. Such action by a father bothered me; he is good for nothing.

When I arrived home, I thought a lot about this, and I prayed to God that I would never act like that with my children. If God continues to give me life, it is better to ask for intelligence in order to help your children.

I give thanks, as usual, for having been given the gift of life.

The Violence in Santiago Atitlán
14 to 22 October 1990

This is what is taking place in our pueblo of Santiago Atitlán, land of the ancient King Tepepul. There is much more violence in this year of 1990 than there was in previous years. Day after day there are more massacres of the *naturales* [Indians] of our beautiful Tzutuhil town. It seems, however, that the two sides are claiming victims and many more than in October of this year. Almost on a daily basis, the Tzutuhiles are killed by the bullets.

Truthfully, I did not witness this. I learned of it through the news on the radio and from the talk of the people living around the lake, both of which condemned the massacre of the six tradesmen who were returning from Cerro de Oro with a truckload of avocados. At the said location, they were all shot, and their bodies were strewn over the road. It is said that one of the assassins, seeing that one of the victims still lived, pulled out a sharp machete and split open his chest and neck. It was said these killers were thieves, although no concrete evidence supported this. What was known for sure was that the six victims were *naturales* and residents of Santiago Atitlán, Sololá. The truck driver was a Ladino. He was able to save his life, although he received many blows. He said he was told to drive the truck to the town, and he did as he was told. It was clear that in our Tzutuhil town of Santiago Atitlán there was no longer any respect for human rights.

The [following] event took place on Sunday, 21 October 1990. In the night, it is said, all the *zajorines* were gathered together in the *cofradía* of Santa Cruz, the same place where they worship Maximón. The *zajorines* had gathered together to perform a *costumbre* to Maximón in order to pray for a miracle to eliminate the violence and killing. Everything was prepared, when suddenly, minutes before the ceremony was to begin, a man with his face covered entered the *cofradía*. This man then asked all those present, with the exception of the *alcalde* of the *cofradía*, Don Martín Quejú, to leave, as he had some business to discuss with the *alcalde*. The *zajorines* complied and went outside. The *alcalde*, Martín Quejú, and the *primer zajorín* [first shaman] remained inside. After a few minutes, shots from an automatic weapon rang out. It is said that the man with the covered face, after having murdered Señor Quejú, calmly walked out onto the street and left.

When the rest of the *zajorines* reentered the *cofradía*, they saw the body of the *alcalde* bathed in blood. He had been killed with fifteen bullet wounds. Also, Maximón had been wounded by gunfire and was half destroyed.

I went to Santiago Atitlán on Monday, 22 October 1990. At 8:00 A.M. the [regional] justice of the peace of San Lucas Tolimán arrived to speed up the proceedings and transport the body as specified by law. The official of the *juzgado* [court] is named Juan. We talked for a bit, since I knew him when he was the [regional] justice of the peace of San Martín la Laguna. It was not he who told me about this affair of the *zajorines;* he merely told me that he had come to this pueblo to pick up the body of a person murdered inside a *cofradía.*

It was other men who told me that it was the *primer zajorín* who was involved in the above case. They also told me the *zajorines* had gathered to perform a ceremony to Maximón to ask protection for the left-wing group. It is also said that those of the extreme right-wing group wanted to do the same thing, that is, to perform the same ceremony to Maximón in the *cofradía* for their protection. Let me clarify by saying that the *zajorines* are divided into two groups. The more powerful *zajorines* are said to be allied with the left-wing group, while the less powerful *zajorines* are in league with the right-wing group. Thus the right-wing *zajorines,* those who are in accord with the military, are helping the military avoid defeat by the leftists.

One day, the *zajorines* of the right wing decided to perform a ceremony in the *cofradía* of Maximón. It is also said the *alcalde* of the *cofradía* of Santa Cruz, Martín Quejú, found out that this group of *zajorines* was collaborating with the right-wing faction. He then decided not to admit into the *cofradía* this group of *zajorines,* since they would perform a ceremony to Maximón. This group of *zajorines* were offended by the decision of the *alcalde.* My friends then informed me that these *zajorines* had undoubtedly gone to accuse the *alcalde* at this meeting of the *cofradía* and that this was what had caused the death of the *alcalde.* Finally, they informed me that soon those committing these murders will be discovered and exposed to the world by Maximón, that is, Don Pedro [de Alvarado]. Don Pedro has never bothered anybody. He is a saint who has performed many miracles to cure the sick, and now he has been wounded by the bullets of the killers. But there is a God in heaven and a God on earth who shall expose these deeds that are happening in our pueblo. This is what my friends in Santiago told me.[35]

Afterward, I said good-bye and returned to my town.

The Violation of Human Rights and the Massacres Continue to Leave More Homes in Mourning in Santiago Atitlán
Thursday, 25 October 1990

The violation of human rights and the massacres continue to leave more homes in mourning. In Santiago Atitlán in the department of Sololá, every day is bathed in blood. The notice circulated through the media and by word of mouth in Santiago that the telegraph operator, Pablo Enrique Camaja, a native of Cunen in the *municipio* of the department of Santa Cruz del Quiché, was shot to death in the telegraph office in Santiago Atitlán. He was living there due to his having obtained a job in Santiago. The notice said that an unknown delinquent staked out the telegraph office and then opened fire on the deceased Camaja with a 9mm pistol. The offender, after having committed this bloody deed, calmly left.

This bloody act was definitely committed in the town, not in the telegraph office. The killing of Señor Camaja took place a block away from the telegraph office. I spoke with some *Atitecos,* and they informed me that the crime was due to personal motives. They told me Camaja married a woman from Santiago, but the woman had a lover in her own town. Her lover became offended because she married Camaja. He then decided to trick her and gain her confidence again. The woman allowed herself to get involved with her former lover. Pablo Enrique Camaja found out that his wife was having relations with another man, and in order to get even with her he also looked around for another woman. However, this woman also had another lover, and it was this man who arranged for Camaja to be killed. Now the people are beginning to ask who is committing these crimes and what are the authorities doing about it, or is it the authorities themselves who are responsible for these killings? This particular killing took place in the center of the town three blocks from the substation of the national police and two kilometers from a military detachment, but they are not helping in the investigation.

Day after day there are killings in the town, and the authorities say the same thing, that the murders are committed by unknown delinquents armed with pistols or automatic rifles. But they say we shall capture those responsible for the killings, when perhaps they should be saying that they are too busy to investigate. What is certain is that many *naturales* have been killed and they treat such crimes as if nothing had happened. Or perhaps we *naturales* are worth nothing. Because of all this, the Tzutuhil people say that in Guatemala there is no authority or justice, and that is why many believe that the authorities are responsible for the killings of the campesinos and the defenseless.

Many of my people abandon their homes, lands, and crops due to fear and repression. If they go to work in their fields, they may be treated as subversives and might well lose their lives and never see their families again.

Many of the *Atitecos* came to these towns around the lake to try to acquire land and construct homes and get away from the violence. This has not been possible, because the prices of the lands around the lake are high, and the only people who can afford to buy them are those with a lot of money, such as the North Americans or the Europeans. For the poor, there is nothing.

Activities of the Political Parties
25 to 26 October 1990

There was a lot of activity on the part of political parties, all offering many things. Here in San José, the party Democracia Cristiana Guatemalteca was active, wanting to appear good to the town. Three years ago, the *profesor* Alfonso Cabrera Hidalgo came to the town to offer the construction of schools and roads and the enlargement of the electrical plant. He also promised to donate 140 *contadores* [electric meters] to those families most needing them. But all this was only a false offer. Nothing concrete ever came of it.

Now, in 1990, Señor Alfonso Cabrera Hidalgo is running again as a presidential candidate. The *directiva* [board of directors] had recorded everything he had promised three years ago, and the townspeople had been upset with his trickery.

Again Alfonso Cabrera came here and promised to supply the *contadores* under the condition that the *directiva* had to negotiate with the Ministry of Development. The *directiva* then took these steps of negotiation. They said the Ministry of Development promised them two hundred *contadores,* but they first needed to compile a list of two hundred persons who represent the needy families. However, in this town, there were not two hundred persons who belonged to this political party. The *directiva* then went from house to house among the people offering their *contadores*. They also came to our house and promised us two *contadores*. We received this offer, not because we are members of their political party, but because the *contadores* are a donation and, truthfully, we have paid many taxes, and so if we want, we can receive two *contadores* when the *directiva* receives them from the *ministerio* [ministry].

On Thursday, 25 October 1990, María went to Quezaltenango with her companions to prepare for their graduation, which is scheduled to be held on Saturday, the twenty-seventh of this month. The truth is I wanted to buy my daughter a ring for her graduation, but it was not possible. The cheapest one cost Q300. She was in agreement with me on this, and we bought her a *corte* for Q200 and a blouse for Q25.

All of us, including my wife, had made plans to go to Quezaltenango on Friday, the twenty-sixth. But because of curiosity on our part to see how the señor from the Ministry of Development was received in our town, we did not leave on that day.

On Friday, 26 October 1990, there was a big fiesta throughout the town. Every family gave a contribution of Q10 for the reception of the minister of development, the lawyer Mario Valenzuela. An engineer represented the Instituto Nacional de Electrificación (INDE), while Dr. Juan Félix Navaro Rodas and *profesor* Viagran represented the candidates. The arrival of Minister Valenzuela took place late in the afternoon, at 3:30. The arrival of the *contadores* took place on the basketball court in front of the entire town. The local branch of the party sponsored a marimba and provided food and many beverages.

The minister, Mario Valenzuela, and the representative from INDE said that there would quickly be a study made concerning the electric transformers and their capacity. Immediately afterward, the *contadores* would be installed at the family residences. The value of the two hundred *contadores* was given as Q40,000.

Obviously, this is a benefit for the town, but this came too late for some people, and they had abandoned their hopes and faith in the party Democracia Cristiana [Guatemalteca], because the government has caused the prices of necessities to rise. This afternoon there was a civic fiesta, but in truth it was only held because the party donated two hundred *contadores*. During the event, *profesores*, representatives, and politicians all spoke. The señores who came from the capital also spoke and exhorted everyone in the town to vote for Alfonzo Cabrera and the other candidates of the party Democracia Cristiana Guatemalteca so that in the future there will be more work and donations for the pueblo.

The two hundred families that benefited from the *contadores* were expected to say words of thanks and farewell. Among them, I was included in having to say these words. In truth, I did not want to participate because I feel I am a simple person, with no obligations to the party, but I concluded that I should since they had expressed their confidence in me.

After all the events, all the señores who came from Guatemala [City] were invited to a special dinner, during which there was much to drink. They left the pueblo almost in a drunken state.

One thing I did not like was the behavior of the local political directors. They went too far and took advantage during the dinner. Instead of serving, they got drunk and ate most of the food.

The two hundred families gave a total contribution of Q2,000. Each family gave a contribution of Q10. Also, the women banded together to make the tortillas and cook the food for the dinner. I believe they worked hard.

María's Graduation
Saturday, 27, to Monday, 29 October 1990
María's graduation was a simple affair. This time there were two *Joseñas* who graduated as teachers of *educación primaria urbana* [primary education in city schools, as opposed to rural schools]. They are Esperanza Julia García Bizarro and María Bizarro Ramos.

A few days ago, Esperanza Julia's father, Santiago García Cholotío, came to ask me if we could hire an automobile to take our families to Quezaltenango. Well, I had to say yes even though I did not want to, because I had no money. In order not to let him hire it by himself, however, I had to agree. Santiago went to Santa Ana to hire the automobile, but things did not work out. He said that the van was in bad shape. We left it at that. Santiago and his relatives hired a car to take them to Xela.

Early on Saturday morning we took a boat to Panajachel. From Panajachel we boarded a bus of the Transportes Morales to Quezaltenango. Only my wife, Ramón, and I went. It was not possible to invite our relatives because of the expense.

At 9:00 A.M. we arrived at Quezaltenango. We then went to the church to find María. We found her with her companions waiting for the start of the mass. Then we went to have a quick breakfast, because we were also anxious to be at the mass, since the benediction followed it.

Everyone was happy when we left the church. Many took several pictures of the newly graduated schoolteachers, but we took only one picture. We then went to the home where María had been boarding to have some refreshments.

At 2:00 P.M. of the same day, 27 October 1990, we went to the Salón Don Bosco, adjacent to the Church of San Nicolás, for the graduation and the handing out of the *símbolos de entrega de título* [symbolic degrees, which are papers tied with a ribbon; the actual degrees are sent after the ceremony]. This was a special event in the national pavilion, with the high educational authorities presiding. There followed the intonation of the sacred national anthem by those present. Then the señor governor of the department of Quezaltenango opened the formal ceremony, and the [ceremony of] *símbolo de entrega de título* took place.

Next was the presentation of awards to the distinguished students. Then the graduating students gave an oath of allegiance of care and loyalty to the flag and a pledge not to bring dishonesty to the profession.

Finally, departing words were spoken by the *profesor* of pedagogy, Renan Robledo Pérez, and everyone left the pavilion. This solemn event was attended by about two thousand persons. The ceremonies of this day ended at 4:30 P.M. Since it was already late, it was impossible for us to return home.

We then went to eat dinner at an inexpensive restaurant. Dinner for four cost us only Q16.

We spent the night at the home of Don Juan and Doña Juana, where María had boarded in 1987, and for an hour and a half we had some drinks with them. We went to bed at 9:00 P.M., since we had to get up at dawn the next day.

At the private school Mixto Liceo Quezalteco there were qualified accountants and *bachilleres* who graduated, but I do not know the exact number. However, the number of graduates from the *sexto [año] magisterio* [sixth year of teacher training] was 79. There were 15 *retrasados* [nongraduates; held back], 94 in all.[36] On Sunday, 28 October 1990, we left Quezaltenango at five o'clock in the morning. We arrived home satisfied and had some breakfast.

I had to attend a meeting of fathers of students to discuss the graduation of the third-year students of the *básico*. I am involved in this because of my son Erasmo Ignacio. I had to contribute Q50 for a small fiesta organized by the fathers of the students.

In this year, 1990, there were twenty-two students in the third grade, twenty of whom passed their exams, while the other two must wait until January 1991.

The graduation of the third year of *básico* was held on Monday, 29 October. All the wives, that is to say, the mothers of the students, worked during this day preparing six hundred tamales.

Everything was festive. The events began at 8:00 P.M., beginning with the entrance to the national pavilion, followed by the recital of the national anthem, and then the distribution of diplomas by the teachers. Next there was recognition of distinguished students. Everything was made more entertaining by the marimba Sonora Joseña. The events concluded at 11:00 P.M., and a dinner was served to the graduates, the members of the municipal corporation, former graduates, family members, the marimba band members, and everyone else who was present.

The money collected came to Q827. In truth, not everyone contributed Q50. This is because some of the families belong to the evangelical church, and they continually protest these things. Perhaps that is why they are called *protestantes* [protestants]. The Q827 did not cover the costs. Some of us had to give an extra donation of Q10 in order for the committee to come out even on expenses.

This is the seventh graduation of students from the Instituto Básico por Cooperativa de San José la Laguna. During this graduation, those named as *padrinos* (teachers selected by the students as most liked or helpful) were the *profesores* Clemente Pelayo Duarte Flores and Luciano Méndez Alvarez.

What Happened to My Nephew, Enrique Eduardo
June to First Days of November 1990

I am now going to describe something that happened to my nephew, Enrique Eduardo. Enrique Eduardo is the son of my sister Julia. They live in San Lucas Tolimán. The boy broke his right leg in an accident. The boy's father is a nurse employed by the government. They noticed that the boy had sustained a serious break. The doctors from San Lucas, seeing that the child was seriously ill, sent him to a hospital in Sololá. The doctors in Sololá put a plaster cast on his leg so that it would heal. But it did not turn out right. When they examined him again, there had been no change, and so they put another plaster cast on his leg. The boy's father had a great deal of faith in the medical knowledge of the doctors, since he is a nurse.

The child's mother began to lose patience and hope when she saw that the boy did not get better. She told her husband that it might be better to look for a bone healer, but the boy's father did not want his son to be examined by a bone healer. For the *niño* [small boy], the plaster cast was like a punishment, because he could not lie down properly. He would spend all of his time sitting and experienced much discomfort when he had to urinate.

My sister, the mother of Enrique Eduardo, is the one who suffered greatly taking care of him. One day, toward the end of September, she sorrowfully brought her son to San José. She then went to summon Señor Ricardo Tziac Sicay, the bone healer.

Señor Ricardo came to my sister's [former] house [that Ignacio had bought] at 6:30. As soon as he entered the house, he knelt down, asking God for the power of Jesucristo, asking that this boy be cured and reciting a prayer in which he said he was a simple man and a sinner but that the power of God in his hands would ease the boy's suffering. I am a witness to this event.

Señor Ricardo, after finishing his prayers, took out his knife to cut the plaster cast. He worked hard at this, and when he finished cutting it off, the boy's leg had a bad smell. Then the señor *curandero* took out a *huesito* [little bone] from his shirt pocket and began to massage the broken bone. The boy hollered and screamed because of the pain that he felt. After the massage, the *curandero* wrapped the boy's leg with avocado leaves. He then tied it all together with a belt and said he would repeat the process the day after tomorrow. My sister kissed his hand and asked him how much he charged for his treatment. The señor said, "It is up to you whether to give me one quetzal or two, but no more because this is not a business. I tell you that your son needs three treatments. After that, his leg will be healed, and he will be like before." My sister was crying, and truthfully, I did not see how much money she gave the *curandero*, but she did give him something.

It seems incredible, but it is true that after three treatments the boy could stand on two feet, but he told us that he still felt pain. At the last treatment, as is customary among us *naturales,* my sister bought *aguardiente* and beer to give to family members and to the *curandero.* The following day they returned to San Lucas Tolimán, but Enrique Eduardo was still sick and could barely walk unaided.

In the first days of the month of November of the same year, 1990, my sister brought her son here to San José to show gratitude to Señor Ricardo Tziac Sicay, the bone healer. Enrique Eduardo can now run, play ball, and get into mischief, as if he had not broken his leg at all. We in the family are happy about this. What is hard to imagine is how this man can do what the doctors cannot.

With apologies, I am not trying to question the medical abilities of the doctors. I merely write this as something that happened to my nephew, the son of my sister.

My Wife Has a Strange Dream
Friday, 30 November, to Saturday, 1 December 1990

In truth, I did not imagine the following dream that my wife remembered upon awakening today. Our son José had problems with his health and had to go to Quezaltenango to receive treatment from a *naturista* [naturist]. When José was getting ready to leave, he woke us up to say good-bye. It was then that my wife began to tell me about the dream she had during the night. She said the dream went like this.

The three of us, José, my wife, and myself, were in a place far from the town. Suddenly, I disappeared, and only José and my wife were there. Then they saw many soldiers arriving, and my wife said to José, "Your father, where did he go?" José answered that I must be around somewhere. My wife then told José, "Let's run away, because these soldiers are going to cause great harm with all their guns." She and José then began to run to a woman's house to hide and be able to see what was going to happen. But the soldiers discovered they were being watched and began to chase José and my wife. In the dream, she was frightened, and they ran into another house and kept looking behind them to see what was happening. My wife then saw in her dream that the soldiers were ready to kill many people with their guns. The soldiers were also following José because they did not want to be observed. With much sorrow she and José began to run from the house where they were hiding and heard many shots and many people screaming. When they looked back, many people were dead, but this was not in our town.

Then my wife said to me, "Be careful, something bad is going to happen." She asked me where I had to go today. I said, at 10:00 A.M. I had to go to Santiago Atitlán on an errand. She told me to be very careful, and I told her thank you. And I told my wife once again, perhaps you had this dream because you were so weary when you went to sleep. I did not think the dream was of much importance, and there the matter rested.

By this time it was 10:00 A.M., and I set off on my errand to Santiago Atitlán, in a tranquil mood, talking with some friends. When we arrived at the pier at the edge of the lake, there were many people going to the market with their goods. These were people from other towns around the lake. It is customary on Tuesdays and Fridays to conduct a great deal of business, although there is commerce every day, but it is busier on these two days.

As we were getting off the boat, a friend of mine from San Martín, Pascual González, called out to me: "Ignacio, go and finish your errand, because the situation is critical. About a half hour ago, there was a shooting near the soccer field. Two policemen were wounded, and it is not known if there were any killed." I told him, thank you, Pascual. We then went disgustedly up to the town.

When we arrived at the market, the tradesmen had all gone to their homes. There was total silence, and the people acted as if they had been struck dumb, unable to speak. I then walked closer to the substation of the national police to buy a newspaper. In truth, one could see the fear on the faces of the five policemen we encountered, and everything seemed to be militarized.

I did not stay longer than an hour in the town, since I could sense the fear, and as we descended to the beach, we saw more army troops arriving. One unofficial version says that the policemen went to the location on orders of the regional justice of the peace. It is also said that the policemen took bribes and that they had driven off in their van to do this, but when they were parked they were shot at from a distance by unknown persons. The result was two policemen wounded and one passenger dead, but truthfully, I did not go to where this took place, since I did not have my identification papers with me.

When we arrived at the edge of the lake, we got into the boat to go

13. *Fishing for black bass on the northern side of Lake Atitlán.*

back home. Apparently the pilot of the boat was very nervous, and he almost killed a fisherman. Luckily, the young fisherman was alert and saw the boat was about to collide with his canoe. He threw himself into the lake and only the canoe was struck by the boat. We were in the middle of helping him out of the water when a boat full of policemen came upon us. They had come to aid the few policemen in the town. They paid no attention to the young fisherman, who might have drowned, but only took down the name of the pilot and told him to present himself in Panajachel. We were all afraid during this accident, but thanks to God, no major trouble occurred.

A strange coincidence [happened] today, Saturday, 1 December 1990. At the same place where we had the accident yesterday, a native fisherman of Santiago Atitlán drowned. The cause of his death, however, is being ignored.

A Massacre in Santiago Atitlán
Saturday, 1 December, to Wednesday, 19 December 1990
This has been a really dramatic day, a day when the town of Santiago Atitlán was bathed in blood by the military detachment stationed in

the *caserío* of Panabaj. All the killings, robberies, assaults, and kidnappings are said to be committed by unknown men who carry guns and weapons, but today it was discovered who has really been committing all these crimes among the Tzutuhil people.

This discovery took place between Saturday, 1 December 1990, and the morning of Sunday, 2 December of the same year. When the town of Santiago Atitlán was isolated, such things could not be imagined. I am sure these events will forever more shape the history of this *Atitecan* town, if not the history of the other towns around the lake, for the whole world to know. The martyrs were shot down by the soldiers' bullets while they were peacefully carrying white nylon flags signifying the need for help and their peaceful protest at what was going on among their people, concerning another kidnapping that the soldiers had carried out in their town.

There are many diverse levels of communication, such as radio, newspapers, and television. All speak of this massacre, and it is certain the facts may get distorted due to the hasty writing about the incident or the different interpretations of any eyewitnesses or even the nervousness of those collecting the facts of the event. The version I am describing is one in which I was not able to actually see the events as they happened, but little by little, as I investigated the incident, people would talk to me about what they had seen without fear, since we are all *naturales*. I was not able to piece together the story until five days after it took place, since in the first few days after the massacre people were very nervous.

The beginnings of the massacre went like this. At 10:00 P.M. an official of the national army from the detachment at Panabaj, along with three other members of the same institution, attacked the home of Señor Andrés Ajuchan with the intention of kidnapping him. Thanks to God, the neighbors were still awake, and they heard the shouts of the Ajuchan family. Some of the neighbors ran to the church to ring the bell and summon the townspeople. The bodyguards [of the official] opened fire and wounded Señor Andrés Ajuchan. The townspeople took advantage of this gunfire and confusion and captured the official in charge of the kidnapping. [The townspeople gathered en masse. The rear guard shot into the air, wounding one native in the leg, but in fear the soldiers ran back to the military detachment.] By this time, a group of more than five thousand Tzutuhiles, led by the current *alcalde*, Don Delfino

14. *Paratroopers on parade on Army Day in Guatemala City.*

Rodas, and the *alcalde*-elect, Salvador Ramírez y Ramírez, had formed.

At first they were going to take the captured official to the front of the church, but after consulting among themselves, they decided to take him to where the army detachment was in order that the captured official's superiors could see what it was like to be kidnapped. Everyone then marched to where the army detachment was located. They were all carrying white banners signaling peace.

When they arrived at their destination, the captured official was rescued by his fellow soldiers. The townspeople were told to be quiet, but they demanded to know why the soldiers had come into town. While this was going on, the soldiers opened fire with automatic rifles against the defenseless campesinos. This occurred at approximately 1:00 A.M. on Sunday, 2 December, the day of the killing of the eleven martyrs.

The big event following this took place during the day on Sunday, when hundreds of *Atitecos* went to San Martín la Laguna to ask *Martineros* to go with them to provide moral support for retrieving the bodies. But the authorities [the mayor] did not do anything within their jurisdictional powers to help them in this matter.

The eleven bodies, watched over by their families, awaited the arrival of the regional justice of the peace. At 1:00 P.M. the bodies were still strewn where they had fallen in front of the army detachment. Some of the corpses were covered with banana leaves while others were covered with native garments. It was not until later in the afternoon that the bodies were picked up. However, they were not taken to the hospital in Sololá because the families of the victims, being humble people, could not afford the costs.

It is said that the official in charge of the kidnapping received blows and wounds, but they would not say his name, so that the people would think he was not a member of the army detachment. On this same day, during the night, that is to say, Sunday, the soldiers from the military detachment at Panabaj were relieved by troops from the same military Zone 14 in Sololá. They were transported on a boat from San Martín la Laguna. This boat is owned by Señor José Sicay, who has been a collaborator with the military since the great number of kidnappings began in San Martín la Laguna. This same man is the father-in-law of the former commissioner, José Méndez. The *Atitecos* are disturbed that this man continues to collaborate and does things he should not be doing.

The eleven people who were assassinated were not taken to Sololá. The judge (justice of the peace) summoned a forensic surgeon from the hospital at Sololá, but it is not known why he did not arrive. The bodies were placed in the municipal *salón* during Sunday night and were to remain there until Monday.

Monday, 3 December 1990. This is to feel and relive a day of sorrow with the people of my race, the Tzutuhiles. Today, Monday, my son José and I were in Santiago Atitlán at 10:00 A.M. In this Tzutuhil town, we observed the pain of watching all the tears that were shed by the people in mourning. Almost the entire town is out in the streets, in front of the church, and in front of the municipal hall condemning the killings. The few people still in their homes are playing funeral music. When we arrived at the town, many journalists and national and international television reporters also began to arrive. We counted more than fifty of them gathering information and taking pictures.

We walked a bit in the town, and all we could hear were the shouts and cries of grief. We then went to a funeral mass in honor of the souls of the dead. After this we went to the corridor of the municipal hall. There were groups of Ladinos, some of them teachers, some not, taking up a collection from everyone in the town to pay for the funeral expenses, or to be blunt, to buy the boxes with which to bury the dead. There were also two groups of *Atitecos* doing the same thing.

It is also apparent that the town is strongly in favor of expelling the military detachment. Many groups of townspeople have circulated petitions and forms requesting the immediate withdrawal of the military unit. By the afternoon, it was known that there were twenty-two thousand signatures on such a petition.

The judge realized that the forensic surgeon had not arrived. As the law specifies, the judge consulted with a doctor, surnamed Bixcul, who then proceeded to release the bodies into the care of the families. This took place about 11:45 A.M. The families were allowed to take the bodies of their loved ones home, but only for one hour, because the bodies had already been exposed too long. At one o'clock in the afternoon each family began to arrive at the church to attend a mass with the bodies of the martyrs present.

We came out of the church for the second time. We went to eat some breakfast. We bought some tortillas and a few ounces of shrimp and ate in the park. It was impossible to eat in a restaurant because they were all closed.

After eating, we again returned to the church to attend the mass. At 2:00 P.M. the ceremony of the sacred sacrifice of the mass was conducted by the three priests of the parish of San Lucas Tolimán. The three priests are North Americans. They are Tomás McSherry, Patricio Green, and Juan Goggin. I should state that they are affiliated with the diocese of Sololá. The eleven martyrs were placed in a single line in the church near the main altar. We stayed for one hour at the mass, because the heat became intense, and we were forced to step outside. However, we waited in the portico of the church. The following is a list of the martyred *indígenas*: (1) Pedro Damián Vásquez, 44 years old; (2) Nicolás Ajtujal Sosof, 25 years old; (3) Pedro Mendoza Pablo, 29 years old; (4) Gaspar Cos Sicay, 18 years old; (5) Pedro Cristal Mendoza, 13 years old; (6) Jerónimo Sojuel Sisay, 10 years old; (7) Juan Ajuchan Mesías, 17 years old; (8) Pedro Mendoza Catú, 18 years old; (9) Felipe Quejú Culán, 53 years old; (10) Savador Damián Yaquí, 50 years old; and (11) Juan Pablo Sosof, 20 years old.

I have not mentioned the number of wounded who were taken to the hospital in Sololá on Sunday, the day of the massacre. They were transported from San Martín la Laguna on a boat owned by Señor

Haroldo Puzul Cotúc. Many of the *indígenas* are grateful to this man for having the courage to perform this action.

Nineteen were wounded. The following is the list: (1) Pascual Nebaj, 15 years old; (2) Antonio Sivij, 45 years old; (3) Nicolás Tziná, 45 years old; (4) Antonio Reanda Coché, 44 years old; (5) Salvador Alvarado, 45 years old; (6) Esteban Damián, 24 years old; (7) Francisco Mendoza, 12 years old; (8) Nicolás Sapet, 25 years old; (9) Gaspar Mendoza, 24 years old; (10) Cristóbal Tacaxoy, 23 years old; (11) Antonio Pablo, 21 years old; (12) Antonio Ajchomajay, 19 years old; (13) Gaspar Tiney, 21 years old; (14) Pedro Cotzay, 25 years old; (15) José Cotzay, 17 years old; (16) Salvador Sisay, 18 years old; (17) Pedro Damián González, 17 years old; (18) Diego Ixbalam, 19 years old; and (19) Pedro Xicay, 40 years old.

Before the mass had ended, we received more sad news. Of the nineteen wounded and taken to the hospital in Sololá, two had just died and four had been so gravely wounded that they were taken to the Roosevelt Hospital in the capital city of Guatemala. This means the number of dead is now thirteen. After the mass the bodies were carried out in single file by relatives or friends. It was obvious that most of the families were poor and humble, because the bodies were placed in simple pine boxes. It was noted that only one family had money, because they had placed their loved one in a casket of great worth, calculated to have cost at least Q2,000.

We accompanied the interment of these eleven sons of God who were massacred by the bullets. We arrived at the cemetery, and many in the crowd looked at us with suspicious eyes. They thought we were members of the army, because my son José has his hair cut short, like the military. What helped me out is that many in the crowd knew me personally, and since we were speaking in our native tongue, Tzutuhil, I was able to explain. We were not able to remain for the burial of all eleven of the deceased because it was getting late and the return boat left at 5:00 P.M. We had to run down to the beach to get there on time. The cemetery is about two kilometers from the town and about four blocks from where the military detachment is located.

On Wednesday, 5 December 1990, the residents of Santiago Atitlán declared in the free press that they had personally asked the minister of national defense, General Juan Leonel Bolaños Cháves, "for the immediate withdrawal of the military detachment based in this town due to

15. *Tourists in Santiago Atitlán listening to a talk about the 1990 massacre near crosses that mark individualized monuments to those who were killed.*

the tragic incident that occurred on the first and second of December of 1990, during which 30 persons were shot. Of these, 13 died, and 17 are so gravely wounded that they may yet lose their lives. If the authorities do not heed this necessary and just petition, the *indígenas* of Santiago Atitlán are determined to stage a march from where the massacre took place all the way to the capital of Guatemala to protest this violation of human rights. At the same time, we ask the approval of all organizations in general, the National School, the Cooperative Movement, and the Union of Workers for their swift approval of these just demands of the town of Santiago Atitlán."

On the same day the president of the republic, the lawyer Vinicio Cerezo Arévalo, stated he was outraged over the massacre of the campesinos of Santiago Atitlán in the department of Sololá and that a commission will be quickly formed to investigate and punish with all the force of the law the perpetrators of these crimes. This declaration was delivered by the vice president of the republic, Roberto Carpio Nicolle, on radio, on television, and in the newspapers.

Also on this day, the syndicate of workers of the supreme electoral tribunal asked in the national press and other media networks that a public petition require the military to leave Santiago Atitlán permanently and that the military detachment be dismantled. This organization asked the president of the republic, in his capacity as commanding general of the army, to immediately suspend those officials responsible for the massacre and have them prosecuted for the crimes they have committed. This same organization, in the same public communiqué, solicited the international community to stand with the town of Santiago Atitlán during its time of sorrow. At the same time that this communication was sent to the government and to the national army, this massacre was condemned before the United Nations in order to get complete agreement from all nations for what [should be done about what] occurred in this *Atitecan* town.

On this same date, the Confederacíon Guatemalteca de Federaciones de Cooperativas (CONFECOP, Guatemalan Confederation of Federated Cooperatives), as representatives of the cooperative movement in Guatemala, on television, on the radio, and in *El Gráfico* repudiated the killing of *indígenas* in Santiago Atitlán, where thirteen campesinos lost their lives and where there were also many wounded. They said that it was not yet known whether those who were wounded would regain their health or remain invalids and that this bloody act had left many families and homes sorrowful and helpless. They declared that the national army should protect the rights of citizens and should not cause harm or distress.

On 5 December 1990 Señor Gabino Quemé, the president of the nongovernmental commission on human rights, sent a telegram to the minister of national defense where he stated his dismay at the bloody events that took place in the early morning on Sunday in Santiago Atitlán.[37] He stated that the Ministry of Defense should publicly declare within seventy-two hours whether it exists for the defense or for the massacre of campesinos and Mayan peoples. The nongovernmental commission on human rights, the Instituto Maya Guatemalteco de Ciencias [IMAGUAC, the Guatemalan Maya Institute of Science], the Comité Campesino Contra Abusos de las Autoridades [CCCAAS, Campesino Committee against Abuses by the Authorities], the Coordinadora Nacional del Consejo de Pueblos Maya de Guatemala [CONACPUMAGUA, National Coordinator of the Council of Mayan Peoples of Guatemala], and other organizations relating to the human rights of the people, issued a communiqué through the newspaper condemning the attack against the inhabitants of Santiago Atitlán.[38] Also included in the newspaper communication was a plea to the minister of defense to engage in a dialogue, since such talk will help people understand. Otherwise, the town feels it should not pay a tax to a ministry that allows defenseless campesinos to be murdered. In conclusion, they stated that the minister is responsible for setting a time and day for this dialogue. The townspeople will be attentively waiting for this. To the contrary, it is better for the minister to resign his post.

Friday, 7 December 1990, I went to Santiago Atitlán on a personal errand, but at the same time I was able to observe what was happening in the town. In truth, it was very critical. The *indígenas* could not stand to see the soldiers or the agents of the national police. The residents, or rather the local authorities, prohibited restaurants and dining places from serving food to the agents of the national police who are stationed in the town. I thought at first this was just talk, but it is true. I watched when the men of the national police came to the market to buy food. They bought tortillas and tomato sauce (*patín con pescaditos*) [small fish in tomato sauce or paste]. I felt sorry at seeing those poor policemen, paying for the consequences of what others have committed. It is true as the saying goes, *Justos pagan por pecadores* [The innocent must pay for the guilty]. Perhaps they have not committed similar crimes, but they are the ones who must atone for the repudiation of the people, and they are viewed as dogs.

On 7 December 1990 the minister of national defense, General Juan Leonel Bolaños Chávez, declared that those who provoke the killing of the *indígenas* in Santiago Atitlán, Sololá, will be turned over to the corresponding tribunals. They are a military reservist, Lieutenant José Antonio Ortiz Rodríguez, in charge of the military detachment, and Quartermaster Sergeant Efraín García González. They are responsible for provoking the incident in the town of Santiago Atitlán, Sololá.

The minister of defense held a press conference concerning the irresponsibility of these two men. He asked that the entire military institution not be condemned. He said it is clear that the national army follows constitutional, moral, and doctrinal precepts. The minister declared and asked that the full weight of the law be applied to those responsible for the massacre of the *indígenas* in the town.

On 7 December 1990, in accord with the orders of the commanding general of the army, the constitutional president of the republic, the lawyer Vinicio Cerezo Arévalo, as a gesture of goodwill, ordered the withdrawal of the Panabaj military detachment from Santiago Atitlán, Sololá. This information was made on the communication channel [on television] last night, repeated from the day before. This declaration was made by the minister of national defense, General Bolaños Chávez. He stated this gesture of goodwill does not signify fear or lack of enthusiasm. The military detachment will be transferred to a place that will be selected within the jurisdiction of the military Zone 14, located in Sololá, since that zone is being threatened by terrorist activities. What was not said was the date this withdrawal would take place.

On Saturday, 8 December 1990, the people of Santiago Atitlán held an open meeting in order that the entire town repudiate the spilling of blood on the first and second days of December. During this open meeting, the *Atiteco* people received the support of national and international organizations repudiating the massacre committed by members of the national army and calling for peace and the immediate withdrawal of the troops of the Panabaj detachment.

In truth, I had knowledge that this public meeting would be held in that *municipio,* but due to a necessity, I could not be there. I had to go to Sololá to buy some feed for our chickens. I wanted to return earlier, but it was not possible. When I arrived, the boat had already left for Santiago. It is certain that hundreds of *Martineros* went, to provide moral support to that suffering town. Only two people from San José went. They got to see all that occurred in the large meeting of this Tzutuhil pueblo. I obtained my information from these two people on the afternoon of the same day.

It is said that all the labor organizations of the country, in addition to foreign societies and groups, were present, placing posters repudiating and condemning the killing of the thirteen campesinos. The meeting began at 2:00 P.M., led by Ramiro de León Carpio, lawyer and president of the organization of human rights in Guatemala, supported by all these groups. They recorded through a notarial act that the town of Santiago Atitlán asked the central government to end the violence unleashed in the southwest part of the country, that the lives of the *indígenas* should be respected, and that the military detachment should withdraw and disappear, in order that the peace that was lost since 1980–82 [the regime of General Romeo Lucas García] be regained.

The townspeople would be in charge of taking care of and watching over the well-being of the town, as they had before the existence of any military detachment. Since the arrival of this detachment, the town has been under heavy repression. It was also recorded that all fathers of families were under a great obligation to put their sons to work; that there be no idleness in the town, because it was from idle sons that subversives can come; that all forms of diversion, such as movies, be suspended; and that all fathers take their hoes, machetes, and pickaxes and work alongside their sons. They themselves would be in charge of guarding the town without the necessity of soldiers or policemen. They would be in charge of capturing all violators and thieves in order to hand them over to justice and have them punished according to the law. They asked for an end to military aid from the developed countries, such as Germany, Holland, and the United States. Only when there was no more money for the military would peace return.

They also asked the government for an indemnity for the affected families. One version says there are more than eight thousand who have been orphaned, that is to say, women and children who are forsaken and abandoned.

On Wednesday, 19 December 1990, the military detachment based in Panabaj, Santiago Atitlán, was withdrawn, but only in part. The entire detachment was completely dismantled on Thursday, the twentieth of the same month. Without doubt this said detachment was taken to the military zone in Sololá. But nothing was heard of this summons in these towns. There were rumors that they would be transferred to these places, but they were all false. What was not known was who were the perpetrators of another crime committed in Pachavac in the same *municipio* of Santiago Atitlán, Sololá. On the night of Wednesday, 19 December, on the same day when the military abandoned the town, a married couple who took care of the chalet of Señor Carlos Bracamonte was riddled with bullets. According to official records, the victims were attacked during the night with 5.56mm weapons [M-16s]. Their names were José Pospoy Mendoza, sixty-four years old, and Juana Coché Tacaxoy, fifty-two years old, a married couple guarding the house of Señor Bracamonte. The man was shot five times and the woman three times. Many say that it was the military, but in truth, it cannot be confirmed. Perhaps it was someone else who took advantage, knowing the military would be blamed.

Police from San Lucas Are Suspected of Kidnapping in Santiago Atitlán

5 January 1991

My daughter María and I decided to go to Santiago Atitlán to ask the señor supervisor of education advice about how María could get a job as a teacher. We went on the launch in the morning, but when we arrived at the pier of Santiago, many people [were] coming to board the launch for the return trip to their towns. A *Joseño* told me, "Ignacio, be careful, there's much alarm and tear gas bombs in the town."

I said, "Thanks, Abraham."

We continued up the street to the town center and on to the house of *profesor* Gaspar Hernández Socorro. We were there about a half hour. Then we went to the market (plaza) to see what was happening. There, nearly the whole population was assembled. I asked some people who knew what was happening, and they gave me the [following] details.

When night fell on 4 January, some residents of Santiago saw an unknown car parked in the place called Tzan Ch'am. These residents went to alert the civil patrol. Then the patrolmen called the vigilantes of other cantons to watch the car. The *aliados de la paz* [allied patrolmen of peace] positioned themselves in the soccer field and covered the road with rocks, blocking the path of the unidentified car.[39]

At 11:00 P.M. the driver of the car was trying to find an entrance to the pueblo, but since the path was blocked, he now could not enter. The *Atitecos* captured the occupants of the car and took them to the police station, where they were identified as five agents of the national police from the police station of San Lucas Tolimán. Then they were taken to jail in the hours of the night.

When the chief of the station at Santiago realized that five agents of the national police were jailed, he radioed to advise the jefe of Sololá. Early in the morning the jefe of Sololá arrived in his car driven by a chauffeur who remained seated in the car. Not until then were the captives taken out of jail and to the police station, which is in the municipality, a *cuadra* across the park from the jail. The jefe of Sololá wanted to take them to Sololá, but the Indians opposed him, asking him to explain why these policemen had come to Santiago at night, since Santiago has its own police station and there is no need for outside policemen to come there. The angry *Atitecos* punctured the tires of the suspicious car as well as the tires of the jefe's car. The chief also became a prisoner, surrounded by thousands of persons.

To me, the whole thing was interesting, and I told Maruca, "Why don't you return home, and I will stay here to see the results of the day."

Then I approached the station. The police had exploded tear gas bombs to make the people disperse, but as there were thousands and thousands of people, the smoke of the bombs did nothing to them. They left by one street to avoid the gas and came back by another street, making sure that not one policeman could leave. Although the police wanted to leave, the mob wanted justice to be served, and they intended to hit them if they tried to leave. Also, the policemen of Santiago were surrounded, along with the five policemen of San Lucas and the chief of Sololá.

The policeman in the most danger was the one who was seated in the car, guarding it with the tires flat while the residents were abusing him. Most of the day this poor policeman sat in the car [with the windows rolled up], tormented by the intolerable heat and the people lifting the rear of the car up and dropping it. One of the surrounded policemen opened the door of the station to throw out another tear gas bomb to disperse the people. But the tear gas had no effect, because one group would leave to avoid the smoke and another group would replace them. For revenge, some of the residents wanted to use their agricultural spray bombs to asphyxiate the surrounded policemen. But there were conscientious people who rejected these measures.

Many shouted that there was a *Joseño* policeman, but the truth was it was impossible to see who he was because the crowd surrounded the cops. It was not until two o'clock in the afternoon that a Guatemalan Air Force helicopter landed on the beach, bringing the *licenciado* Ramiro de León Carpio, procurator of human rights, and the *licenciado* Oliverio Castillo Rodas, the president of the commission of human rights of the congress of the republic.[40]

The señor procurator talked to the chief of police, but since they are both Ladinos, they ignored the voices of the residents. Then the police were taken from where they were surrounded and set free. The procurator said that the five policemen were on a mission, looking for a fugitive thief who escaped from jail in San Lucas Tolimán. The car that they were driving actually belonged to the mayor of San Lucas. The procurator, without listening to a word from anyone, climbed to a higher place on the steps of the Catholic church and began to condemn the residents. He said that they were drunks and that they didn't have reason to capture the police and that if they continued with these things, soon the military detachment would return. The residents asked to be heard, but they were not allowed to speak.

It was suspected that the five policemen came to perpetrate a kidnapping because three were uniformed and two were in civilian dress. And if they were looking for an escaped thief, why didn't they communicate by radio with the police station in [Santiago] Atitlán instead of entering the town at night? Among those five policemen, there was indeed one *Joseño* named Andrés.

At 5:00 P.M. the five policemen were delivered to their jefe, who conducted them in a launch from San Martín toward Panajachel. Well, it could be seen that the police had been beaten because their faces were blue and their uniforms were dirty.

One thing the procurator told the people of Santiago was that the five policemen will be taken by their jefe to Guatemala [City] and held for questioning by an appropriate tribunal to see whether they had committed a crime. Those of the town were grateful to the señor procurator of human rights. But this was a lie of Señor Ramiro de León Carpio, because the next day the *Joseño* policeman was happy with his family as if nothing had happened. [An investigation would have taken at least two or three days.]

Finally, when the policemen were descending the path toward the launch, they were ridiculed and reproached by the *Atitecos*. Ricardo Sisay told me, "Look Ignacio, your compatriot (the policeman) killed many of our people. [He and his] Sicay brothers acted with the military and kidnapped many men."

I answered him, "Ricardo, the truth is I don't know anything about the lives of the policemen, and moreover he is a native of San Martín." Only in this manner could I calm the nerves of my friend, Manuel Sisay [by letting him know that the bad policeman was not a native *Joseño* and that not all *Joseños* were like him].

I witnessed everything that happened during the day. The residents wanted revenge from all that they have suffered from the loss of their kin. Also, I observed the nervousness of the police and the señor procurator, who did not value the native people and who reproached them.

On this day I arrived home at 6:30 P.M.

The Second Round of Presidential Elections and Local Elections
6 January 1991
This day is called the Day of Kings or the Day of Gifts [Epiphany]. On this date the elections for president and vice president of the republic are held, that is to say, the second round of elections.

Don Jorge Carpio Nicolle lost the votes of the second round to his political adversary, Jorge Serrano Elías. The loser belongs to the UCN party and the winner belongs to the MAS party. In November 1990 Jorge Carpio Nicolle won the general elections, while the engineer Jorge Serrano Elías took second place. Don Jorge Carpio thought he would completely win the votes of the Guatemalan people by spreading dirty (false) propaganda. Jorge Carpio, who is Catholic, knew that the majority of Guatemalans are also Catholic. He paid for false advertising against Jorge Serrano, who is Protestant. The candidate of the UCN [Carpio] advertised in the papers and on radio and television that the candidate for the MAS [Serrano] is Protestant and that if the people vote for Serrano, the Catholic Church will close, that the traditions and the customs of the villages and of all Guatemala will be terminated, that all Guatemala will be obligated to belong to the Protestant churches, that masses will be terminated, and that the priests will be suspended.

Then the people realized that these publications were just lies because the constitution of Guatemala says that there is freedom of religion. Article 36 says that the exercise of all religions is free, that every person has the right to participate in his or her religion or faith in public and in private, and that he or she can teach, worship, and observe their faith, as long he or she maintains the public order and respects the dignity of other faiths. Also, Article 37 says that the legal standing of the Catholic Church will be recognized.

Then the people realized the falseness of the publicity that Don Jorge Carpio generated. Don Jorge Serrano Elías was like the cat waiting for the mouse, making unexaggerated advertisements talking about the problems of Guatemala and saying what is needed to achieve true peace and democracy (although his words too seem to be lies). The people saw and heard that this man said nothing about religion, and they confirmed that the other [Carpio] was a liar. On 6 January the people voted overwhelmingly for the engineer Jorge Serrano Elías.

In one medium it was predicted that if Don Jorge Carpio Nicolle lost the election he would die of a heart attack within a few days. This was erroneous.

[As far as the local election is concerned] the mayor-elect of my town is from the *aldea* of Patzilín—the first time in the history of this town that a native of an *aldea* won the mayorship. He is Señor Ricardo Demócrito Sicay Hernández of the Quiché race.

But some townspeople were angry. They didn't want him to take possession [of the office of mayor], saying that on the inauguration they are going to attack him because as a man of the mountains he does not know the town's customs and doesn't respect the town's elders. But their position was weak because before the law, everyone is equal.

An Attempt to Reemploy the Military Reserves in San José
8 January 1991

Today the mayor and the military commissioner went announcing through the streets of the town that tonight there would be a meeting before the municipality regarding the reimplementation of the organization of the obligatory military reserve of all men from eighteen to thirty years of age. The commissioner said that he had been pressed by the commander of the military reserve to deliver the list of the population without consulting them or the mayor. The commander said to the military commissioner, pointing to his pistol, "There are no jefes other than our weapons" (suggesting that if the commissioner didn't want to provide a list, the commander could have him eliminated with arms.)

At 7:00 P.M. a group of residents, including myself, went through the main streets of the town calling to the townspeople for a meeting with the military, refusing the execution of their plans. At 8:00 P.M. the military presented themselves on the basketball court, and at the same time the whole town arrived, including men, women, and children, not wanting to listen to the military. The residents began to shout, saying: "Out of the town, military assassins, kidnappers—remember how many people you killed in Santiago Atitlán, remember the massacre of 2 December."

When the jefe tried to talk, the citizens began to sound noisemakers and make even more of an uproar. What wasn't known was who turned off the transformer switch for the electricity. For a moment everything was in darkness. Feeling they had been overcome by the will of the townspeople, the military left running from the town looking for the dock. The truth is the men of arms suffered bad treatment.

After the soldiers left, the townspeople met and signed an *acta* that totally rejected the formation of a voluntary military company in the jurisdiction of this town. Now San José la Laguna has demonstrated before the entire world that it has been a peaceful and hardworking town and that it has not had the bloody problems that Santiago has had and that it never wants to live as Santiago Atitlán has lived.

Also, the commissioner Santiago Juan Puzul Puac suffered a good deal from the people's mouth. He was treated like an animal, and they asked that he renounce his post. It was observed that there were also two other persons who wanted to be commissioners, but the townsfolk didn't support them.

My Daughter Gets Her Teaching Credentials
9 January 1991
My daughter María traveled three times to Quezaltenango for her school records. Not until today did they deliver her general certificate of studies. Now she is a teacher of *educación primaria urbana*. The truth is that we feel very proud of her, but also it is a great sacrifice for the children of a poor person to study. If my friend Jaime D. Sexton had not been helping, it is certain that I alone would not have been able to do something for my daughter.

More on the People Rejecting a Military Reserve Unit
10 January 1991
A certified copy of the memorandum drawn up on January 8 was sent. The copies were sent to the commander of the military reserves, to the señor procurator of human rights, and to the assistant of the same lawyer, the *licenciado* Eduardo Delfino Gutiérrez, whose headquarters are in Sololá. The memorandum drawn up on the eighth was signed by 504 residents.

A New Mayor Takes Over
14 to 15 January 1991
All of the adults in town were invited to attend the inauguration of the new mayor, Ricardo Sicay, and his corporation. Religious dignitaries of the *aldea* of Patzilín made the invitation, not the directors of the

party, since the mayor-elect is from Patzilín.

From October to November 1990, the politicians fought a lot. In San José there were many parties that ran candidates for the mayorship, including the following: Unión del Centro Nacional, Cornelio Humberto López; Partido Socialista Democrático, Gerardo Mendéz Batz; Alianza Popular, Santiago Alberto Vásquez Bizarro; Movimiento de Liberación Nacional, Bernardo Coj Mendoza; Partido [Democrático] de Cooperación Nacional, Orantes Cuc (*aldea* Patzilín); Democracia Cristiana Guatemalteca, Ricardo Demócrito Sicay H. (Patzilín); [Partido] Revolucionario [Guatemalteca, PRG], José Sandoval Coché; and Movimiento [de] Acción Solidaria, José de León Tuc (*aldea* Pachichaj).

José de León Tuc had problems when he registered as a candidate for mayor. He says that he and his family were registered in the Democracia Cristiana [Guatemalteca], a party that gave his son a teaching position. His family felt obligated to the party Democracia Cristiana. When Jose's wife learned he had switched to the Acción [Movimiento] Solidaria, she became angry and left him and went to live with some relatives in Sololá. Juan de Dios Puac, candidate for mayor, remained in Pachichaj without his wife and without the support of his children. And more comical for many, this señor suffered two mortal blows. Unaware of the electoral laws that say citizens who register for the post of mayor must be able to read and write, he was discovered to be illiterate. Shortly after he registered, the supreme electoral tribunal examined the applications and found a fingerprint [instead of a signature] of Juan de Dios Puac. Immediately, they rejected the MAS candidate. Without recourse, Juan de Dios also was dismissed by the party. This señor first was thrown out by his wife, then by the supreme electoral tribunal, and finally by the party.

The Movimiento Acción Solidaria had to undertake the battle of finding another candidate. That was when they found and registered Señor Humberto Sic of the village of Tzarayá.

On 15 January 1991 Ricardo Sicay received the municipal staff of office from the hands of the politician Juan Mendoza. Juan Mendoza, the outgoing mayor, wanted to perform the ceremonies in the mayor's office so that none of the residents would see that the staff, which is the symbol of the power of the office, was being handed over. The truth is that many of us went to see and to hear the transfer of power.

Thus I wrote a note that said:

Señor Ricardo Demócrito Tuc H., mayor upon taking possession:

We the townspeople desire and ask that the solemn act of taking possession be done outside in order that the entire community be cognizant of such a sacred event.

A resident of the *aldea* took this paper to the office. They tell me that the mayor read it in a loud voice. The truth is that I didn't see him do it because many people were there.

After reading the paper, the present corporation left the office, and the mayoral staff was passed to the new mayor on the basketball court. There I observed that not all the townspeople were happy with the new mayor, but the townspeople of the three villages expressed joy and enthusiasm in their faces. Two days ago the mayor-elect and his councilors had gone to the house of the *principales,* the persons who deserve respect, to facilitate the transfer of office. Afterward there was a delicious lunch in the home of Jaime Ramos y Ramos, the syndic.

I went to the lunch and attended the transfer of office. In the afternoon there was a marimba, but I didn't go in the afternoon. In truth, everything went well.

My daughter María has now graduated as teacher of *educación primaria urbana.* She wants to continue studying in the university for a higher degree, but I told her that I cannot [support it] because I have no money and studying in the university in the capital or in Xela requires a lot of money. I have many [financial] obligations with the other children, and Ignacito also needs to study. Then my wife and I thought about it, and we told María that if she wants to continue studying, she must do so in Sololá, where the faculty of the Universidad de San Carlos offers extension courses in pedagogy on Saturdays for Q20 each weekend. Contentedly she went to Sololá to register in the university on Saturday, 19 January 1991.

Ignacito Registers in the Instituto Normal
21 January 1991

Ignacito and I went to Quezaltenango, to register his name in the Instituto Normal para Varones de Occidente [INVO, Teachers' Training Institute for Young Men of the West]. The truth is he wanted to study in the capital, but I told him no, because to live in the capital requires more money. Thankfully, he understood me and we went to Xela.

By the time we arrived at the city, it was already late, and they told us that the last day [to register] would be tomorrow. We stayed in Xela to look for a house where he can live. We went to three houses that take boarders, but they were expensive. Finally, we arrived at the house of Señora Nicolasa de León. Then we talked with her and arranged that Ignacito would stay in her house for Q150 a month for only meals and a bedroom. The boy has to wash his own clothes, however.

We spent the night with a nephew of mine, who also is a student. At 2:00 A.M., 22 January, we got up and rushed to INVO. When we arrived, there were already five people in line. We took the number six. It was cold, and not until 6:00 A.M. did they begin to give out admission tickets. Then they told us that we had to present a request in writing on stamped paper to the director and that it was our responsibility, not the institute's, to get the stamped paper and write the request.[41]

Because of the cold and the early hour, all the establishments where the *papel sellado* [official paper] was sold were closed. Then we paid a taxi Q20 to [go to] the house of the *licenciado* Simón Juan. He indeed had the *papel sellado,* and he also wrote the application for us without charging anything. By 8:00 A.M. we were already back at the INVO. After registering Ignacito, we went to Panajachel and then back to San José.

Attempted Assassination of Jorge Serrano Elías
30 to 31 January 1991

When the constitutional president of the republic, the engineer Jorge Serrano Elías, had barely completed fifteen days in office, there was an attempt on his life. When he made a trip to Petén, Flores, to do fieldwork, the URNG guerrillas fired machine guns at his air force helicopter.

On the thirty-first of January it was officially announced that the señor president of the republic was miraculously saved, despite several bullets hitting the helicopter. The president issued a press release, providing the details about the attempt on his life and the cost of the repair of the aircraft, which will be Q350,000.

An Account of Violations of Human Rights
Thursday, 31 January 1991

The señor procurator of human rights, the *licenciado* Ramiro de León

Carpio, gave an official report on violations of human rights. During 1990, there were 589 persons brutally massacred, 144 persons abducted with their whereabouts unknown, 146 persons threatened with death, 188 persons illegally detained, and 48 persons abused by the authorities. This is what is called peace and democracy in Guatemala!

My Wife's Distant Kin Make Trouble for Me
Thursday, 10 February 1991

Two women, distant kin of my wife and both named Juana, arrived. What I don't know is why they came to visit us at night. We noticed that they had been drinking liquor. First they offered us a beer to drink, but my wife and I didn't accept it because we were ready to go to bed. Then we told them, "No, thank you, another day."

When they saw that we didn't want to drink, one of them began to insult me, saying that I was not a man, that previously she had sexual relations with me when she was young, and that I didn't want her now that she has a husband.

I just remained listening and surprised at the mouth of the woman. My wife kept looking at me; she thought that it was true, but all of it was a lie.

I thought that these women were purely of the devil. What this woman wanted was to cause trouble in our home. I told my wife not to reply to her, and like this it went. The two women left the house, and we stayed in our house. I told my wife that this woman was doing the work of Satan.

The woman and I are not the same age—I am fifty years old and this woman is barely twenty-eight. Thanks to God my wife knows my self-respect and deportment. Never before in my town have things like this been said to me. The truth is that this event bothered me a lot.

The Second Commissioner, Geofredo Bizarro Bizarro
31 January to 13 February 1991

Who knows at what time during the week the assault on the food cooperative called Flor Joseñera took place. Friday, 1 February, the directors and members of the said cooperative went to San Martín la Laguna to place a demand before the justice of the peace.

[He is] the stupidest justice of all time! Instead of conducting an investigation to find out who robbed the store [of the cooperative], the justice went to the municipality with the directors of the cooperative and drew up a memorandum in the municipality, stating that after 10:00 P.M. no person could be on the streets of the town. A resident found on the streets after 10:00 P.M. would be taken to jail and turned over the next day to the judge in San Martín to be sentenced.

This memorandum was bad news for the young people as well as the adults, who might need to go out to look for medicine or call a midwife. What happened? Today, Friday, the ignorant commissioner ordered the guards to capture whomever they find on the streets after the curfew.

At 10:30 P.M. the baker Haroldo Zacarías Ramos and his assistant were captured. After their exhausting work in the bakery, they went out to drink some beers in a *tienda*. Before arriving at the store, however, they were captured and taken to jail. Without asking them a single question, the guards imprisoned them.

On 2 February Haroldo Zacarías and his helper were sent to the judge in San Martín, but he was not in his office. Without advising or listening to them, Andrés Cholotío, the official in charge, fined Haroldo Zacarías and his helper Q40.

Through the night of Saturday, 2 February 1991, there was a lot of persecution of young people after 10:00 P.M. No one could walk around to do their necessities. One young man, Ambrosio Quic Pérez, slept on the porch of a house until dawn, for fear that they would take him to jail. The guards saw this boy enter the *sitio* to ask for help, and the guards and the municipal police waited for him to leave. But the boy didn't leave until the sun came up.

On Sunday, 3 February, Fernando Timoteo Ramos Castro, the third municipal commissioner and a former military commissioner, a man who likes to annoy people, began to take his turn. My wife and I went with Ignacito to Xela to buy things for his studies at the INVO. On this day I spent more than Q400 buying shoes, clothes, a bed, and other things, apart from the expenses of food and the trip.

On Monday [4 February] we left our son at the institute and returned to our town, but first we had to pass through Paxtocá, Totonicapán, to visit our friend Juan Diego. At 9:30 P.M. we arrived at our town.

My children told me that the situation in town is very serious, that during the night of the previous day five men were captured and taken to jail and today they were fined Q30 each. We had dinner, and by that time it was 10:00 P.M. Having finished dinner, I went outside to wash my hands. When I was at the faucet, a group of people shined a flashlight in my face. I asked them what they wanted, but they didn't answer me. Not until I opened the door of the house did I recognize that they were members of the patrol. I asked them why they were abusing me by shining a light in my face when I was inside my own *sitio,* and I told them to look for robbers and not to persecute honest people. They didn't answer me.

I decided to talk to the [head] commissioner of the patrol because he is a respected man, but it did no good. To the contrary, they sent a report to the judge, saying that I had insulted the guards and municipal police. My son José appeared in the report. In the dispatch they asked for a sentence for both of us.

On 11 February 1991 I went with my beloved son Ramón Antonio to Paxtocá. He told me that he needs to master the art of weaving so that he can have work. Earlier I had talked to my friend Juan Diego [a weaver], and he promised that he is going to teach Ramón how he works.

When we went this morning, we had a disaster on the road. When we were going uphill from Panajachel to Sololá, the assistant of the bus driver didn't tie up the suitcase and a radio fell on the road. The radio was destroyed, and the truth is I got angry.

We had breakfast in Salcajá, and then we paid a taxi Q10 to go to Paxtocá. Then we talked a moment with Juan Diego. Ramón stayed with Juan, and I had to return in the same taxi to Salcajá.

Never is man perfect; sometimes his consciousness goes to sleep on him. What happened to me on this day? Always I've said that I am a little smart, but the truth is that always there are shortcomings in oneself. In Xichal I bought thread and dye, and I arranged the *bulto* [bulky load]. I spent a good amount of time waiting for the bus. I boarded a bus of the Veloz Quiché line, told the driver to let me off at the mountain crest, and handed over my *bulto* to the assistant.

Well, I went happily thinking about my business, and en route I read the newspaper a bit. When we arrived at the crest of the mountain, the driver stopped the bus and I left slowly with the others. The assistant shouted, "Those who have cargo, tell me which ones they are [on top of the bus]." The others didn't have any cargo, but I did. But because I didn't tell the assistant to lower my *bulto* to me, realizing nothing had been said, the driver continued his journey. About ten minutes later I remembered and said, "Oh, my *bulto!*" But the bus was now headed to Los Encuentros. I was like a madman spinning around to see what I could do to recover my *bulto*.

I signaled the driver of a pickup, but he did not stop. Luckily a small car was approaching [with a driver and a passenger]. I spoke to the driver, the car moving and I running and shouting. Finally, the man in the car took pity on me, stopped, and asked me what I wanted. I told him, "Señor, do me the favor of taking me to Los Encuentros; it's that I forgot to take down a *bulto* of thread from a bus."

The good man told me to get inside and he accelerated the motor, but when we arrived at Los Encuentros, the bus had already left. The señor of the car didn't let me off in this place. He continued on the road that went to Santa Cruz del Quiché. At last we caught up with the bus, and the driver of the car went out in front and told me to ask about the load. Well, the assistant lowered my *bulto,* and we put it in the car and went back to Los Encuentros.

The driver asked me, "What is your name?"

I told him, "Señor, my name is Ignacio Bizarro Ujpán of San José la Laguna. What is your name?"

He told me that he is called Alvarez Mendoza and that the man accompanying him is his brother. Señor Alvarez Mendoza was only going to Los Encuentros to drop off his brother who was going to take the Rutas Lima bus to the capital. When we were in Los Encuentros I wanted to take out my *bulto,* but he told me, "Watch the car while I go with my brother to the other side of the road." I stayed guarding the car, and soon the señor returned and said, "Let's go." On the road he told me that he was a native of the capital and that he has a chalet in Santa Catarina Palopó, always going there because he prefers to live on the shore of the lake. Also, he said that when I had time I should go to his house to chat. This Señor Alvarez Mendoza left me at the beach [in Panajachel] where one catches the launch to cross the lake. This man did me a great favor. May God give him many blessings.

On Wednesday, 13 February, my son José and I had to appear before the judge [with regard to the patrolmen]. I entered the office at 9:30 A.M. The judge told my son José and me that on 5 February we had insulted the guards and municipal police when they made their rounds. I said to the judge, it wasn't the fifth, this event took place on the fourth at night, but it was only with me, José was already asleep. It is true that I protested to the guards and the police because they were shining a light in my face, but I was inside my *sitio,* and because of this I told them to look for robbers and not to pursue honest people. The angry judge told me that this was a consideration but that the patrol is authorized to capture and arrest anyone found in the street after 10:00 P.M. He told me if I insulted the patrolmen again, I would be sentenced. I told the señor judge:

> We are not strangers to be taken to jail; we are working people and natives of San José, not suspects. Besides, this is a time of peace, not war, yet you want to impose a curfew on us. Please go to San José and tell the patrolmen that the working people will not be persecuted, that they should look for robbers and apply the law to them.

The judge sent an order that nullified the memorandum and that stated that the patrol is not to abduct the youngsters and that all will be peaceful. Not until then was this matter settled. The truth is that the youth are now grateful.

Later information about the robbery of the cooperative came to light. They say it was an inside job planned by two members, the managers, who knew that the treasurer had not collected money from the sales for four days. That is why they knew that there was money in the *tienda.* The total amount of the losses was Q1,200.05 cash and a little bit of merchandise.

The Mayor Resigns
15 February 1991
Ricardo Sicay, the mayor who took office last January, resigned on 15 February 1991. The motivation for his resignation was that he is from the *aldea* and he was pressured by the *concejales* [councilmen]. He only lasted thirty days. [He said it was] a lot of trouble for him. He said that he paid Q250 a month for food and Q150 for a place to sleep but that as mayor he only earned Q300. For this reason, he resigned.

A Mobile Military Detachment Arrives in Town and Religious Leaders Fight Each Other
Wednesday, 20 February 1991
A military detachment arrived at this town and camped on the soccer field, but it is said that it is a mobile detachment. First it was in Santa Ana, and from there it was in Patzilín. Now it is here in San José.

The religious people are never at peace. They always create problems for themselves. They fight to have posts as directors. They say they are faithful and obedient sons of God, but it is a lie. They don't do what they say, because when a group is in power they hold the other groups up to their standards, and they say it is better to be the good ones, not the others [who are not in power]. But who knows which of them is the best?

These days the *cofrades* are going out to the homes of the people to collect food for the parish priest. It is clear that the towns that make up the parish of San Martín each month provide assistance of funds or supplies for the upkeep of the priest. Well, the four groups of *cofrades* of this town arrived to collect Q300 to Q350 plus the supplies on the first Sunday of each month. They say that one of the pettifoggers, José Horacio, talked with Father Diego to ask him if they are delivering to him the upkeep that the *cofrades* collect each month. José says that Father Lucas said that the president of Catholic Action only gives him Q80 each month, and who knows where the rest of the money goes. To be more clear, the *cofrades* take up the collection and then they hand it over to the president of Catholic Action and this same president hands it over to the parish priest. On 16 February this pettifogger sent a letter to the jefe of the *cofrades,* who is the *alcalde* of San Juan Bautista. This letter caused a big problem among the groups that are in the Catholic church. Father Diego did not advise the towns of his parish that he was going to vacate his post. He just said he was going to leave for a few days, but he didn't return.

Becoming Godparents
Sunday, 14 April 1991

This was one of the most beautiful days in our lives. The whole town knows that my wife and I are poor, but we enjoy the respect of many, thanks to a living God. This is a gift from heaven that many yearn for but few achieve.

My wife and I became the *padrinos* [godparents, coparents] of a beautiful godchild named Laura Bizarro Vásquez, daughter of the couple Abraham Bizarro Cojbx and Paula Vásquez Temó. The baptism occurred in the church of my town.

After the mass our *compadres* invited us to their house. We sat down and ate with them. We also drank some beers that my wife bought. She only drinks on special occasions. After the meal we chatted for a good while, and then we said farewell. We arrived home, giving thanks to God Almighty.

Samuel Jesús's Birthday
Monday, 22 April 1991
It was the birthday of our son Samuel Jesús. This child turned seven years old; he is truly loved by his brothers and sisters. My wife and I were not thinking about celebrating, but the children told us that we should do something for the child. Then my wife and the children made tamales.

In the afternoon when the tamales were cooked we sat down in a circle on the floor, not at the table. We ate the tamales, and the family gave him a present. We spent his birthday peacefully.

Peace Talks between the Government and the URNG
The Month of April 1991
The peace talks between the government and the URNG were carried out in Mexico. The mediator between the groups is Señor Obispo de Zacapa, Rodolfo Queza Toruño. This meeting was announced in the paper, on the radio, and on television. In the dialogue they said that peace had been achieved. Those of the Right, that is, the government, say that if the guerrillas lay down their arms there will be peace. Meanwhile, the guerrillas say they will not lay down their arms while the government doesn't honor the agreements in past negotiations. The truth is nobody knows what they have negotiated.

In Guatemala there is always talk of progress toward peace. It has been talked about for many years back, but it has not been achieved. The conflict is because of the lack of social justice. If there were social justice there would not be so much violence. To us, poverty is difficult, but little by little it could end. What saddens us each day is the spilling of the blood of our brothers. What a pity they have lost their lives! The truth is I do not blame only the soldiers or only the guerrillas—the two forces are the cause of the violence in Guatemala. They are responsible for the spilling of blood of thousands of [innocent] Guatemalans, blood spilled to the point that the earth cries out to God, asking forgiveness for those who have cut down lives and asking peace for their wives and their children who are orphaned. But peace is like a cloud—the wind carries it away. It does not last.

The jefes of the army and of the guerrillas need to try harder to reach an agreement. There has been enough blood shed. They have already met in Geneva and other countries on several occasions. The big jefes of the two factions just eat and drink in grand hotels, while their members spill their blood. This should not be.

In April 1991, in Mexico, a guerrilla commander gave an interview on television to the director of Channel 7. The guerrilla commander uses the pseudonym Gaspar Ilom, but his real name is Rodrigo Asturias. And he has the title Doctor. Some say that he is the brother of the deceased writer Miguel Ángel Asturias, but Gaspar Ilom (Dr. Rodrigo Asturias) is his son. Gaspar Ilom is the name of the protagonist in a work titled *Hombres de maíz* [Men of Corn], a work by the deceased master Miguel Ángel Asturias.[42]

The Day of San Pedro the Apostle
29 June to 6 July 1991

[Today is] the day of San Pedro the Apostle. Many people went to the fiesta. We in my family did not go.

On this day I had to go the village of Tzarayá. A friend had requested a calf from me, and when I arrived his wife told me that the friend would not return until the afternoon. Because there was a lot of rain, I had to return without doing business.

When I returned I cut corn husks for the *tamalitos* [little tamales]; I also cut mulberry herb. When I arrived at the house, I told my wife that the trip did not work out. My wife cooked the herb and made tortillas and we ate lunch.

On 6 July 1991 I sold a calf to Señor Pascual Ixtamer of the village of Tzarayá, for the price of Q1,200. I sold this calf out of real necessity.

The following day I had to go to Quezaltenango to pay the debt [Q300], and I exchanged the other part of the money for thread to be able to work more [at weaving].

Señor Tomás Ixtamer Is Robbed
26 to 27 August 1991

Thieves entered the house of Señor Tomás Ixtamer, who lives in Panajachel. They say that the thieves broke into his house at 11:30 A.M., wounded his neck, and stole Q11,030 from him. This news reached San José because the señor was a native *Joseño*.

On 26 August 1991 Señor Tomás Ixtamer went to the military Zone 14 in Sololá to ask protection for the town so that the robberies would not continue. Don Tomás says that the señor commandant offered to watch over the entire town.

On 27 August 1991 I received a check from the sale of the books *Son of Tecún Umán* and *Campesino*. I cashed this check in Panajachel on the same day.

I was able to visit Señor Tomás Ixtamer, and he told me that there is no worry. The military will take responsibility for all of the thieves and murderers.

Our Granddaughter, Rose Josefa, Has a Birthday; a Wedding; and Señor Ixtamer and the Military Zone
27 to 29 August 1991
On the afternoon of 27 August our granddaughter, Rose Josefa, turned three years old. My family prepared a dinner, and at 7:00 P.M. we all ate. By the grace of God we are content, not as we were three years ago when we were having a problem with my daughter María.

We were invited to a wedding. The young Leonel Cipriano Hernández Puzul and Juana Dominga Pur Sicay were married. My wife and I had to accept the invitation, always giving thanks to God for the respect we get.

As things go, Señor Ixtamer went to the military Zone [14] to ask for protection for the town, and the commander promised to take care of the town of Panajachel. What a disgrace, when on the twenty-ninth of the same month, three days after having communicated with the jefe of the zone, the thieves returned to rob the house of the wife of the same Ixtamer. The thieves, after the robbery, left the woman seriously wounded from firearms, and three days later she died in the hospital in Sololá. Both the police and the army acted as if nothing had happened.

Watching a Soccer Game and the Announcement of Cholera
Sunday, 1 September 1991
As usual, I gave infinite thanks to God for one more day of life. We are accustomed to rising early. Even the small children get up early since they are used to it. I went to Xebitz early to take a load of beans. When I returned I ate breakfast.

At 11:00 A.M. my wife and I went to the soccer field to see the match. On this day there were two matches because it was the anniversary of the Blue and White Sport Club. My wife and I always go to the soccer field when we have time, since during the week we feel tired from so much work. On Sundays is when we can rest for a few hours.

In Guatemala there is a serious problem. They say there is cholera morbus. There is a lot of alarm because they say that in Mazatenango and in Coatepeque people are dying. Mainly it is alarming for the Ladinos. For us, the *indígenas*, there is nothing. The doctors and the authorities prohibited us from eating fish, crayfish, and any shellfish. Also, they prohibited the sale of fruit, saying that nobody is to go to the towns to sell fruit. Many of the merchants lost their sales because there are no buyers.

Well, we Indians [are still] happily working in our fields. And the women are content with their warping and weaving. We hardly paid any attention to the order. When we ask to buy fish or crayfish, we eat it without a problem. [Besides,] beans and herbs are the best meals for us poor people.

Although the fear of cholera has been in the news since August, it was the month of September that it was covered in the media the most. As a precautionary measure against cholera, the anniversary of national independence [15 September] was not celebrated in the entire country. This was bad, however, because there was no cholera. There is diarrhea, but there always is diarrhea, mainly among the small children. From negligence, adults get it. In my town, though, there is no cholera.

The Earth Shakes
18 September 1991

When we were peacefully sleeping, suddenly an earthquake gave us a fright. We got up, opened the door, and took the children outside. In my town there were no injuries, only fright, and then we were afraid to sleep. This earthquake hit at 3:50 A.M. When I turned on the radio to listen to the news, all of the broadcasting stations were off the air except the Mazatenango station, Radio Victoria, known as La Venadita.[43] They said that the antennas located on the Alux Hill, San Lucas Sacatepéquez, suffered damage.

In [the department of] Sololá there was not much [destruction], but the National Hospital of Sololá [in the departmental capital] suffered damage. In San Carlos there were two dead and wounded. The roads from Santiago Atitlán to San Lucas and from San Lucas to the coast were closed [because vehicles could not pass]. The radio said that in Mazatenango one side of the church in Samayac collapsed and that also homes suffered damage.

Those who suffered the most are our "brothers" [countrymen] in San Miguel Pochuta in the department of Chimaltenango. Official notice said that besides the dead they found beneath the debris, twenty-three thousand people were affected and 85 percent of the housing was destroyed. Because of the large collapses, San Miguel Pochuta remained without communication. The wounded were taken out by Guatemalan Air Force helicopters. Our "brothers" suffered a lot, and we [in San José] could do nothing directly for them [because they are too far away and we had no means]. In all of the towns of Sololá, help was collected in the Catholic churches. The bishop and the priests worked arduously. What made the calamity in this town even sadder was that there were only eleven days until the celebration of the titular fiesta of the town.

Another Fatal Accident
15 October 1991

Life is a dream. *El que amanece no anochece y el que anochece no amanece* [He who greets the morning may not meet the night, and he who greets the night may not meet the morning].[44]

José Abelino Puzul calmly drove his car on Tuesday to visit his brother, Héctor, a lawyer and notary who was the regional justice of the peace in Santa Clara Tecpán. He stayed in Tecpán on Monday. Then on Tuesday, the fifteenth, Abelino and Héctor arranged to travel to Quezaltenango. With the two of them went the secretary of the court. Peacefully, the three of them ate lunch in a restaurant, and afterward they headed back to San Martín. But they did not arrive alive. Between Salcajá and San Cristóbal an intercity bus, Transportes Sibilia, hit them, and they died instantly. José Abelino Puzul Cholotío was an urban primary educator, but he resigned when his father, Haroldo Puzul Cotúc, founded the company Martinera [a boat line]. Abelino resigned as a teacher and became a pilot of the boat named *Tzutuhil*. Also these two young men, Abelino and Tosh [nickname for Héctor], were very good to the poor people. The two neighboring towns, San Martín and San José, were very sad.

Thieves Steal the Image of San Miguel Archangel
15 October 1991

They say that the robbers even took the statues. Some thieves broke into the side door of the church [of Tzarayá] at night and took San Miguel Archangel, the patron saint, from its place on the altar. After the robbery they very quietly closed the church and left.

When the people in charge of the church arrived, at first they did not notice the empty altar. When they began to sweep at 8:00 A.M., they noticed and sounded the alarm. But they could not find out who stole the image. Some think it was Protestants who took the image out of pure religious spite, but it is not known if this is true.

In this month of October the cholera situation is more serious, but really it is serious in words only. They said that no one could buy fruit, that both the vendor and the buyer would be punished. There was also the order that no one eat fish or crayfish. The doctors of Santiago Atitlán and San Martín ordered that no one drink water directly from the spout, the river, or the lake. Before drinking one must add chlorine—he who does not will die.

We in San José heard about the order, but we did not do anything. In Santiago Atitlán they drink water from the lake, and the doctor and the mayor require the people to mix chlorine in the water. People poured chlorine in the water but without measuring the proper amount. This was what gave them an intestinal infection; many people of Santiago Atitlán got dysentery. To look good, the mayor and the doctor said that it was cholera, but this was a lie. What happened was they did not explain to the people the right quantity of chlorine to add to each gallon of water.

Because of the cholera, they suspended the celebration of all activities, in the town, in the district, and in the *aldeas*.

Celebrating the Day of San Miguel in Tzarayá and News of Death
29 September to 25 October 1991

My family and I have faith in San Miguel the Archangel, and we decided to celebrate the day of San Miguel in the *aldea* of Tzarayá. My wife, Susana Julia, Anica Catana, and I went to Tzarayá to hear the mass.

It was sad. They didn't celebrate mass. They said it was because of cholera and because Father José didn't want them to have a fiesta. A program was planned, but it was not followed. The priest said mass and did the baptisms and first communions on Saturday, the twenty-eighth [because he said that was the only day he could do them].

Well, for us everything was fine. We ate lunch and returned to San José, passing by the milpa that we have in Chuchalí. We arrived at our town somewhat content. We picked wild herbs for our meal.

As things go, no one knows what tomorrow brings. "Our days are numbered," says the Bible. This is certain. When death arrives, it doesn't ask age, position, or sex.

Two and a half years ago three young *Joseños* went as *mojados* ["wetbacks," illegal immigrants] to the United States because it is said that there one earns more than in other countries. The young men were Calixto Puzul Temó, José Temó Asturias, and Abraham Manuel Velásquez Bizarro. The three are related. The parents of these three boys made a great sacrifice to raise Q3,000 each. It is said that they gave Q2,000 to the *coyote*—in other words, a smuggler of people. Altogether, the three gave Q6,000 to the *coyote*, a señor from Totonicapán named Francisco Hernández. They gave to each young man Q1,000 for his expenses on the road. The truth is no one knows how many days they traveled to reach North America. What is known is that the parents of these boys sold their land in order to send their sons.

Calixto and José stayed in the United States only a year and a few months before returning to their hometown. But Abraham Manuel continued working in Florida, U.S.A.

Abraham Manuel was born on 12 October 1973. They say that minors are not permitted to work in a company. Without doubt Abraham Manuel wrote, asking his parents to get a certificate of age retroactive three years. The father struggled to get a birth certificate saying that the boy was born 12 October 1971, son of the married couple José Velásquez Cholotío and Dominga Bizarro Vásquez. With this certificate the boy obtained work in a company.

The parents of Abraham Manuel celebrated a mass in the church on Sunday, 13 October 1991, to give thanks for the boy's eighteenth birthday. But in the United States he said he was twenty-one years old. His parents and relatives had a party without knowing what the next day would bring.

On Tuesday, 14 October, Dominga, Abraham Manuel's mother, went with other women to the capital for a course in *comadrona empíricas* [midwifery]. His father received a telephone call informing him that his son Abraham Manuel collided with a bus when he was riding a bicycle. The impact threw him several feet in the air, and he was seriously injured. He was taken to a hospital, where he died Tuesday.

The father began to mobilize [to get money together, to ask for ideas, to decide what to do, and] to communicate with [the authorities in the] United States, but each three minutes [on the telephone] costs Q67 in San José. The father was told that the person in charge is the ambassador of Guatemala and that the ambassador will send the cadaver to the international [air]port, La Aurora. From the airport, parents or relatives could conduct the body to San José. On the phone, they said that the body would arrive on Saturday, the eighteenth, but it was not true. From Miami, Florida, they sent notice that the body will be delivered to the parents on the twenty-first or twenty-second.

The cadaver of Abraham Manuel arrived on 24 October 1991. The burial was on the twenty-fifth. The town was filled with mourning—the young man who died was really well liked, and he was from a good family. About two thousand people attended the funeral.

Reconciliation of Factionalism in the Catholic Church
27 April to 1 November 1991

In the Catholic church there has been a tremendous division, the large group and the small group hurtling insults at one another. Neither side gave in.

On 27 April 1991 there was a meeting for the towns belonging to the parish. The purpose of the meeting was to plan a trip to the capital of Guatemala to request a priest specifically for the parish, because the priest that came to substitute for José McCall was loaned and came only on Saturday and Sunday and then returned to Panajachel. The two groups from San José participated in this meeting. I was invited to it, but I saw that the two groups did not like each other, although they were from the same town. After we returned from San Martín, I talked with my two friends José Haracio and Bernardo. We decided to talk with the leaders of the small group about a reconciliation with the large group, to urge them to forget all that had happened in the church, so that they all could become one family.

That night we met with the leaders of the small group, and they said that they agreed to reconcile but that they wanted to be respected by the others because for years they have been suffering marginalization and bad treatment. Then they told us that we should meet with the head of Catholic Action so that he would meet with the people to see if they want reconciliation.

Then we asked for an audience with the president of Catholic Action, and this señor told us that the first meeting would be on 7 May. This day arrived, and we brought up before the leader the need for a reconciliation between the two groups, because the discord, which has been going on for almost four years, is bad for the town. Then they told us that first they have to talk to the rest of the people to see if they agree to a reconciliation, and they promised us that on 15 May we would have our next meeting to find something positive.

When 15 May arrived we met again, and they told us that it was possible to have a reconciliation but only if the small group would agree to tear down the shed that served as the oratory and if they would hand over the benches and other things that were in their possession. If they would do these things, everyone, including the adults and children in both the small and the large group, would have a fiesta and the matter would be settled. After we left this meeting we made our way to the leaders of the small group and we told them what the other group had promised. They then began to dismantle the *galera* and hand over the benches and other things.

The director of Catholic Action and we decided that our next meeting would be at the end of May, to determine the day when the reconciliation would take place. It was decided that the reconciliation would take place in the presence of Monsignor Benando Gálvez and Father José McCall.

Also, the president of Catholic Action predicted problems because many of the people did not want to reconcile, and he had to find a good way to appeal to the conscience of the people. On 22 July the president called me for a secret meeting in his house. He too is an enthusiast for unity. We agreed that he soon would ask Monsignor Gálvez for the celebration of the liturgy on Thursday and the exposition of the Santísimo [Holy Sacrament] on Friday. Monsignor Benando Gálvez reauthorized Señor Juan Bizarro to administer the Holy Eucharist. Everything was set.

Monsignor sent a letter to the head of Catholic Action, to the heads of other groups, and to us. The people began to come again to the church. But when we arrived, those from the small group did not arrive. Our planned meeting didn't take place and, finally, we had to leave. The bishop sent a letter to Señor Andrés Ramos Toc, owner of the *sitio* where the *galera* is constructed, but this man was disobedient and didn't respond.

It was a complicated matter. Some in the small group now did not want reconciliation because they didn't want to dismantle the *galera* and hand over the benches. But finally the unification with the majority was accomplished, even though ten people of the small group refused.

The reconciliation took place on 1 November. There was a solemn fiesta. Mass was celebrated by Monsignor Benando Gálvez and Father José. Father Alberto was not present because he had to say mass in San Jorge.

Some people are indeed bad. A day before the reconciliation, five people from San José went to Panajachel to tell the bishop that the reconciliation would not take place because a group is against it and that group might make an attempt on his life. The bishop called by telephone, and we told him that it was a lie, that there was no group of such evil persons. Nevertheless, the bishop sent Father Ciro to investigate, but the priest found no evil.

All the people were feeling festive, waiting for the day of the reconciliation. Thank God all went well, and now in the town the majority of people are united. The truth is that some members of the both the large group and the small group are egotistical. I will always believe that this reconciliation is worthwhile so that the young people can see that there is forgiveness. As we forgive our brothers, God forgives us. We made this effort of reconciliation for the good of the whole town. We suffered insults and contempt, but God pardons those things.

A New Year and My Sons Are Called to Municipal Service
1 January 1992

We are beginning a new year, a gift of the Almighty. It is certain that no one can buy a day of life. Without money one must thank God for life, for the air, and for the sun. We must love one another as brothers, a lesson that the teacher of teachers, Jesucristo, taught us when he said, "Love one another as I have loved you." God loves us equally. Many times people read [about love in the Bible], but they don't love their fellow man. For Christmas and for the New Year, people here embrace in the streets, in their homes, even in the church, saying, "Merry

Christmas, Happy New Year, peace and love be with us."

I have seen people who are easily offended and say harsh things about their fellow man, quickly forgetting what they said at Christmas and New Year's Day. Perhaps I am the only person who doesn't hug at Christmas and New Year's Day, but indeed I respect and always feel love for the rest of humanity, even those who say and do bad things to me. Then I remember the prayer:

Our Father [who art] in heaven, hallowed be thy name. Thy kingdom come, thy will be done on earth as [it is] in heaven. Give us [this day] our daily bread and forgive us our sins, as we forgive those who trespass against us. Lead us not into temptation, but deliver us from evil.

This prayer is from the mouth of the King of Kings, Jesús.

Well, as always, with my family on this New Year's Day I said the blessing: "Thanks to God we are of good health. We are a united family, caring about our work and struggling to make life a little better."

On 1 January 1992 my two sons José Juan and Ramón Antonio were both called into unpaid service in the municipality. José is a *guardia municipal* [municipal guard], and Ramón is an *alguacil*. They take a weeklong turn every two weeks. To be more specific, [their pattern] is to work for two weeks for themselves and then to work for one week for the municipality. During the day, they run errands or make citations; at night they stay in the commissary to guard it or to attend to emergencies of any kind that may happen in town.

Many refuse to do this service, but I told my sons that it is better to be obedient and that it is necessary to serve and to respect, so that in the future they will also be respected. My sons took my advice. The truth is they did not volunteer for this service—the municipality selected them.

Harvesting Coffee and the Day of the Lord of Esquipulas
2 to 15 January 1992

We were picking ripe coffee, working eleven days and finishing on 14 January. We did not pay helpers. We in the family did it because there is not very much to harvest and the price is very low.

The fifteenth of January is the Day of the Señor de Esquipulas [Lord of Esquipulas].[45] My mother celebrates this day, making tamales and buying beverages. She invited us to have lunch with them. We felt like we had to accept. During the lunch, they drank their drinks, but we did not because my wife doesn't like to drink. We only ate.

Harvesting Corn
22 to 24 January 1992

At 5:00 A.M. I got up. I did not eat breakfast; I just took some tortillas with me. On my back I carried a seventy-five-pound load of nets and other things necessary for the corn harvest. The climb up the slope from Pachitul to Tzarayá was difficult. When I arrived, I ate the tortillas. Then I went to harvest the milpa together with other native field workers from Santa Ana.

My helpers stayed working in the field while I went to town to look for drinking water and for a shelter where I could store the corn. In the afternoon, the *muchachos* went back to their hometown, and I stayed guarding the corn against thieves who might like to steal it.

I left the milpa at 8:30 P.M. and arrived home at 10:00 P.M. It was cold in the cornfield, and when night fell I drank a lot of coffee, which caused my stomach to hurt. Thus when I arrived home, I didn't feel like eating anything.

On 23 January my wife and daughters Susana and María prepared the tortillas and other food to take with us to the cornfield. I got up at 4:00 A.M. This time my brother Geraldo went with me to Tzarayá, and we took the horse.

When we arrived, we built a fire and gathered around it to warm and eat the tortillas. The *muchachos* from Santa Ana began to harvest the corn, and my brother and I carried it to Santa Ana. We looked for an easy path to take to carry the corn to a place where it could be loaded on a truck. The work was very tiring, and we did not arrive home until 7:30 P.M.

In the morning of Friday, 24 January, José went to San Martín to look for a truck to transport the corn. He returned at 7:30 A.M., and then I left for Tzarayá. Erasmo Ignacio and Geraldo had already gone ahead. This time I took a very steep shortcut under the hot sun.

I made bundles of corn that weighed 3 *quintales* each. When the truck arrived at 4:00 P.M., I started to load the heavy bundles on it. Loaded and on the road, the truck driver, Homero Salaj, and I recounted our earlier work in the cotton industry. We recalled the suffering we endured working on the *finca* Caoba.

We also talked about the problem of alcohol, and he told me that he had suffered a lot from it. He said that he had gone fifty-eight days, drinking day and night. Homero played a tape of marimba music as we traveled. It was pleasant.

At 7:00 P.M. we arrived at San José. Homero and I ate bread and drank coffee. Afterward I was exhausted, so I went to bed.

The Patron Fiesta of San Jorge and Prostitution
25 January 1992

The patron fiesta of the town of San Jorge sets people in motion. Fiestas are to have a good time but not to go over the limit. In this fiesta of San Jorge there were a lot of problems in many of the homes of these people and also in neighboring towns.

It happened that a citizen of this village contracted a marimba and brought in prostitutes, who were the downfall of many men. They fought with their wives and lost money, and some even sold their land, resulting in adjudication.

In my town of San José a very serious incident happened. A townsman named Jorge Erasmo got involved with these women. Undoubtedly, from so much *guaro* he became crazy, and when he arrived home he began to beat his wife. He told her that in San Jorge there are women better than she. Since it was night and she was sleepy, the poor woman was not able to defend herself, and she asked her daughter to help her. Because the crazed husband was trying to kill the woman, her daughter grabbed a stick to defend her mother and hit her father on the head until he fell to the ground. To save her mother, the girl almost killed her father, inflicting a big wound on his head. They took Jorge Erasmo to the hospital in Sololá, but the doctors wouldn't accept him there because his situation was very serious. They sent him to Roosevelt Hospital in the capital city.

When Jorge Erasmo left the hospital, his wife didn't tell him that it was his daughter who hit him. Instead, she simply told him that he had fallen and hit his head on a rock. This happened in San Jorge, and because of such incidents, people are losing their respect and their culture.

María Is a Teacher
26 January 1992

Our daughter María is a teacher; she graduated in 1990 as teacher of urban primary education. In the year 1991 she was helping the students of the *instituto básico* with a course in typing, starting to work at 5:00 A.M. and quitting at 9:00 A.M. They give her a small salary of Q100 per month. But as I have said, the salary of the *básico* teachers is not paid at the end of each month but sometimes every two or three months. She studies Saturdays in Sololá. So we think she can find work in the *cabecera,* which will help to support her and allow her to continue to study. She went to speak with the director of the Santa Clara School to see if he would hire her to teach the children. This was 23 January.

She said that the director told her to show up on the twenty-seventh to begin to work. On the twenty-sixth María went to Sololá, and my wife and I went with her to carry her bed and clothes. In Sololá we rented a house from Señor Bartolo Batz.

We left home at 12:00 noon and arrived at Sololá at 3:00 P.M., and we spent the afternoon arranging things. At 9:00 P.M. we arrived back home. The truth is that María only earns Q300 per month, but we are happy because now she is able to take care of herself and continue studying to earn a higher degree, teacher of secondary education.

María is lucky. Three days after having gone to Sololá we received a note from the president of the project Visión Mundial Cristiano [World Christian Vision], saying that she should present herself to sign a contract to teach the children in the school. But that is not possible because she is already teaching. I had to thank by letter Señor Gregorio Tzaj, president of the project, for his good intentions for my daughter. Gregorio is a good friend; we were working in the crews on the coast weeding and picking cotton, and now he is better off because he has a salary working on the project. This project is concerned with supporting poor people and with education and development. [The project] constructs houses, provides fertilizer at low prices, and even combats malnutrition in children. They say also that this project is funded by evangelicals, but they don't say of which church.

Ignacito Continues His Studies
27 January 1992

Today, Monday, Ignacito went again to live in Quezaltenango to continue his fifth year of study in the Instituto Nacional para Varones de Occidente.[46] Ignacito concluded all of the courses successfully. Three of his colleagues failed courses; they lost out on the exams. My son was advanced to the next grade, and I begged and asked God to give him enlightenment to have peace and tranquility with his teachers. Now we must struggle to pay for what he needs in his studies, always with God's guidance.

Six Indians Are Massacred
9 February 1992

A bus was returning to Santiago Atitlán from the coast. It was carrying merchants, *Atitlanecos* [people of Atitlán] who had been on vegetable business in Mazatenango, San Antonio Such[itepéquez] and Chicacao. Still in the jurisdiction of Suchitepéquez, the passengers were content. As the bus approached the boundary of the department of Sololá, close to the finca Tarrales, a group of men armed with automatic rifles forced the driver off the paved road and onto a dirt road. Most of the bandits were off the pavement, a little inside the bushes. They made all the men and women get off the bus. They robbed them of their money and their possessions, taking their rings and watches.

Resenting that they had stolen his money, one of the young merchants grabbed a rock and landed a solid blow in the face of one of the armed men. The bandit fell to the ground, and his companions carried him off on their backs. But some [of the outlaws] remained behind to shoot six merchants. In this place six citizens of Atitlán were murdered.

What is unknown is who it was that massacred the six *indígenas*. Many say it was the guerrillas, that is to say, the people of the other towns. But the citizens of Atitlán say that they were angry soldiers who don't like the people of Santiago. Earlier they killed *Atitecos* in the town of Santiago Atitlán; now they were killing them on the road. The truth is this crime is bad for humanity.

In Guatemala there is a procurator of human rights, but he did nothing about investigating this bloody event. He didn't say a word. It seems to me that the *licenciado* Ramiro de León Carpio is pressured by the two groups. "Yes," he says to the Right; "Yes," he says to the Left. And [it's] the indigenous people who end up massacred by the assassins. The señor procurator has the protection of the two powers—he has his safe life and the rest get murdered. This is what is happening in my Guatemala.

An Evangelical Dies from Insanity
Monday, 10 February 1992

I went to Totonicapán to visit my friend Domingo Toc Cojox. He sent me a telegram telling me about the death of his sister, but I wasn't able to go [immediately]. It wasn't because of a whim. Rather, I've been in bad health with an infection of the mouth, which made it difficult for me to eat for ten days. The infection was cured, but then I caught the flu.

Still sick with the flu, I went to Totonicapán to console my friend Domingo. He told me that his twenty-seven-year-old sister had died. The illness from which she had suffered was insanity; that is to say, she became crazy for some months, and they took her to doctors in Quezaltenango. But they say that the doctors said they didn't have a cure because it was an illness of the mind.

Well, Domingo told me that they belong to an evangelical religion and that when they pray to God they shout loudly and beat their hands, their feet, even their heads on the ground or on the walls, so that their prayers will be heard by God. The family had been three years in this religion, Prince of Peace, and the pastor ordered that everyone had to shout in order to be heard by God. Domingo said that his sister Berta went crazy from shouting so much, and she couldn't be cured. He was sure it was because of the religion.

Then Juan Domingo and his family changed churches. Now they belong to the Seventh-Day Adventist Church. He told me that it suits them better to be in this church because it is more peaceful than before.

After the chat I had to help Domingo, just as a little sign of affection, because he spent a lot of money, as much to pay doctors as to pay for the burial of his sister. This friend suffered a lot.

In the afternoon of this day I returned from Totonicapán with a high temperature and a headache. The illness is complicated—at night my arms and fingers ache and I don't sleep peacefully. I don't believe that I'm suffering from old age but from the effects of work when I was young.[47] What's more, I'm not taking medicine or vitamins from a pharmacy. I'm only eating food, that is to say, tortillas, herbs, beans, fish, and, once in a while, meat.

We Sell a Bull
Wednesday, 26 February 1992

We sold a bull for the price of Q1,175. We had bought this bull for

Q650 in August 1991 when he was small. It was my beloved son Ramón who fed him and cared for him for six months, but as extra work. He got up at 4:00 A.M. to get hay for him, and he also fed him in the afternoon.

Ramón is the best of the kids for field work, for weaving, and for making *jaspes*. He is obedient. When we bought the calf, we conferred with him. He agreed to take care of it if we gave him some of the profit when we sold it.

When we sold the bull, I gave him a little money to spend on something he wanted. I was in favor of our agreement in order to teach him to love to work. Besides, it doesn't pay to lie to a child because that is when resentment is born.

Profesor Matea Offers María a Job and Señor Enrique Santos Montufar Criada Has Connections with the Ministry of Education
Monday, 2 March 1992

I went to Santiago Atitlán to say hello and to thank *profesor* Roberto Zacarías García Matea for his good will toward my daughter María. Roberto Zacarías was María's teacher when she was in her second year of primary school. When he learned that María had graduated as a teacher, he sent us a letter saying that she should present a photocopy of her degree in order to secure a position as a substitute in the official [government] school in the canton Pasajquim of the same *municipio*.

As I always say, friendship and respect are the most valuable [things]. When Roberto Zacarías was working in San José, he earned our affection and respect. He told me we would be friends until death. Indeed, Roberto sent us the notice that my daughter could work in Pasajquim. But she is working in Sololá with a small salary, and it would not please me if she gave up the school in Santa Clara. It's true that in Santiago Atitlán she would earn a regular teacher's salary, but it would be a shame to be unfaithful to the director of Santa Clara. Because of this, I had to go to Santiago Atitlán to thank the noble *profesor* for his love toward us.

Also on 2 March I talked by phone with Señor Enrique Santos Montufar Criada. On Monday, 21 February, this señor had been here in San José for some discussions with the Catholic Actionists to reconstruct the church. He told them that he has connections with a branch of the Ministry of Education so that he can secure permanent positions with the government [public schools in Guatemala are run by the federal government]. Then the president [of Catholic Action] called to tell me what the señor had told him.

Later I met with this señor Enrique Santos, and he told me that he could get positions for teachers and that he is good friends of high-ranking personnel [in the ministry]. He told me, however, he needed money for the procedures. "Begin now and the position will be available in 1993," he said.

Since I knew nothing, he convinced me that he needed Q100 to begin the work. At the time I didn't have Q100. José lent me the money, and I gave it to the señor without receiving a receipt. The truth is I didn't know if it was the right thing to do or if it was a mistake, but I trusted the señor because he seemed upright and because they said he was religious.

Today, when he called me on the phone, he told me that he was certain about what we had discussed. I hope to God that he is right.

A Doctor and Health Workers in My Town, San José
15 to 16 March 1992

The doctor and health workers, with the support of the municipality, built a ward behind the municipal *salón* a month ago. It's the place where cholera patients are quarantined. Also, there is an order from the minister of health that people who die of cholera must go from the ward to the cemetery without rituals or wakes.

On 16 March it was said that cholera was in San José. They said that on Sunday, the fifteenth, the couple José Temó Velásquez and Isabel Bizarro Velásquez went to San Martín and ate fruit. That night the woman began to have diarrhea and to vomit, and around dawn the husband also came down with diarrhea and vomiting. To signal an alert for prevention, the doctor and the health workers announced that these two persons were in the ward.

What is a little comical is that these two persons are evangelicals from the Assembly of God [Church], and when they became sick with diarrhea, the children went to the home of the pastor to tell him that they were sick. But they say the pastor told them that he could not go to pray for them because they suffered from a dangerous illness.

Getting Firewood in Haunted Patzunoj
Monday, 16 March 1992

Four of us—Don José, Abelino, Chago [diminutive for Santiago], and I—went to the mountain Patzunoj to fell trees for firewood with Chago's chainsaw.

Before beginning to cut down the trees, I had to perform a *costumbre,* as my ancestors had done when they were about to begin to work in a place. They had to burn myrrh and *copal* [incense] in order to ask permission of the *dueño del santo mundo* [lord of the sacred world, earth].

I am not a *zajorín* or *brujo,* however. I am only a man who retains the customs of his fathers, grandfathers, and the ancient Maya.

Well, on this day I prepared for and performed a small *costumbre,* and then we began to work.

What kind of costumbre *did you perform?*

In addition to using myrrh and incense, I performed a *costumbre* with sugar, candles, and an eighth of a liter of *aguardiente.* The combination of sugar, incense, and myrrh gives a favorable aroma. The rum is for the *dueño* and the spirits of the dead ancestors. I asked for permission to take the trees from the *dueño* and for protection while I was working, because I was doing damage to the area and there are creatures such as three-meter-long snakes that can harm the workers.

Patzunoj is a haunted place. One hears the voices of men and the yelps of dogs. On a November afternoon of last year, my brothers and first cousins, ten of us, were taking a rest before returning to our homes. We were sitting in a circle telling jokes when near us we heard men talking and dogs yelping. These sounds attracted our attention, but when we tried to find out where they were coming from, we saw nothing. My relatives were frightened. What they say about the place—that it's haunted—is true.

The Madness of Alcohol
Tuesday, 17 March 1992

According to his family, my neighbor, Domingo Tuc García, left last night to visit some uncles who were sick. Who knows why he began to drink liquor. When he went home drunk, he hit his wife. After the craziness he slept.

They say on waking up at two o'clock in the afternoon, a small child told him what had happened to him. Then Domingo began to look for his wife, and he saw that she wasn't there and thought that the woman had abandoned the house. Domingo became desperate, and, as he had alcohol in his brain, he drank an *octavo* of insecticide called Malathion. They took this seriously ill friend to the hospital. The incident was expensive because they spent a lot of money to save his life.

Working in Patzunoj
18 to 22 March 1992
Together with some boys from the coast, I was working in Patzunoj, splitting firewood with an ax. The work of making firewood is hard because it requires much strength and practice.

On Saturday, 21 March 1992, we were working in Patzunoj. Ramón, my son, Chago, the owner of the chainsaw, and I were cutting firewood in the forest. During the day, the chainsaw was managed by the owner. We were the assistants. Chago cut five and one-half *tareas* [jobs, pieces of work that can be done in one day.] He earned Q55. He told us that the limbs are hard [dry] and that he was unable to do anymore. He said when the limbs are soft [green], he can cut ten *tareas* in one day. I did not pay Chago until Sunday, 22 March. I gave him Q105 because I owed him Q55 from last week.

Trying to Secure a Position for María
Sunday, 22 March 1992
My wife and I think about our daughter María a lot. It is true that she is working, but we want [something better] for her in the year 1993, to see if she can get a permanent position. And if we are not able to, it won't be because we didn't try.

At 10:00 A.M. María, my wife, and I went to Santiago Atitlán on an errand. We had heard about a vacant position in this town and went to inquire about it. But they said one first must earn the confidence of the director, of the parents' committee, and of the mayor. But I haven't even met these people.

What I did was to leave my wife and María in the park while I went to the home of my friend Alejandro Chavajay to tell him what I needed. This friend told me that the director was his first cousin and that there would be no problem with the mayor. This friend offered me his help.

Then we went to the home of the director, who received us. We chatted with her and told her the purpose of our visit. She offered to help us, saying she would tell the committee and that they should consider my daughter. She said she would inform María, who was in Sololá, by telephone. It is not certain that María will obtain a job; it's only a hope of ours.

Land Problems with the Tuc Brothers and Some Relatives
Wednesday, 8 April 1992

On Patzunoj mountain there is a piece of land that my grandmother told me belonged to her husband, Ignacio Bizarro Ramos. When their house burned down in 1946, she said the deed to the property also burned. About thirty years ago my grandmother showed me where the boundaries were; she even showed me where they tied up the dogs for guarding the corn because there were many animals in the area.

I didn't work the land because it required a lot of money and, besides, there was no document to protect me. Every once in a while, my grandmother told me that the piece of land was ours. The truth, however, was that I was afraid to use the land because the landowners, the Tuc brothers [Juan Benando Tuc and Roderico Tuc], also said that this land was theirs.[48] Thus I was afraid to claim this land because the Tuc brothers forgive no one.

Well, when I was in the cooperative in 1983, a group of us people of the poorest class who lacked land went to the municipality and asked the mayor and vice mayor to grant us the communal land with the right of usufruct for the cultivation of coffee, maize, and beans. The municipality took into account the [religious and civil] service that we residents had freely given to the town as volunteers.

In a municipal agreement they swore solemnly that we fifty residents could work the land as usufructuaries, and when we grow old we could leave it to our children.[49] The only thing was that we would not have the right to sell it.

In an official document, it says I was one of the fifty residents, and I drew section no. 4. So it is in a document that the municipality gave me the right to work thirty *cuerdas* of land in Patzunoj.[50] It was like this with all of us. There is one notable thing that we fifty campesinos had to contend with—the pieces of land are not in one place but scattered in different places but in the same jurisdiction; also, some of the pieces of land are ten *cuerdas* in size, others twenty, and some even forty.[51]

The parceling of the land was done in February 1983. Those who have the land in Patzunoj are only Antonio Cholotío Canajay, Santiago Alberto Vásquez, Eduardo Flores Sicay, and I. Actually, these three persons have land adjacent to mine. The location of their land is really called Pachitez.

So we tried to cultivate this land in 1983, but it wasn't possible. It is a pity that it is close to the mountains. The people said that the guerrillas passed through my piece of land, and at times they stayed there to sleep. Then I was too afraid to work this land. Who wanted to lose his life for a piece of land? And they said that the army continuously passed through there. Even more frightening, in this same year a Guatemalan Air Force plane flew over the area, shooting rounds of automatic rifle fire and dropping bombs.

I didn't see the airplane do it, but Santiago Alberto, Antonio Cholotío Canajay, and Eduardo Flores did. They indeed had planted coffee, but they abandoned their fields. Since I never cultivated this land, I didn't go there anymore. In November 1991, however, I had thought about preparing this field for planting maize for the year 1992.

But thirty *cuerdas* of land is a lot, and for me it would require a lot of money. Seeing the need of my poor relatives, I thought that all of us were children of [the same] God and were of the same flesh and bone. We had the same needs. All of our lives have a beginning and an end, and I didn't want to be inconsiderate.

As my grandmother Isabel had said, this same land belonged to my grandfather Ignacio Bizarro Ramos, who planted corn on it. He died on 10 August 1950. This land, then, had actually always been ours. So my uncle Bonifacio, who is now an old man of eighty-five years, is poor, and he has adult children who don't have enough land to cultivate. They have some *cuerdas* of land, but they are in rocky areas. Like them, my brother Jorge is short of land.

One day I called Uncle Bonifacio and my brother Jorge to tell them that we would divide into three parts the land that belonged to my grandfather, Ignacio. Ten *cuerdas* would go to Señor Bonifacio, ten *cuerdas* to Jorge, and ten *cuerdas* to me. I told them that I have a copy of a document in the municipality in which I am assigned as an usufructuary. And I told them that they could work it the same way, without being able to sell the land.

Well, my uncle Bonifacio was grateful and he told me that although he could no longer work because he was too old, his sons could prepare it to plant maize. At the same time, Manuel was also grateful. He told his father what we had discussed.

We began to work together and measured the land, coming up with thirty-two *cuerdas*. But eight sons of Señor Bonifacio arrived, and they thought that ten *cuerdas* [to divide between them] was very little. So I was conscientious with them; I gave them sixteen *cuerdas* so that each one would have two *cuerdas*. Of the remaining sixteen *cuerdas,* eight were for Jorge and eight were for me. Preparing my eight *cuerdas* for cultivation cost me a lot of money—about Q80 per *cuerda.*

The Tuc brothers and sister are the only big landowners in San José, because their father was a thief and invaded a lot, but really a lot, of land.[52] Then members of the Tuc family [Rita, who married Danny Hi, Juan Benando Tuc, Roderico Tuc, and Tanya Tuc] ordered me [at four different times] to the municipality, saying that the land was theirs. I told them to present the written [document] so it can be examined. They told me that it is in the real estate registry in Quezaltenango and when they have the deed they will show it. Like this it remained; it was not a major legal problem for me because they did not have a title to the land.

As things go, there are people who are opportunists. On Wednesday, 8 April 1992, we were doing the final work and the land was almost ready for planting.

A group of brothers, [this time] from the Bizarro family, claiming that the land belongs to their father [Diego Bizarro Ramos], wanted to fight us. They wanted to take the land with brute force. They are Humberto Bizarro, Daniel Bizarro, Andrés Bizarro, Carlos Bizarro, Gilberto Guido Bizarro, and Mario Bizarro. I didn't want to provoke them; I told my cousins and our helpers to continue preparing the land. I returned to register a complaint in the municipality, to say that they wanted to take the land away from me when I have already prepared it [for cultivation].

On the afternoon of Wednesday, 8 April, Humberto, Daniel, and Andrés were summoned because I only gave the names of these three in the verbal complaint. It was because Andrés was the *alcalde* in the year 1983 and he signed the *acta* whereby the municipality gave plots of land to the townspeople to cultivate. It is the same Andrés and his brothers who now want to take it from me.

In the municipality they said to Señor Andrés that he should be more careful because he was committing a crime. They told the *alcalde* that they would continue working the land, until they planted it. They are stupid. The *alcalde* told them to no longer go on this land, but these idiots said that they would continue doing it.

The *alcalde* gave me a written order so that the justice of the peace would intervene in this matter. On 10 April I went to leave this order with the justice in San Martín.

The justice of the peace told me to present myself on Monday, so that he and the official will go to the Patzunoj to capture the implicated brothers and send them under arrest to Sololá. What the señor justice told me gave me great sorrow; never in my life have I put people in jail, nor do I want to.

I thought a lot about them being my relatives, and I thought it better not to present myself on Monday. I considered abandoning the land and leaving it to them, but I have spent a lot of money on it.

For a few days I didn't go to Patzunoj. What these relatives did hurt me a lot. But when they realized they could go to jail, they no longer went to the land to plant it. Later, I planted this piece of land, but I don't know how this will all turn out.

Tarea Hunajpú: What Happened in the Early Morning of the Day
10 April 1992

The students at the University of San Carlos were making preparations for the parade on this day, Sorrowful Friday, preparing the float for the comic parade that always happens, year after year.

The *muchachos* were working through the night, and they say four of the students went to a store to buy cigarettes. When they left the store, a group of armed men in a pickup truck chased them. The truck had personal license plates; that is, they were policemen, and the police vehicles didn't have official plates so that they could confuse anyone who saw them. The students ran toward their companions. The murderers opened fire on the students with automatic rifles where the students had been working on 1st and 2d Avenue of 12th and 13th Streets of Zone 1. There the university student Julio Rigoberto Cú was riddled with bullets, and the university professor Julio Felipe Sajché was seriously wounded; what's more, [there were] seven wounded who were treated in the Centro Hospitalario.

The assassins are members of a government group that has the name Tarea Hunajpú.[53] This group is composed of members of the national police, *guardia de hacienda* [semimilitary border patrol who are armed treasury police], the *militar ambulantes* [roving military police], and army soldiers. It is said that this group is the best for ending delinquency and violence. But this is not true; they are the criminals.

An official communication said that the group Tarea Hunajpú that had committed this bloody deed has thirty-two members. The attorney general and public prosecutor officially declared that upon confirming the ones responsible for this criminal act, the death penalty will befall them. But things like this they only say and never do. There is no justice, and because of this each day Guatemala goes from bad to worse.

Holy Wednesday
Wednesday, 15 April 1992
Twelve neighbors and I bought fruit and prepared a decoration; that is to say, we made an *arco* [arch, a special decoration made of fruit or flowers] totally of fruit in order not to forget the tradition of Holy Thursday and Friday. We are the people who live close to the intersection where the procession will pass. We made the *arco* completely of fresh fruit: bananas, peaches, pineapples, *pataxtes* [white cacaos], and oranges.

Holy Friday
17 April 1992
In the afternoon we prepared a carpet using sand as a plain base and then, with paint or with flowers, drew figures of the people, crosses, and Santísimo, depending on the ability of the people doing it. It was expensive for those who used paint, because the sand soaks up a lot of it. As the proverb says, *El hombre propone, pero Dios es el que dispone* [Man proposes, but God disposes]. We planned to make the best carpet of all, but halfway through our work we had to stop because it rained and a stream washed away all of it. The rain stopped, and we spread out dry sand. We began again, and the rain fell again and for the second time washed away the carpet. Since we humans are weak, with this second instance of bad luck we dispersed and went home. I went to bed to sleep.

I thought we would not do it again, but Pascual came to tell me that we shall work again to make another carpet. I had to agree, and we went together again to begin the work.

The procession passed through our street at 11:30 A.M. After the procession went by we had coffee and bread at my house, and then my companions left to go to bed. We also went to bed.

On the afternoon of this day, Easter Sunday, 19 April, we dismantled the *arco* and divided the fruit among all of us. It was nice. We were all happy, and we said that, God willing, 1993 would be a little better than this year. But who knows, because the truth is we don't know what could happen tomorrow.

A Boat Capsizes on Glorious Saturday and Samuel Jesús's Birthday on Easter Sunday
18 to 19 April 1992

Many people come from many places to enjoy a rest during Holy Week, especially in Panajachel. As the proverb says, *Todos sabemos donde nacemos pero nunca sabemos donde morimos* [We all know where we are born, but we never know where we are going to die].

Well, this Glorious Saturday in Panajachel a group of people who found themselves in the seaside resort hired a boat for a ride on the lake. The boat, the *Tzutuhil,* is large, and it is owned by Haroldo Puzul of San Martín la Laguna. They say that more than two hundred people, men and women, were squeezed into the boat. They left the dock happily, but in the middle of the lake the pilot felt the boat was unbalanced, so he turned it back in the direction of Panajachel. The weight of the passengers was too much on the second level and not enough on the first level. They almost reached the dock.

In the lake, however, close to the dock, a señorita was drowning and the lifeguards were helping her. The passengers, curious to see what was happening, crowded together on one side of the boat, without realizing that they too were in danger. The boat capsized and sank into the lake.

This fatal accident claimed eight lives. Of the eight bodies, only seven were found. In addition, there were people injured. Four of the dead were *Sololatecos* [persons from Sololá]. A deceased couple from the canton Cacsiquan, Sololá, left eight [surviving] children, and among them there were minors. One *muchacho* had a girlfriend. The young man asked and received permission of the girlfriend's father to take the girl to Panajachel to spend time at the beach. The girl had a sister who also wanted to go to Panajachel, and the father also gave permission to the other daughter to accompany the sweethearts. What bad luck that the girlfriend and her sister drowned! The boyfriend, who survived, returned alone to Sololá.

The boat was pulled out by cranes on Sunday the nineteenth. The recovery of the boat cost the owner Q2,000. The owner handed over to the relatives the bodies of the dead, and he paid for the funeral expenses. The pilot and the assistant were taken as prisoners to the jail in Sololá.

When the accident happened, the people who were here [in San José] in the beach area of the Chuitinamits went to their villages. Sunday is a day of much activity, but this time people weren't at the Chuitinamits; there was much fear because of what had happened in Panajachel.[54]

A Friend and His Wife Are Assaulted in Their Store
Monday, 20 April 1992

Today I went to Sololá to accompany my *compadre* Juan and his wife. The reason for our trip was to inform the justice of the peace what they suffered on 8 April of this year. They had a store in San Benito la Laguna, and they were assaulted in the middle of the night. Both were wounded. The patrol of the town managed to capture a thief by the name of Roberto Tzaj Temó, and they sent him to the jail in Sololá. In a declaration before the justice of the peace, he confessed that he entered the home of Juan Ramos, but he said it was because he was drunk.

The father of the thief is a man of means, and with Q3,000 he bribed the judge of Sololá who set the delinquent free on 14 April—with no justice and without applying the law. Many times I say, in Guatemala there is no justice; moreover, if there is money the thieves and delinquents can kill and rob honest people and nothing happens to them. They pay off the officials.

The San Benito Fiesta and Dyeing *Jaspes*
25 April 1992

At 5:00 A.M. my son Ramón and I went to the mountain with two beasts [horses] to bring firewood. We returned at 10:00 A.M.

After lunch my wife and the children went to San Benito to see the town fiesta. They went by boat and returned at 8:00 P.M.

On the afternoon of this day Ramón and I dyed forty-six pounds of *jaspes;* we finished at 7:00 P.M., tired. This work is very hazardous to one's health. First one works with boiling water and then with cold water, and the acids are dangerous.

The Craftswomen of San José, Sololá, Central America
1987 to April 1992

The women weavers are part of the Mayan culture; they warp and weave the traditional fabrics of the southwest region of beautiful Lake Atitlán. They use multicolored thread, and that is what makes these beautiful shirts, jackets, blouses, and other articles of clothing look so good.

In the beginning the women of my town did not use foot looms; these days there are some twenty-five foot looms. But there still are more back-strap looms. They are called back-strap looms because the *Joseñas* support their weaving with the back strap and weave seated, always smiling and intoning the music of the dances of our ancestors or some religious songs that they know. (They intone the music as if their voices were the musical instruments. They are not singing the words. They hum the music such as "El Rey Quiché.")

The little bit of money that the *Joseña* earns with her weaving helps to support some of the expenses of the home and pays some of the children's school expenses, because if the father doesn't have the money to buy a notebook or a pencil the mother can buy it with the little money that she earns with her weaving.

The women of my town were exploited for a long time, for years, as they say. Those who took advantage of the work of the indigenous women were the big Ladino middlemen who exported the weavings to foreigners, scarcely paying anything, just a low price. Many take advantage of the work of the indigenous women, and it is a shame that in my town there is a majority who do not speak Spanish, especially the women of twenty years of age and up. They don't know how to read and write, and that is why the Ladinos of Panajachel earn good money, buying cars and land and living happily with their families, while the indigenous women are poorer each day. The middlemen never think about paying a fair price to the needy people. There is a saying, *Dios tarda pero no olvida* [God may be slow, but He doesn't forget]. This is true now that the women of my town are well organized and they themselves sell their products to the foreigner without the need of middlemen.

The women's association Artisans of San José began in the year 1987 with the help of the *licenciada* Rose Marie Lexington, a North American. She was working with projects aimed at raising the value of the work of the indigenous women of Guatemala, especially in Antigua, Guatemala. Rose Marie Lexington knew a *Joseña* señorita named Fedora Pur Bizarro who was studying in Antigua. By chance Fedora and the *licenciada* came to this town of San José la Laguna to study the suffering of the *Joseñas*. This was when Rose Marie Lexington began to chat with the women about organizing themselves with the help of the artisan Alejo Rafael Bizarro Pérez. Then the *licenciada* and Alejo managed to assemble about twenty women, analyzing the problem that was confronting these women.

Rose Marie Lexington is a good-hearted person. When the women began to work as a group, they didn't have the money to buy the raw material. Rose Marie donated $50 so that the women would be able to make some samples of their work. When the samples were prepared, the same *licenciada* sent them to two stores in the United States of North America.

When the stores realized that the women's work was of high quality, they ordered a dozen jackets and a dozen blouses for each store. Then Rose Marie and Alejo Rafael laid out before UNICEF the situation that the women were facing for lack of funds. Then, through UNICEF's program, they obtained enough donations from the United States for training, labor, and buying the raw material.

As the group was growing, more orders came from the United States. When the women provided the samples, it was the *licenciada* who went to show them in the stores. But when more foreign orders came for articles of clothing, the women did not have the machines to fill the orders. Thus they went back to UNICEF to ask for sewing machines, and the representatives of UNICEF in Guatemala resolved the problem by donating them. They also received donated machines from organizations in the United States. Then the women began to make the traditional clothing.

The women realized that this program benefited themselves and their families, and more of them began to enroll. One hundred fifty of them joined.

The women also bought foot looms and increased their knowledge of the work. They bought the raw material in Salcajá, Quezaltenango. When the project began, warpers were paid Q2 for each piece warped and weavers were paid Q4 for each piece woven. All of this was done in the years 1987, 1988, and 1989 before they were recognized legally as a group, although they had petitioned the pertinent governmental officials.

During the three years mentioned, the women suffered because of

16. *Woman weaving on a back-strap loom that is tied to a tree next to a* temascal.

the meetings they had beneath the sun [outside] in the *sitio* of Ignacio Cojox Puac. Ignacio also helped a lot to organize the women because he is the father of Señorita Fedora, but this señor (Ignacio) noticed the irregularities in what Alejo was doing with the women's money, and Ignacio Cojox Puac withdrew from the group. The women no longer came to Ignacio's *sitio*.

This is how it was when the meetings were then held in the *sitio* of Alejo Rafael Bizarro Pérez. When the women were just beginning to organize themselves, they confided a lot in Señor Alejo, without knowing later what would happen. They named a provisional board of directors who were the following: president, Alejo Rafael Bizarro Pérez; secretary, Berta Guerra; treasurer, Berta Temó de Quic; pro-secretary, Juana Rita Velásquez, who is in charge when the secretary is not there; and committee members, Rubidia Puac Velásquez and Berta Ramos.

On 22 November 1990, the association of women, Artisans of San José, was recognized by governmental authorities under the register number 2299–50 of the president of the republic of Guatemala. Their headquarters were situated in the municipality of San José la Laguna, Sololá, on the shore of Lake Atitlán. Their main objective was the manufacture

17. *Woman weaving on a foot loom.*

of textiles that were authentically regional, indigenous designs and that were a legacy of our ancestors of the great Tzutuhil kingdom. After obtaining legal standing, the members of the provisional board were sworn in to their original positions.

What changed was the location of the store and warehouse; that is, Señor Alejo constructed two chalet-style houses a few meters from the lake. What also changed was that the women received bad treatment and lower wages, under the oppression of the president. From then on the women felt deprived of their rights because they no longer had a voice or a vote in the meetings. If the women tried to say something, they were suspended from their work. The president of the association became like a king or a dictator. The women suffered a lot. The man, Alejo Bizarro, became self-serving because every aspect of the project was under his hand and he thought there was no one else who could do it.

The women suspected that the president was spending the association's money for himself, but they could not prove it. The women's suspicion was reinforced because they could see that Alejo bought two machines to fabricate [concrete] blocks and a new re-frigerator. He also built two quality houses and bought land. His house was furnished like the house of a rich man. Before his involvement with the association, however, he had nothing. Since he became president of the association, he was making an exorbitant amount of money.

The women asked the president to make a declaration of the amount of money he had received from institutions as donations and how much he had invested and how many stores he has outside [the association]. But their request was a big problem for this man. He became angry, and he didn't want to explain the status of the accounts. His answer was that the rest of the board didn't have to know anything about this matter; the only one who needed to know was the president.

Many of the women were dismissed from their jobs, simply because they asked for a meeting to clarify the reason that the money had run out. [To try] to calm the situation, he gave the rest of the women a small raise of Q3 for each piece to the warpers and of Q5 for each piece to the weavers. The women accepted the raise, but they still were not happy with the situation.

[Also] with the assistance of UNICEF, the women had bought a *sitio* so that they could construct a nursery for their small children. To buy the new *sitio,* UNICEF provided a portion of the money and the women raised the other portion. They bought the *sitio,* composed of 1,430 square meters, for the price of Q7,000. The deed for this *sitio* is in the name of the Artisans of San José. The women said, however, that Alejo Rafael had used all of the sand of the *sitio* to fabricate blocks for his personal business without consulting with the board of the project. This was the [nature of the] abuse of Señor Alejo, and because of it the women wanted nothing more to do with him.

On 15 March 1991 the general assembly voted for a change. They elected Berta Temó de Quic president of the Artisans of San José. She had been the treasurer, however, and it was said that she was conspiring with the ex-president. Nevertheless, the electorate kept this woman as president of the association, because there were no other qualified women for the duties: 95 percent of them were illiterate.

Alejo, the former president, did not want to leave. He tried many tricks. For example, he offered money to the rest of the board so that they wouldn't accept the new president. Through money, the ex-president divided the women into two groups—a small group in favor of Alejo and a larger group in favor of the new president. Then there was trouble at work between the two groups. The large faction backing President Berta saw the small faction supporting ex-president Alejo as bad, and the small faction viewed the large faction as bad. For a while it was like this, with misunderstandings between the women, because Alejo said that he could cancel the project.

In the month of April 1991 the women wanted to leave the house of the ex-president, to gain more freedom, to communicate better, and to work with more enthusiasm. The women tried to find places to rent where they could do their work, but the man told them that if they were thinking about leaving his house, he would cancel all the contracts with the outside stores because everything was in his name and he was the only person who could manage the association's money.

When the women heard these things, they became really worried and called Señora Berta Moreno, representative of the store in the United States. They asked for her immediate help to resolve the problem that the women artisans of San José were confronting.

Señora Berta Moreno arrived in San José on 17 June 1991. There was a general meeting with all of the women who worked together on the project and with Alejo Rafael. Señora Berta Moreno agreed that the women were within their rights and, in order not to continue losing time and money, it was necessary to change locations so that the women could work in peace and harmony. In this meeting they drew up a memorandum, stating everything that had been said in favor of the female artisans.

In the months of June and July 1991, the new board of the Artisans wanted an audit because the resources of the project were almost depleted. But they could not do anything since they didn't know how to proceed.

On 6 June 1991 the board of the Artisans of San José drew up another memorandum; that is to say, those assembled unanimously asked to change the location of the association because they no longer could tolerate being in the house of the aforementioned man. Alejo Rafael granted their request. He told them to remove immediately from his house all of the things that belonged to the association, because he said he no longer wanted to see them there.

At once the women began searching for a new location, but no one wanted to offer them a house because they were afraid of the ex-president. Finally, a rich family offered them a large house but at a high monthly payment of Q300. Since they had no money, they could not pay this amount.

On Sunday, 7 July 1991, my wife and I went to the soccer field to watch some of the game. On the road we met two women who were members of the board of the association and who invited us for a chat in the home of the new treasurer, Enrique Guerra Velásquez. We went to his house and saw that there was a delegation of women, but I told them that the chat had to be brief because we were on our way to the soccer game. Then they asked me whether I would rent them the house [a duplex] that I have in the center of town—one apartment for the office and the other to store their work. Well, I thought hard about them because my wife also works in this project as a warper, and I told them that within three days I would give them a response. On the third day we went to inspect the two apartments and the women offered to pay me Q100 a month for them. I agreed, telling them that they could occupy the apartments, each with its own bathroom, a while without any problem.

Today, 16 July 1991, is an unforgettable day for the women, Artisans of San José. On this day men, women, and children had a fiesta, and they gathered together to move all the things out of Alejo's house to the places they had rented. The houses that I rented to them weren't large enough for them, however, and they had to rent another house from my sister-in-law that served as a store for them. When they finished hauling all the things that belonged to the association, they set off *bombas* and firecrackers as signs of joy for having obtained their freedom, because it is certain that the women had been oppressed by the aforementioned man. I was not with them on this day because I had to go to the *aldea* to spread fertilizer on my milpa.

On 20 July 1991, the board members and the associates had their first meeting in their new headquarters with the participation of Alejo Rafael [the former president]. They told him that he could work on a fixed salary as coordinator and head of design but on the condition that he no longer manage the funds and that the checkbooks [accounts] have to be in the name of the new president who will immediately have her name registered in the Banco Agrícola Mercantil. At this meeting, this man accepted the women's proposal, but with ill will. A few days later he began to look for ways to annoy the new president of the project. He was not in agreement that the women should work democratically.

On 31 July 1991 he convinced Doña Berta Moreno, the representative of international marketing, that he was the only person who could direct the future of the association, that all the women supported him, and that the women withdrew from the project because they were not in agreement with the new president, Berta Temó.

Berta Moreno came to San José on 31 July and met with Alejo Rafael. In this confidential meeting that took place without the presence of the women artisans, they agreed that on 10 August of the same year he would be reinstated as the president of the women's association. There is, however, a saying, *Hay que tener cuidado para hablar porque hasta las paredes tienen orejas* [You must be careful of what you say because even the walls have ears]. Everything that Alejo and Berta Moreno discussed, the women already knew by the afternoon of the same day. Thus they knew that within ten days the current president [Berta Temó] was to be removed from office. Once again the women became worried. This authoritarian man didn't want to let them work in peace. He continued to be threatening, foolish, annoying, and abusive. Again, he wanted to be president of the association, but the women could no longer stand him.

On 8 August 1991 fifteen of us men, husbands of the women who work in the project, met. Our purpose was to offer our support and prevent the removal of the president [Temó]. Moreover, she had been elected by the general assembly in accordance with the statutes. The meeting took place in the home of our friend Martín Puzul Cholotío. We decided that on 10 August, when Berta Moreno came back to town, we men would have to gather to support the women so that they could work in peace and put an end to their marginalization and maltreatment. We agreed that the women have the same rights as men. Without doubt, there was among us a spy for the aforementioned man. The following day Alejo sent a message, telling Señora Berta Moreno not to come because something bad would happen to her. Thus she did not come, and our plan was undermined.

Today, 10 August 1991, four residents of San José were threatened with anonymous letters, telling them to keep out of the problems of the women, and if they don't heed this warning they will see what will happen. The four who were threatened are husbands of women who work in the project. The four letters were done on pink paper, and for this kind of threat they blamed a stepson of Alejo and one of the women who supported him. But nothing was certain; no one knew for sure who had made the threats. Those who received the threatening letters were Benjamín Peña Cholotío, Jaime Vásquez Alvarado, Gaspar Vásquez Alvarado, and Martín Puzul Cholotío.

On 11 August 1991 some important people from the United States and from Guatemala City came to San José to show appreciation for the work of the women and to give them moral support, offering assistance and financial aid so that their work—the warping, weaving, and fabrication of the traditional weavings of the region—can continue. They said that the women should forget about what had happened, that they should think about the future, and that they themselves can direct the future of the association in such a way that they are not exploited and marginalized by men, as had occurred in the past.

This day was a day of celebration and much happiness for the women and their husbands. There was hope that in the near future the project would improve and again have sufficient funds. The truth is that I only spent about an hour with them, observing their actions and hearing the words of encouragement. I had to leave this meeting because I had previously received an invitation from a sports group to join them at the soccer field.

On a Friday in the month of August 1991, on a day I failed to note, two señoritas who were students arrived in our town to conduct research on the work of artisans. The two señoritas first met with Alejo Rafael, the former president, to interview him, and then they met with Señora Berta Temó, the current president, to interview her. When the two señoritas arrived at the house of Alejo, he happily prepared breakfast for them. In doing so, he gained their confidence. He told them that he had done nothing bad and that he had been the best person in town to run the project. Without him, the women would not have been able to start the project. He told the two students that they should convince Señora Berta Temó to give the position of president back to him so that the town would not lose the project and so that the women would keep their good jobs. The two students believed everything the man told them.

In the afternoon the students went to the house of the artisans to convince the president to give the position back to Señor Alejo. In the afternoon Alejo Rafael also came to find out the results of the meeting. This was about three or four o'clock in the afternoon.

The students who meddled in this case of the women artisans of San José told the president to give the position back to Alejo but without the president's consulting with the general assembly. The students said they could make the change between the two of them so that the association would function better, because a man has more know-how than a woman.

The president responded that she had been elected by the general assembly and only they could remove her from the position, not individuals who are not even artisans. The president got angry with the students and with Alejo. At the same time, Alejo felt a moral blow and left the women, saying that he would never go back to work for them. The anger of the president subsided, and she chatted again with the two señoritas until she enlightened them on the man's bad attitude.

Afterward, Alejo organized another group of women weavers, that is to say, the women who remained with him when the association divided into two groups. He made his own textile workshop, and for a while he paid the women weekly. He competed with the association. What is not known is where he got the money to pay the women.

Alejo took advantage of the women. In the month of September 1991, he received a white car. They say he had solicited it from an institution in the name of the women's association. He had made the request when he was president, and they granted it to him after the women had expelled him from their group. When he was asked how he was able to buy the car, [he gave conflicting explanations on different occasions]—that a friend gave it to him, that he won it in a lottery, and that they gave it to him for the work he had done with the women. He didn't want to tell the truth. The women knew very well, however, that the car had come in the name of their association and that this man seized possession of everything registered in his name so that he could do anything he pleased with it for profit.

At an automobile dealership, he received Q10,000 for the white car as a down payment on a corinthian red pickup. His intent was to confuse the people by having a different car, so that no one would speak ill of him.

In December 1991 the women artisans of San José contracted with auditors in Quezaltenango for Q3,000 to determine the amount of losses the association had suffered. At the end of December, the auditors said that they couldn't finish their job until January. They could say only that they knew a lot of money had been embezzled, but they couldn't say how much. They told the members of the board that in January they would deliver the official report.

But the months of January, February, and March passed. Not until April [1992] did the auditors come from Quezaltenango to inform the entire association of all the losses suffered. They gave this information in the parish meeting room.

They said Señor Alejo Rafael Bizarro Pérez inflicted a lot of financial damage on the women, enjoying a lucrative business at the expense of the poor women, who didn't know how to read and write. The seamstresses, the weavers who worked with the foot looms, and the weavers who wove with the back-strap looms all suffered. The board of directors had agreed to pay each woman who worked with a back-strap loom Q15 for two pieces of fabric [or Q2.5 per yard] and to pay each woman who worked with a foot loom Q2 per yard. What wasn't said is what they paid the seamstresses. But the president, in collusion with the association's bookkeeper, the certified accountant Bartolo Ixtamer Velásquez, paid the women with a false set of account books and took advantage of the money with another set of account books. Notice was given that the embezzlement of salaries from 1990 to 1991 was Q40,746. They said they paid the back-strap weavers Q8 per yard [not Q2.5 per yard] and the foot loom weavers Q10 [per yard, not Q2 per yard, and they kept the difference]. That is how the ex-president and the certified accountant took advantage of the women's money.

The auditors found only one receipt for a donation from the year 1991 for Q23,362.61. The women of the board said that during 1991 they received more money than that, but an account of it did not appear in the documents. Also, the auditors found a false document that said that the president of the women's association had donated to La Esperanza Primary School the amount of Q6,000. And they found another false document that said the president of the women's association had given a loan of Q2,000 to the owner of a *cédula* that had the order number G-10 [the number identifying the town of San José] and the registration number 9691 [the number assigned to a person within the town], but the name of the person doesn't appear on the document.

They found the receipts for the costs of communication, that is to say, for postage and telephones (GUATEL). During 1990, the sum of Q850 was spent. This system, or list of numbers, was accepted by the board of directors because it seemed to be normal; that is, the listed expenses for the telephone seemed to be okay for this year, but the following year the phone costs were highly exaggerated.

For the year 1991 they found false documents stating that during this year an exaggerated amount of Q11,192.20 was spent on mail and telephone calls. Everyone said that it was not possible to spend this amount on such expenses and that, during a year, there should have been an expense of only Q30 a day, including Saturdays and Sundays. It was confirmed that this money was stolen.

It also was confirmed that during the year 1991 the women of the Artisans of San José produced 2,092 jackets, and they only sold 1,497 jackets. Five hundred ninety-five jackets were missing or lost. It was a loss of Q53,550. When they heard this information, the women of the board said that all the jackets had been sold.

What the auditors didn't mention was the number of fabrics made with foot looms. They didn't say how many of them were sold or lost. I had my doubts, but because I was only an observer of the situation I didn't want to ask what happened to the rest of them. I didn't want to get myself mixed up with other people's problems.

The truth is that it can't be said whether the board also took part in the embezzlement of money. They say that only Alejo Rafael was the thief. But it has been observed that the woman who was the treasurer and who now is the president has been buying many pieces of land and *sitios*. What I think is that whoever is responsible for these financial and other loses will be held accountable before God, will always have a stained conscience, and will await the law of compensation. It is written in the Bible that for what the father does, the children, grandchildren, and great-grandchildren will pay, to the third and even to the fourth generation.

To me, it is bad to seek a lot of money. The truth is that money is important, and it is a major part of the lives of human beings. Without money we can't live, but we should not steal it. One must earn what one can honestly. I feel sorry for what has happened to these poor women. They worked a lot and lost a lot of time to make only one person happy. With pain in my heart, I say this is a pity, caused by illiteracy. It's a shame that the women are uneducated and that they are the ones who suffer the consequences. But it is a greater shame that a man exploited his own people.

Now Alejo Rafael lives happily with his family. He lives the life of an exploiter, and he is proud of being a member of the Evangelical Church of Central America, paying no attention to what he did to the poor people. *Ay* [*púchica*, my goodness], [he has] a blemished conscience. Damn the man who knows better yet does evil.

José Gustavo Velásquez Velásquez Dies in the United States
28 April to 9 May 1992

The entire town heard the news of the death of José Gustavo Velásquez Velásquez who died in the United States. José Gustavo, together with his son Abraham Timoteo [Velásquez] Bolaños, went two and one-half years ago as *mojados* to North America [the United States] in search of wealth. Many say that there one earns more, but sometimes greed is great. José Gustavo said he didn't earn much, but he earned better than we campesinos because he was a qualified construction worker [contractor] for the INTECAP [Instituto Técnico de Capacitación, Institute of Technical Training]. His preoccupation was to make more, but everything was to the contrary. The son sent a notice through GUATEL that his father had disappeared on Sunday, 22 March. They say that José Gustavo went for a ride in his car, but from there he didn't return. They say Abraham Timoteo reported to the authorities that his father was missing. But they told him not to advise the family in Guatemala until they had some evidence.

The truth is that Abraham didn't say when the body of José Gustavo was found. On 28 May the news arrived here in San José that he was sending the body from the United States to Guatemala. But they said that the family had to do whatever was possible to pay for the undertaker expenses from Guatemala [City] to San José. But Gustavo's wife, Señora Juana Bolaños, said that she had no money, her husband had not sent money, and who knows what he did with his money?

On Monday, 4 May 1992, Juana Bolaños was accompanied by the gentlemen of the municipal corporation and a citizen named José Horacio Temó. They went through the streets of the town, asking for financial assistance in order to transport the body of her husband. She said that without the help of the people she could do nothing and that she was putting her faith in her people.

I helped them a little, and by nightfall the townspeople had contributed Q500. But I think more than that amount was given, because many people went to the *casa de duelo* [house of mourning, the wife's house] to help financially.

José Gustavo's wife is angry with the mother of the deceased because she insisted that her son go to North America [the United States] to earn money. They say the son didn't have the money to cover the expenses of paying the *coyote,* or guide. But the mother told him to sell his *sitio* to cover the expenses and when he had a job in the United States he could recover [the money] and buy another *sitio.* His wife is angry because she has no *sitio* in which to live and she has no money as a result of his work. What angers her most is that José Gustavo left a car in the United States. And she says who wants a car when there is no food for the six children.

On Thursday, 7 May 1992, Abraham Timeto came from the United States to give notice that the body of his father would arrive on Friday, 8 May.

The cadaver of José Gustavo arrived at San José la Laguna at 11:00 A.M. on 8 May. It was carried to the little house where his wife lives.

The parents asked for permission to take the body of their son to their home. But the wife didn't want that. José Gustavo's body was put in a *panteón* on Saturday, 9 May 1992. The *panteón* where they placed his body was constructed and donated by the bricklayers of this village, as a demonstration of love.

There is still a *Joseño* in the United States, but who knows if he is alive or dead, because the parents say that the last letter they received from him was in June 1991. The name of this young man is Abraham Joj Asturias, son of Abraham Joj Chávez and Isabel Asturias.

A Brutal and Savage Event
10 May 1992

When a bus of Santiago Atitlán was coming from the coast to Santiago, by the Tamales farm between Patulul and San Lucas Tolimán, they say, two men accosted the driver, and he had to obey them. They made him leave the pavement and drive on a dirt road but not far, about five *cuerdas* from the asphalt. There a group of armed men waited. They made the passengers get out, and they stripped them of their watches and necklaces and took their money. On this bus were riding two very pretty women, one traveling alone and the other with her husband. These two women were raped in this same spot. All the passengers had to lie face down so they could not see what was happening.

The husband wanted to help his wife, but he could not because he was tortured by two of the villains—one held him on his back and the other on the back of his neck—and the rest [of the outlaws] violated his wife. After the armed men committed these violent acts, they disappeared into the bushes, and little by little the passengers went back to board the bus. The two [violated] women, however, cried a lot.

But one of the passengers picked up a *carnet de indentificación* [identification card] that belonged to a squad leader [a corporal]. What was not revealed was of which group—the Right or the Left.

Why couldn't the culprit be identified with the identification card?

Without doubt the man who found the military identification card didn't want the owner's name revealed because he was afraid that the owner would come back and kill him. Only the army is so organized, and it most likely was not the guerrillas, because they don't carry around official military identification cards.

What was certain was that it was sent to the señor procurator of human rights. But this señor of human rights did nothing to investigate this deed. The raped women were from San Lucas. They know to which group the violators belonged.

If the women knew which group it was, why didn't they say so?

Many people say the group was the army, but without doubt the women didn't want to identify them because they were afraid the violators would find them and kill them. At this time there was a military detachment between San Lucas and Patulul, and the event took place just below the position of the military detachment. Until last year, when I last went to the coast, the detachment was still there, but I can't be certain that it still is. The press reported this event in vague terms. Perhaps they too were afraid of reprisals by the military.

A Most Horrible Crime in San Martín
12 May 1991 to 18 May 1992

A most horrible crime committed in San Martín la Laguna happened on 13 May 1991 to Jesús Quic Pur, a man in the business of selling fertilizer. On Sunday, the twelfth, he went to Quezaltenango on business and returned the same day. That night his wife told him that he had to go to sleep in the house they had above the town and on Monday he would have to make a trip to the capital city. He left his house at

8:00 P.M., and Jesús's family remained sleeping peacefully. On Monday Jesús's family was confident he had reached the capital.

In the morning a plastic sack shoved inside a net appeared. Thinking it was garbage, neighbors went to throw it out. But the dogs wanted to tear open the net since they sensed something bad inside. People gathered, and a child near the net saw a man's finger. The people called the magistrate to see who it was. When the magistrate ordered the net and bag cut open, they discovered the mutilated body of a man. His hands, legs, and head were cut off. His spine was severed, and his testicles were cut off and put inside his shirt pocket, and his penis was cut off and shoved in his mouth. The cadaver was recognizable only by its clothing and the bare feet, because he didn't use shoes.

The family was alarmed. Then they took the cadaver for a medical autopsy in Sololá. On 14 May they buried it. These wealthy people gave money to bring the *policía de asuntos criminales* [*judiciales,* or judicial police, criminal police] to investigate and to capture the murderer. The police came on the fifteenth, only to investigate if he had had problems with someone. The family said that Santiago García Estrada owed him Q5,000 and that he didn't want to pay. Then the police went to Santiago's house. One version, although I don't know if it is true because people like to gossip, is that in Santiago's house they found signs of blood. This man was captured at 4:00 P.M. on 15 May when he returned from work with his two sons. One of them had been studying in the capital and had come home to San Martín only to see his mother because it was the Month of the Mothers.[55] The three were arrested.

There was a lot of criticism by the people of the two towns, even insults between *Martineros* and *Joseños.* Santiago had been born and reared in San José, but for about forty years he has lived with his wife in San Martín.

Seeing that there was much criticism and insults from the mouths of the people, that night I gathered my children and my wife and told them not to get mixed up in other people's business and not to say anything bad. They too had noticed that the people were speaking badly about this murder. I told them that we have to be very careful and that we should not get involved in these things. If Santiago and his sons were the murderers, they would pay with justice, and if they weren't, God would free them from jail. Then we lit some candles and a little incense and we knelt at the altar where there is a statue of the crucified

Christ. We asked God to pardon our sins, to give us understanding, and to bring peace to our "brothers" who are dealing with such difficulty, as much for the family of the deceased as for Santiago and his family. This was the prayer of each one of us. Then we went to sleep.

At about three o'clock in the morning I had a revelation in my sleep. For me this dream was strange. I will not forget it as long as I live. In the dream I was on the road that goes to San Martín. Almost there, we encountered a man by the name of Alejandro Cholotío, a respected señor. He told me: "Ignacio, you are a friend. Walk with me to my house!"

"Okay, Don Alejandro," I said, and I followed. When we were entering the village I saw water that was running in the town, but the water was running upstream.

Don Manuel said, "Ignacio, do you see this river?"

I said, "Yes."

Then he told me that I have to cross over this stream. "You also are going to cross as I cross and without dirtying your shoes."

Like this it was; the señor passed over the stream without dirtying his shoes, and I also crossed the same way. Passing to another street, it was the same thing, and Don Manuel said the same thing: "You see this stream of dirty water? We are going to cross it without dirtying our shoes." And we did.

After crossing the stream the señor said, "People's mouths are like this dirty stream of water." And he said again, "Ignacio, you're going to leave me at my house."

"Fine, Don Alejandro," I said, and we went.

When we arrived he opened the door of his house, but the house of this señor was like an evangelical church—there were flowers on the altar, a lot of flowers. And he said, "Ignacio, here I am staying," and he offered me his hand. He remained seated in a chair between the flowers.

In the dream when I sensed I was already in Santiago Atitlán I said, "What am I doing here alone? There are no people."

I went up to the town and again I said, "What am I doing here," and I saw Santiago García Estrada, the one who had been arrested. He was seated in a chair in front of a man.

The man was like a judge or like a chief of police, and in front of me they said to Santiago: "Confess if you killed Jesús Quic. Why did you kill him?" Again he asked, "Why did you kill him, Santiago?"

But Santiago did not want to answer. The two were face to face. The judge, or chief of police, said to the arrested one, "Say if you committed the crime, and I will deal with defending you, but confess."

Santiago answered, "Señor, if you say that I killed, you don't know. I know that I have [committed] no crime. I am not guilty." They said these things two or three times, and finally the judge, or chief, was silent. The two remained seated without speaking.

At that point I saw Santiago's body transform into a body of a young man. His face, his hands, his whole body was like that of a handsome young man of sixteen or seventeen. Even his hair shined, and his eyes were strong, like the eyes of a handsome child. I saw him like that in my dream. I stopped dreaming and thought about what it meant. It was a strange dream—the face of a man who is fifty-five years old changed [to appear] like the face of a young man.

I told my family about this dream when I woke up. Then I told my friends and Santiago García's relatives about the dream, and I advised them to continue to pray to God because Santiago may be set free.

May, June, and July passed. The rich people of the town paid lawyers to ask for the death penalty for Santiago and his sons. On 14 August, at a public sentencing, Santiago García and his two sons were sentenced to twenty years in prison. Then I told my family that my dream was meaningless. Because Santiago's enemies paid for false testimony, he and his sons received a sentence of twenty years.

But for God nothing is impossible. The magistrates of the court of appeals examined carefully the trial and the sentence dictated by the judge in Sololá. Without doubt they found fault with the trial because on 18 May [1992] they decreed liberty for Santiago García and his two sons.

Well, then my dream did come true but not until a year later. My family, my friends, and the relatives of Santiago know about this dream. What I said was, "If Santiago did the crime, he will pay with justice, and if it was not him, God will free him from his enemies."

Santiago was facing possible execution, and he was freed from a twenty-year prison sentence. Now, he, his wife, and his two sons live in their house, but poor, because they lost a lot of money. They were merchants who had bought many *cuerdas* of onions to harvest and sell, but when they were imprisoned the wife fell sick to her heart, and she lost the onions.

Agreeing to Accept the Office of Alcalde of San Juan Bautista
March 1993

I am a Tzutuhil Indian, and for that reason I like serving my town.[56] In the month of March 1993, I received a summons from the señor president of Catholic Action, and I had to go at that moment. The president greeted me with a lot of respect, asking me if I would accept the office of *alcalde* of the *cofradía* of San Juan Bautista. He told me that the last service I would have to perform before becoming a *principal* of the town was to receive the image of the predecessor of Christ in the month of July of this year of 1993. Then I told him that I would give him a response within the next eight days because I first would have to discuss it with my family. [If I accepted] everything would be done with much respect because San Juan is nothing less than a saint and the patron of the town. In this manner, I said good-bye to the señor president of Catholic Action.

When I arrived home, I told my wife the reason for the summons, that we needed to talk about whether we are capable of accepting this *cargo* [office]. By the grace of God, my wife encouraged me and said that we would accept it because we are the right age for this *cargo*. We could not let the traditions of our ancestors die since it was part of our Mayan culture. My children encouraged me in the same manner. With their smiling faces, they told me to agree to receive the saint in our house.

Five days later, I returned to the office of the president of Catholic Action to give him a positive answer. I told him I would accept the *cargo* of the *cofradía* with much pleasure. The president was very appreciative, because it is true that only a few of us are conserving the *costumbres* of our fathers. The religious people and the catechists want to end the *cofradías*. The truth is that I don't understand them; they like to walk in the processions, but they don't want to serve in the *cofradías*.

Then the president of Catholic Action asked me to designate the person I would like for *juez* [vice-*alcalde*] of the *cofradía*. I told him that I didn't know anything about choosing the person that I would like because we are all equal in the eyes of God and that I couldn't discriminate against anyone. I told him that it was his discretion to select the persons for the *juez* and the *mayordomos*.

In a few days I received the following list of people: *juez,* Lucas

Velásquez Agustín, native of Santa Rosa la Laguna who lives in this town because his wife is *Joseña;* first *mayordomo,* Diego Gerardo Ramos; second *mayordomo,* Gerardo Sicay Tuc; third *mayordomo,* Bartolo Toc Xico; fourth *mayordomo,* Arnoldo Velásquez Velásquez; fifth *mayordomo,* Alejandro Ramos Ramos; and sixth *mayordomo,* Edgar Alvarado Velásquez.

The following day I went to the house of the *juez* to meet him and to tell him that we were the designees to receive the *cofradía* of San Juan Bautista. He answered that he indeed had agreed to be *juez.* I gave him a list of the names of the *mayordomos* since the custom is that the *juez* goes to the houses of the *mayordomos* to tell them when we would meet to get to know one another and to determine how to pay the expenses. I told Señor Lucas Velásquez that our meeting would be on Holy Thursday, 8 April 1993, at 5:00 A.M. Three days later the *juez* came to my house to tell me that he had complied with the errand to tell them when we would meet.

Our First Meeting as a Cofradía
7 April to 9 May 1993

On Holy Wednesday, 7 April, my wife and I arranged to welcome the members with refreshments. So on this day we baked bread. On Holy Thursday, my wife got up at 3:00 A.M. to make coffee. At 5:00 A.M. the *juez* and *mayordomos* arrived. As is the custom, they kissed my [right] hand, and we began to chat. I told them the reason for the meeting:

> In the name of God, who is the heart of heaven and heart of earth, in name of our fathers, who have given us a heritage, we ought to preserve and take care of our Mayan culture. Our fathers have bequeathed our culture in place of themselves—they have gone and have turned into dust, but their spirits are always with us. Also, we are going to die, but it will be our sons and our grandsons who will serve the representative of the heart of heaven and heart of earth, who is San Juan Bautista, patron and guardian of our town, a saint of god of the clouds and of the rain, who also is *dueño* of the origins of rivers and hills, a saint of god who also is *dueño* of the storms. And the image of this saint is what we are going to serve for a year.

Then we served them coffee and bread. As is the custom, we had to send something to their wives. So after we ate bread, I told the *juez* to tell the *mayordomos* to take the bread to their houses but to interchange houses; that is, the first *mayordomo* would carry the gift [of bread, although it could be something else, such as tamales or meat] to the house of the *juez,* the second *mayordomo* would take the gift to the house of the first *mayordomo,* and so on.

We decided that our next meeting would be 9 May, Sunday, to [discuss] decorating the house and [doing] other things we will need to do for the reception of the image, including making the traditional *atol* of the *cofradía.* After everything we said good-bye.

Preparing the Cofradía
20 May to 22 June 1993

On 20 May we bought paint the color of sky blue. The *mayordomos* painted the house [one room, inside and out], but three days earlier we had washed the walls and the loft with water. On this day my wife and I provided lunch for the *cofrades.* I told them that on 13 June we would begin to collect the decorations but that it would be in the afternoon because we also needed to work in our fields.

Thus it was. The truth is that we liked preserving a little of our heritage. The *juez* bought the *bombas* and the *manteles* [tablecloths], and I obtained the flowers to decorate the area where the image of the saint would be placed. The nineteenth of June I went to Santa Ana to buy the *pox lak'* flowers.

What kind of flowers are these?

They are small yellow flowers that grow on a plant that has small leaves. They can last sixty to ninety days without water. Since Ladinos don't use them, I don't know their name in Spanish.

They are flowers that our ancestors used in the past. In Santa Bárbara, we asked for them at many houses until we finally found them. But because there wasn't enough of them, we had to pay a *mozo* to look for more flowers in the mountains.

On Sunday, 20 June, we began to tie special white sticks (used by our fathers) in grids under the part of the ceiling that covers the altar of the holy image. We planned to attach aromatic leaves and flowers to the grid. We finished at nine o'clock at night on 22 June.

Then I went to the mountain to look for some aromatic leaves that in the Tzutuhil language are called *c'o jotz,* but I don't know what they are called in Spanish, since only we natives use them. By the grace of God, everything went well.

I was on the mountain alone when a woodpecker arrived to sing. We Maya worry when a woodpecker sings on the left side of a person, which is considered a bad omen, but when it sings on the right side of the person, it is considered a good omen, or sign of good luck. Thus it was when a woodpecker blurted out a song above in a tree that was directly in front of me, not to the left or to the right. The truth is that it troubled me and I said, "Woodpecker, guardian and *alguacil* of the world, are you giving me good or bad advice? May the god of heaven and earth bless you and me."

The bird sang only one song. After picking the leaves, I walked slowly down the mountain because it was steep. At three o'clock in the afternoon I arrived home.

Our First Procession and Receiving the Image of the Saint in the Cofradía
23 to June to 2 July 1993

The twenty-third of June begins the *novenario,* which is nine days of praying, saying the rosary with hymns, and signaling with *bombas* and firecrackers that the arrival of the patron saint is near. The *novenario* ends on the first of July, the day that the image arrives in the new *cofradía.* The images that are brought to the new *cofradía* are those of Juan Evangelista [a smaller image], who was a disciple of Christ, and of San Juan Bautista [a larger image], who was the precursor of Christ.

The same day, 23 June, was our first function. We all left together in the procession, but we [new members of the *cofradía* of San Juan] were just guests of the old members of the *cofradía.* We walked with them as they carried the image of San Juan Bautista from the house of the outgoing *cofradía* to the church, where it stayed one night.

We did the same thing on 24 June, when the image of San Juan Bautista was paraded through the main streets of the town, accompanied by the images of the Virgen María and Santo Domingo Guzmán.[57] The image of San Juan Evangelista remained in the outgoing *cofradía* until 1 July.

As is the custom, it was a joyful celebration with the explosion of *bombas* and firecrackers. There was a marimba, and men played the traditional drum and flute. Also, the church bells were rung, giving thanks to God.

The twenty-seventh of June we met at 1:00 P.M. in the *cofradía* and finished some work. The *mayordomos* touched up the paint job on the house. Then the *juez* and I went to the houses of the *principales* of the town to pay homage to them. We had to spend fifteen to twenty minutes with each *principal*. On this day we went to only twenty houses. The following day we went to the remaining thirty-seven houses. There was a lot of rain.

To prepare the food to be eaten by the *cofrades* and by the invited guests on 1 July, it is the custom that the wife of the *alcalde* of the *cofradía* find at least five women to help her. It is difficult work. On 30 June we bought the meat.

All of the preparations are made on 30 June. On this day corn is cooked to eat and to make the *atol* [to drink].[58] All night long the women do not sleep. At ten o'clock at night they carry the corn to the mill, and then they begin to wrap the *tamalitos* and cook the meat. By four o'clock in the morning everything is prepared. During the night, as is the custom, some *traguitos* [little drinks] must be given to the women because they suffer from much weariness, but only a few drinks, not enough for them to get drunk.

At four o'clock in the morning the *mayordomos* arrive. The *juez* explodes two or three *bombas* that signal that the new *cofrades* of San Juan Bautista have arrived. Also, the catechists arrive together with a chorus, which plays and sings religious hymns. Then the *novenario* is concluded, and at that point breakfast is served to everyone—a lot of food, *tamalitos* and the traditional *pulique de res* [meat with chili], *achiote* [a shrub whose reddish seed is used for food coloring], tomatoes, and rice with vegetables.

After breakfast the wife of the *alcalde* prepares the earthenware jars to fill with *pulique* [beef seasoned with salsa of corn or bread, tomato, garlic, onion, apazote, and salt] to put inside the cane baskets along with the *tamalitos*. Then the *mayordomos* carry the food to each other's house.

At 7:15 A.M. on 1 July we marched to the church to the accompaniment of the flute and drum to take possession of the insignias of office. The most important hour of this day was when Father Juan Peña sprinkled holy water on the new *cofrades,* who were seated, and on the outgoing *cofrades,* who were standing in front next to the father with the insignias. The two staffs for San Juan Bautista (one for the *alcalde* and the other for the *juez*) had the image of the Santísimo Sacramento [Eucharist]. Then the father took the insignias and gave them to the *juez* and to me. This service took place with a lot of respect.

At nine o'clock in the morning, we took out the images of San Juan Bautista and San Juan Evangelista, carrying them through the main streets of the town. The truth is that I felt a little happy and a little sad.

While service as the *alcalde* of San Juan Bautista is the last [religious] service that one must perform for the community [before becoming an official *principal*], no one earns a salary. He does earn, however, the respect of the majority of the townspeople. They pay homage to the *alcalde* with ancient words that our fathers used, and for that reason it is required that the *alcalde* of San Juan act with much respect, dignity, and wisdom. It is a serious commitment to the community. We Maya respect the elders a lot, and we kiss their right hands as a sign of reverence for conserving the customs of our pueblo.

At 1:00 P.M. we went out again in procession. *Principales, cofrades, madres de familias* [mothers of families], and members of the municipal corporation escorted the images to the church. Although it rained, there was a lot of joy among the people. They exploded *bombas* and firecrackers, celebrating the patron saint of the town. (The spirit of San Juan is in heaven with God and here on earth with us. He represents the Heart of Heaven and Earth, guardian and protector of our children. He is a saint who passes through the air and in the clouds. The creator conferred on him the power of being a saint, and for this reason, his name is San Juan Bautista.)

When the image of San Juan Bautista arrived at the new *cofradía*, that is to say, in my house, the *principales* and the rest of the group sat down. Then came the most sacred part when I, the new *alcalde*, welcomed the *principales*, paying the homage to them that they deserved. Thus I said:

> In memory of our deceased fathers, whose bodies are now the dust of the earth but whose spirits are with us. They are with us watching and listening. They are with us here in spirit through the medium of the air and through the medium of the aroma of myrrh and *copal*.[59]
>
> Now you *principales* are the cement and the foundation of our race and our traditions, the fighters, defenders, and

conservators of our Mayan *costumbres*. You are the ones who take care of our culture, from our birth and growth until we reach the age where we are your followers and successors, if the creator and maker, Heart of Heaven and Earth, wills it. Now, on this day, we are receiving the patron saint, [with] you *principales* of white hair and white beards [that you have] as a gift of God and of the patron saint, San Juan Bautista.[60] We, your children, are disposed to conserve and continue what you have sown and what you have cultivated. We can neither forget nor abandon our *costumbres,* our traditions, which is what forms the bastion of our Mayan culture.

After drinking the *atol,* the *principales,* Catholic Actionists, *madres de familias,* and chorus said good-bye to the new *cofradía* and went to the church, and from the church they dispersed to their houses. That is to say, the fiesta was over.

But for the departing *alcalde* the night is most sad. Generally, at 8:00 P.M. members of the old *cofradía* carry the wardrobe and the big clothes chest of San Juan Bautista and San Juan Evangelista to the new *cofradía* (my house). They also bring the materials needed to perform the burials for those who die during the coming year.

Before leaving, the outgoing *cofradía* drinks brandy, beer, or sodas. Thus the *mayordomos* carry all these things when they are a little intoxicated. The wife of the outgoing *alcalde* and the wife of the outgoing *juez,* with their incense holders in their hands, position themselves to walk in front. They cover the street with the smoke of incense to the accompaniment of the sad sound of the drum and the flute.

When they arrive, the members of the new *cofradía* receive them with *bombas* and firecrackers. Then they carry all the things in order, so that the new *cofrades* can take an inventory. The outgoing first *mayordomo* reads the list of items, and the incoming first *mayordomo* accepts each item. When all this is finished, drinks are given to those who drink—beers to those who want them and sodas to those who don't drink alcohol.

So went the first day of service for us.

The second of July 1993, we met again with the *juez, mayordomos,* and families. At 10:00 A.M. we changed the clothing of the images, as always with a lot of respect and incense. Every little while, the first *mayordomo* was the one who was in charge of spraying the house with incense.

We collected the clothing and put it in order in the chest, and then my wife and the girls prepared lunch. When we were finishing arranging the clothing and the materials for burying the dead, we looked for a place to put the shrine that we use to carry the image in procession because one has to put it away. When this was all finished, we all had lunch, and after lunch, we agreed that, for the year, Saturdays would be the special days for us to offer to God, San Juan Bautista, and San Juan Evangelista a Holy Rosary [*santo Rosario cantado*], sung at seven o'clock at night. We also agreed that our visits to the Santísimo Sacramento in the church would be on Tuesdays and Fridays at five o'clock in the afternoon. Thus was our desire as *cofrades*. One has to be obedient in everything.

The Beheading of Juan Bautista
20 to 28 August 1993

The twentieth of August began the *novenario* of the beheading of Juan Bautista. Also, this *novenario* is the responsibility of the *cofradía* of San Juan.

To be a *cofrade* of a saint, it always costs money. The *novenario* ended on the twenty-eighth in the morning. The day before the [celebration of the] beheading [of Juan Bautista], I invited the three groups of *cofrades* of María Concepción, Santo Domingo Guzmán, and San José. Also, I invited the members of Catholic Action, singers, and some catechists. I gave all of them breakfast, and then we went to a mass in the church. The mass is the responsibility of the *alcalde* of San Juan.[61]

At eleven o'clock in the morning, the wives of the *juez* and the *mayordomos* arrived with *atol*. They voluntarily brought two big jars of *atol*.

At two o'clock in the afternoon, the *principales* of the town, Catholic Actionists, and the people in general came to the *cofradía* to drink *atol*. As always everyone had to be appreciative of the presence of the *principales*. Then we carried the image of the said saint in procession to the church, exploding *bombas* and lighting firecrackers and singing sad hymns because we were remembering the saint's death. In these processions, when San Juan Bautista leaves the *cofradía*, San Juan Evangelista remains in the middle of the altar, occupying the place of the patron.

Problems between the Catechists and the Priest
29 August 1993

This 29 August there was a small problem between the catechists and the priest, but we *cofrades* didn't get involved with them. The problem was that on the twenty-ninth of August a group of catechists set up a marimba in front of the church, but this day was not the day to set up a marimba with loud music. Rather it was a day only for meditating and reflecting on the death of our patron.

Father Juan Peña did not want to celebrate mass because the catechists set up the marimba. Then I told them that it was the same to me if the father celebrated mass or not or if the catechists set up the marimba. I believe that God pardons all of us because everyone has faults. I told them that we can't judge anyone.

Finally, Father Juan Peña was convinced to celebrate mass. After the mass we took out the holy image of San Juan in procession, carrying him through the main streets of the town. After the procession with the flute and drum, we went to the *cofradía* and left the saint in the church for three days.

The Celebration of Independence Day
14 to 15 September 1993

On 14 September I received an invitation from the señor municipal *alcalde* to meet with the four groups of *cofrades* and *principales* and with the municipal corporation to participate in the celebration of our independence. I had to talk with the other *cofrades* to tell them that we had to accept the invitation.

On 15 September we had to march with our insignias in hand. It was an enormous parade; a lot of groups participated: the cooperative of the association of Artisans of San José; Grupo Ramos [a group of kin who also are artisans but not associated]; BANDESA; DIGESA; Programa Vivamos Mejor; Visión Mundial; students of the evangelical primary school, La Esperanza; and students of the *instituto básico*. The parade began in the place called Xechumil and ended in front of the basketball court. After all these acts, the mayor, Santiago Alberto Vásquez, and the corporation gave us lunch. When lunch was finished, the mayor thanked all the *principales* and us *cofrades* for the participation of each one and said good-bye to each of us.

18. *Ignacio offering incense to the image of San Juan Bautista.*

Celebrating All Souls' and All Saints' Day

5 October to 2 November 1993

The fifth of October we met the group of *cofrades* in the *cofradía* of San Juan Bautista to decide what we were going to do on the first of November because it would be All Saints' Day and the second of November because it would be All Souls' Day. On the second we would celebrate the day of the dead, and we would be the ones in charge of making the preparations not only in the church but also in the cemetery. We agreed to do these jobs on the twenty-eighth and twenty-ninth of this month of October. Also, we agreed that during the night of 1 November until it dawns on the second, we were going to have a wake. It was the *costumbre* of our fathers, and we could not omit it. Thus we all agreed that we were going to do the wake in the *cofradía* of San Juan and that each group would have to give Q20 to buy chocolate, plantains, and sweet potatoes. This would be about Q2 per person in each of the four *cofradías*. We agreed that the first *mayordomos* would be the ones in charge of buying the things for this day.

When only five days were left until the twenty-eighth, I asked the first *mayordomo* if the other three *mayordomos* had already given their contribution, and the first *mayordomo* of San Juan told me no. Furthermore, he did not know what had happened.

On the twenty-eighth the *juez* of the *cofradía* told us that the other *cofrades* didn't want to perform any more *costumbres,* that they weren't coming, and that they didn't want to make *atol* on the day of the saints. For me it was bad news because they had broken the agreement that we had made on 5 October.

I ordered the first *mayordomo* to call the three groups of *cofrades* to ask what they thought. When the first *mayordomo* went to call the other *cofrades,* the *juez,* Lucas Velásquez Agustín, told me that he was retiring voluntarily from the *cofradía* and that he didn't want to spend the day of the saints with us. I told him to wait for the groups so that they would know that he was leaving the *cofradía.* And I told him that we had barely had finished four months [of service]. [Nevertheless] the *juez* left, and I had to deal with the *mayordomos* alone.

In the afternoon of this day, 28 October, the *cofrades* of Santo Domingo Guzmán, María Concepción, and San José arrived to tell me that they were in agreement with continuing the *costumbres* on the days of the first and second of November and that the enemy of our *costumbres* was Señor Lucas Velásquez. But they said that now that he has left, we will continue.

The twenty-ninth of October was the day when we were in the cemetery preparing a large shed where the mass would be celebrated on 2 November. We four groups worked. But there is one thing: the materials that we used were contributed by each of us. Some gave pieces of sheet metal, while others gave wood.

The *cofradía* of San José was in charge of performing the *costumbre* on this day, buying sodas and bananas as refreshments for the four groups of *cofrades* who worked in the cemetery. It was pleasant. After we finished putting together the shed, the *alcalde* invited us to his *cofradía* to give us lunch, but he served some *tragos* beforehand. This man is respectful and likable. He is a son of a *principal* of the town.

We four groups of *cofrades* were always united, and we worked to conserve the *costumbres* of our fathers. On 31 October corn *atol* is made in the three [main] *cofradías,* but it is not made in the *cofradía* of San José. At two o'clock in the afternoon all the *principales* and *cofrades* left the church to go to the *cofradía* of María Concepción to drink *atol,* but beforehand the *alcalde* [of María Concepción] had to pay homage to the *principales*. We took the image out of the *cofradía* of María Concepción and carried it in procession to the *cofradía* of Santo Guzmán, where we drank *atol*. Then we carried the images of the Virgen María and Santo Domingo Guzmán to the *cofradía* of San Juan, where we drank more *atol*. From the *cofradía* of San Juan we carried all three images to the church with much respect and reverence.

During the afternoon and night, while the images were in the church, the *mayordomos* guarded the church so that no thief would enter, because on the head of San Juan was a *splendor* [halo] of pure silver and in his hand a banner of the same material. Also, on the head of the Virgen María was a crown of pure silver. And on the statue of Santo Domingo was a *splendor* of pure silver. In addition, there was a plate of pure silver for the offerings in the fiestas. We *cofrades* knew the value of these things. They were antique objects, and if they were lost, we would lose the respect of the people for not having guarded what our fathers have bequeathed to us.

On 1 November, the main day of the saints, each group in each *cofradía* had its own expenses. At five o'clock in the morning when the *mayordomos* arrived without the *juez,* I received them contentedly. First we had bread and chocolate while my wife and her companions were preparing meat and *tamalitos*. At 6:30 A.M. we went again to the table to eat what is called *cortesía* [present, gift] of San Juan because he is our patron and father. When we were eating, my wife prepared the gift (food and *tamalitos*) that the *mayordomos* took to their houses, always interchanging, one going to the house of the other. When they returned, [it was customary] for them to go to the kitchen to give back the earthenware items to the wife of the *alcalde*. They said, "Many thanks, señora," and they kissed her right hand.

When this was finished, we went to mass. After the mass, there was the procession in the principal streets of the town as a manifestation of faith, reviving our *costumbres* and conserving the images of the saints because they are friends of God. Mainly on this day, 1 November, we honored and venerated the saints for guarding our pueblo, children, and ourselves. We *cofrades* on this day asked our patron saint San Juan Bautista, the representative of the Heart of Heaven and Earth who is our God, to not allow violence in our community, to prevent our young people from being tempted by evil, and to protect our children from illness.

At six o'clock in the afternoon of 1 November is the allegorical [happy] hour of us *cofrades* at the head of the procession toward the cemetery. We carry nets of pine needles, leaves of *pacayas* [palm fruit whose flowers are also edible], and different kinds of a whole lot of flowers to adorn the cemetery where the bodies of our mothers and grandmothers and our fathers and grandfathers rest. They were the ones who served [earlier] as *alguaciles, mayordomos, jueces,* and *alcaldes* of *cofradías*. Also, they were the [former] *principales* of our town. For that reason, the *cofrades* are obligated to adorn the cemetery as homage to the spirits of our dead.

In this procession with the flute and drum, we were accompanied by members of the municipal corporation, the catechists, *principales,* Catholic Actionists, and other people of the town. After adorning the [entrance to the] cemetery, it was opened, and the people began to decorate the tombs of their dead kin.[62]

The municipal *alcalde* and his corporation, upon seeing that the cemetery was decorated, set up a marimba in it. It was a pure marimba without other instruments [such as the saxophone]. Also, the drum and the flute were at the entrance of the chapel thanks to the *cofradías*.

We returned to the *cofradía* of San Juan to cook ears of corn, *güisquiles,* sweet potatoes, plantains, and coffee. It wasn't my wife who cooked these things; she only was directing and providing the material such as the big earthenware jars and jugs because what was going to be cooked was for more than forty people.[63]

Those in charge of cooking were the *mayordomos* of the four *cofradías*.[64] When everything was cooked, they put it in a big basket and placed it in front of the altar. We believe the moment that such a pleasant aroma emits from the basket is the moment that the spirits of the dead visit us in the *cofradía*. For that reason, we offer the basket of food, but only so the spirits can sense the smell of the ears of corn, *güisquiles,* sweet potatoes, and plantains, which is what they ate when they were alive and is what we still eat.

And that's the way it was with the *alcaldes, jueces, mayordomos,* and their families. We ate our fill of what was cooked, and the rest we divided among ourselves to take home to our houses. Then we went to the cemetery again to give *tragos* to those who were playing the marimba and the flute and drum.

At four o'clock in the morning on 2 November, we went again to the cemetery, all of us carrying the big table where mass was celebrated, the glass flower vases, the silver candle holders, and the flowers.

After the mass we *cofrades* are able to take a little rest, each group in his *cofradía*. Those who want to drink do so; those who do not wish to drink don't. No one is obligated. There is democracy in our *cofradías*.

Celebrating the Fiesta of María Concepción and Las Posadas, a Tradition in My Pueblo

7 to 24 December 1993

The month of December is when the fiesta of María Concepción is celebrated. Those in charge of celebrating this fiesta are the members of the *cofradía* of María Concepción. We in the *cofradía* of San Juan are only invited to attend at night to say the *novenario*.

The seventh of December is when we took out the image of the Virgen María from the *cofradía*. The *alcalde* and the *juez* who finished the year were Samuel Luciano Tuc and Domingo Quic Puzul. In the morning they served us breakfast, and in the afternoon we took out the Virgen in procession from the outgoing *cofradía* to the church.

The eighth of December is the main day of María Concepción. We of the *cofradía* of San Juan Bautista received a special invitation by those of the incoming *cofradía* of María Concepción to accompany them for the reception of the image of the Virgen María during the day and for the reception of the clothing and the other things that pertain to the image—silver crown, gold necklace, and jade necklace—during the night.

All of this has to be done in the presence of the *alcalde* of San Juan Bautista because it is he who holds the highest-ranked] *cargo* of all the *cofrades*. The new *alcalde*, Señor Cholotío Yojcom, and the new *juez*, Wilfredo Ernesto Ujpán Oliva, of the *cofradía* of María Concepción bought special drinks like champagne and Sello de oro Venado Especial.

The *alcalde* of San Juan is the one in charge of the rest of the *cofrades*. He has to see what needs to be done for the fiesta. Thus we *cofrades* worked on the fifteenth and sixteenth. First we made two *ranchitos* [small *ranchos*, or huts] of cane and straw in which to carry the [images of the] Virgen María and San José for *las posadas* [the ceremony of taking out the images of José and María in their *ranchitos* before Christmas]. Each day for nine days they would be carried to a different house. The images that serve for *las posadas* are the small ones that are kept in the *cofradía* of San José.[65]

On 16 December, at seven o'clock at night, we took out *las posadas* [the guest houses, or *ranchitos*]. There were two groups, and each had a platform on which they placed the images of the Virgen and José. The first group was composed of the *cofradía* of San Juan Bautista and the *cofradía* of María Concepción. The second group was composed of the *cofradía* of Santo Domingo Guzmán and the *cofradía* of San José. Each group was accompanied by a large choral group of singers and players [18 to 20], catechists, *principales*, and *madres de familias*. *Las posadas* in the pueblo were solemn.

The first night we carried our *posada* to the *cofradía* of San Juan Bautista. The other group carried their *posada* to the *cofradía* of Santo Domingo Guzmán.

Each *alcalde* decides whether to give something to drink to those who accompany *las posadas* during the visits with the people. The gift is that of corn *atol,* or *caliente,* which is what we call a cooked drink made of pineapples, apples, plantains, and peaches, which are minced with a knife. Then cinnamon, orange leaves, and sugar are added. The whole mixture is cooked in water and served hot. It is tasty. On this occasion my wife and my daughters prepared *caliente* and gave it to those who accompanied *las posadas*.

One thing more, this kind of drink is served in *jícaras* [cups made of gourds], but only in the *cofradías*. *Caliente* is a stimulant for the body. The adults are asked whether they would like to have a little *aguardiente* in it. This drink is given to the children but never with *aguardiente*. We make *caliente* because in the month of December it is really cold, but upon drinking this kind of beverage, the body warms up.

That's the way it is in San José. *Las posadas* is a time of much joy for both adults and children. The twenty-fourth of December is when the processions with *las posadas* end. But before going to the *cofradía* of San José, we four groups gather and form just one group in a procession, always with the two *ranchitos* of San José and María. We march until reaching the *cofradía* of María Concepción. When we are in this *cofradía*, it is the *costumbre* for the *alcalde* of this *cofradía* to thank the *alcalde* of the *cofradía* of San Juan for his participation during the nine days of *las posadas*.

Since I was the *alcalde* of the *cofradía* of San Juan, I answered, "It is our duty and our commitment before the people of the community; it is the tradition and custom of our Tzutuhil town."

On this night the *alcalde* of María Concepción offered each adult two *tragos,* and he served children and adults hot tamales.

At 11:00 P.M. we left the *cofradía* of María Concepción, again with San José and María in procession toward the church to be left there at midnight in order to remember and celebrate the birth of the Savior Jesús.

On the twenty-fourth the images of María Concepción, Santo Domingo Guzmán, and San Juan Bautista were carried from their *cofradías* to the church. Each *cofradía* prepared its *atol* to give to the people who accompanied them in the procession.

Since the *juez* had resigned earlier from the *cofradía,* the *mayordomos* and I prepared for the reception without him. I am not going to say that the office of *juez* is worthless. The *juez* is an important person—he is the second in command. He calls the *mayordomos* to attention, corrects those who are not behaving well, and buys the flowers at the end of the week. He also buys some of the candles and helps with the *atol.* I felt a little sad because we had to meet all the expenses, but with the help of God and San Juan Bautista, we moved forward, because when one makes a vow he has to fulfill it before God and the community. There is a phrase in the Bible that says: *vuestro sí, sea sí, y vuestro no, no* [Your yes should be yes and your no, no (or do what you say you are going to do)].

Christmas Day and Celebrating the Birth of San Juan Evangelista
25 to 27 December
Christmas, 25 December, for us *cofrades* is a day for a little rest. Each group stays in its *cofradía.*

We in the *cofradía* of San Juan ate with the *mayordomos,* and we sent a little of the food of this day, the traditional tamales with meat, to their houses.

The twenty-seventh of December is the day that the birth of San Juan Evangelista is celebrated. There is a fiesta only in the *cofradía* of San Juan. One day before, the *alcalde* invites the three other groups of *cofrades,* the Catholic Actionists, the chorus of singers and players, and the *madres de familias,* and they arrive at four o'clock in the morning for a Holy Rosary sung in honor of San Juan Evangelista, to remember his birth, because he also was a faithful disciple of Jesucristo.

Thanks to God, everyone who had been invited arrived. After the Holy Rosary, they all were given chocolate and bread. We said good-bye to one another happily.

Day of Three Kings
6 January 1994
The hard work in the *cofradías* is on 6 January, the day of the celebration of three kings, Gaspar, Melchor, and Baltazar. On this day we divide into two groups and go to all the Catholic houses of the town, carrying the images of the child Jesús.

We left at 6:00 A.M. and did not finish until 6:00 P.M. The people kissed the image of the child Jesús and gave an offering for him. The *mayordomos* and I worked hard, and we became really tired.

Those in charge of taking care of the money are the señores of Catholic Action. We *cofrades* never touch a single centavo. We are just in charge of the image of the child and of the *asofate* [round gold platter with a gold cross in the middle] where the people deposit their offerings.

At night officers of Catholic Action counted the money; we were only witnesses. The amount that the people gave to the infant Jesús was Q1,430.80. The Catholic Actionists kept the money for the maintenance of the church.

After the money was counted, we carried the images of San José, the Virgen María, the child Jesús, and all their adornments for Christmas and New Year's Day to the *cofradía* of San José. The *alcalde* and *juez*, Juan Oliva y Oliva and Santiago Polaz Bizarro, had prepared *aguardiente* for everyone. Out of respect and from much weariness almost everyone drank. When I realized that it was eleven o'clock at night, I had to say good-bye, and [at that point] everyone went to his house.[66]

Lent and Holy Week
2 February to 3 April
All the work of the *cofrades* during Lent is under the direction of the *alcalde* of San Juan. This *costumbre* is begun on the day of Candelaria [Candlemas], the second of February. We open the church at 4:00 A.M. The *cofrades* of Santo Domingo Guzmán, María Concepción, and San Juan have to get up at 3:00 A.M. As a sign of respect, they have to go to the *cofradía* of San Juan to fetch its *alcalde*. Then they all go in procession to the church, beating a sad

sound on the drum that announces to the population that it is time to begin Lent.

At 6:00 A.M. the four Nicodemos [young men named after the man Nicodemus who lowered the body of Jesus from the cross] arrive and light their large candles in front of the sacrosanct image of the body of Jesús. They open the urn, and with much respect and care, clean the face and the body of the image of Señor Jesús with a velvet cloth. Then they close the urn and put it back in its place.

The *alcalde* of the *cofradía* of San Juan thanks the Nicodemos and asks them to keep doing this work during the seven Fridays of Lent.

On the first Friday at 4:00 A.M. we open the church, and the *mayordomos* beat the drum. Then we *jueces* and *alcaldes* adorn the platform with flowers and ears of wheat where they place the image of Jesús Nazareno. It is a big platform that requires eighteen to twenty men to carry it. At 7:00 A.M. each *cofrade* goes to his house.

We of the *cofradía* of San Juan are in charge of the procession of Jesús Nazareno. The procession generally leaves at 8:00 or 9:00 P.M. and enters the church around 10:00 P.M.

Each Friday for five Fridays we take out the image in procession. On the sixth Friday there is no procession. Instead, we begin to make the decorations to be used for Holy Thursday and Friday.

On Holy Tuesday we make a wooden frame that we use as the monument. On Holy Wednesday we hang the fruit with *pita* (maguey fibers) from the top of the monument. We make what looks like a small church inside the big one. We make the small church like a *galera,* or shed with *relón,* or small boards. It is rectangular, but the entrance, or door, is arched above the roof, and this part is called the "cerro [hill]." We tie a lot of fruit and flowers to all of the walls and the roof. The fruit that we put in the monument include pineapples, plantains, peaches, cacaos, melons, and *pataxtes,* and the flowers that we use are the beautiful *corozos* flowers.[67] The air fills with the scent of fruit and flowers.

On this Holy Week, we spent Q700 just on the flowers and fruit that we put on the monument. Catholic Actionists bought the fruit. We *cofrades* were not able to pay for it because we have our expenses in the *cofradía*. The municipality contributed for some of the fruit, but I don't know what the value was.

During the morning of Holy Thursday, each group was in its own *cofradía*. The *mayordomos* and I ate breakfast happily; we ate chicken, *pulique,* and hot *tamalitos,* as is the *costumbre.* Also, as a gift, we sent some of this food to the houses of the *mayordomos.*

The image of San Juan Evangelista left in procession on Holy Thursday, accompanied by the [life-size image of] Jesús Nazareno [bearing a cross] and the [image of the] Virgen María. We took them out at 9:00 P.M. and brought them back to the church at midnight.

Carrying the images of the saints in procession is something of a sacrifice, but it is a commitment that the *cofrades* have with the community. A *cofrade* never leaves in the middle of a procession even though he is tired and sleepy. He has to do what is possible. He is only excused when he goes on a trip or is sick.

During the day of Holy Friday, there is not much work for us *cofrades.* The Nicodemos are in charge of the religious services such as the crucifixion of the image of Jesús. The Nicodemos take out the image of the Santo Entierro [the image of Jesús that is in the coffin] and crucify it with ancient nails. The catechists and singers are in charge of the adoration [of this image].

During the night of Holy Friday, we do participate to make sure that all goes in order, that the [image] of the body of Jesucristo is carried with much respect, and we do the same for the images of San Juan Bautista and María Concepción.

In all the processions and religious services during Lent and Holy Week, [overtly] drinking *aguardiente* is not permitted. One can do it privately, however.

Sunday of the Resurrection is the day on which Lent and Holy Week ended. The priest celebrated mass. Immediately, we took out in procession the image of Jesús Resurrected, but we did this only in the *atrio* of the church.[68]

This procession is pleasant. The image of Jesús Resurrected goes out accompanied by the *cofrades* of San Juan Bautista and Santo Domingo Guzmán and by a group of singers. Likewise, the images of San Juan Evangelista and María Concepción are accompanied by the *cofradía* of San José and María Concepción. When they leave the church, the group with the image of Jesús Nazareno goes out the front door in a half circle to the right while the other group goes out the door with the other images in a half circle to the left. When the two groups meet on the opposite side of the circle, they unite and act as if Jesús meets his mother and his dear disciple. The *texeles* [low-ranking female members of a *cofradía*] of María Concepción and of Santo Domingo Guzmán begin to cover the faces of the images with flowers, a lot of flowers. When the *texeles* begin to throw the flowers, the procession stops for a moment. After this both groups go back to the church in a procession through the center of the circle they had made while leaving. They walk in a straight line directly through the door of the church, and then this procession is all finished.

We carried the image of San Juan Evangelista to our *cofradía*. By the grace of God, we had fulfilled our responsibility. Then the *mayordomos* and I ate lunch, and afterward they went home.

The Closure of Our Tenure with the Cofradía of San Juan
16 June to 2 July 1994
Time goes by like the flowing water of a river; one can't stop it, although one would like to. Thus it was with us. We didn't want the image of San Juan Bautista to leave our house, but my wife and I knew that everything has a beginning and an end.

Well, we reached the month of June, which is the month that we would have to deliver our *cargo* in the *cofradía*. My wife and I thought about giving a gift to our patron saint, San Juan Bautista. The saint didn't ask for anything, it was our free will. Our sons Ramón Antonio and Erasmo Ignacio did the *labores de jaspe* [works or adornment of tie-dyed thread or yarn], and they did the dyeing. My wife warped and wove. I told her that we could have another person do it because I could see that it was a lot of work for her. She said no, that she would work during the nights. She was able to prepare the new suits of San Juan Bautista and San Juan Evangelista.

The sixteenth of June began the *novenario* of the birth of San Juan Bautista. The people greeted us, saying, "Thanks to God you have managed the year, doing everything required with only the *mayordomos* and no *juez*. But you will have something good in the future." And they kissed the hand of my wife and me. I felt something that you can't buy—the respect and appreciation that our Tzutuhil people have for us.

The twenty-second of June 1994 arrived. My wife and I prepared and bought everything needed for the *costumbre* that we thought would be our last service in life. Our son made the bread. All night long my woman and her helpers worked, preparing the *tamalitos* and other food. The twenty-third dawned, and at five o'clock in the morning the *mayordomos* spread pine needles in the house [on the floor], and they arranged the candles.

On the twenty-second we had to decorate the *atrio* and clean the walls of the church. At six o'clock in the morning we ate our breakfast, and then my wife told the first *mayordomo* to carry these little gifts of tamalitos with chicken to their houses, now that these were the last days and that we were going to complete our service. The first *mayordomo* thanked her, and they did what she asked. When they returned, they left the utensils in the kitchen.

At one o'clock in the afternoon the *mayordomos* arranged the shrine with the flowers that I had bought in Sololá on the twenty-first. From Sololá to Panajachel, I had to carry them and eighteen *bombas* on foot because cars weren't allowed to pass where there were many pieces of machinery repaving the road.

That's the way it was. At 3:00 P.M. the *principales,* Catholic Actionists, catechists, and visitors from other towns arrived at my house to drink *atol.* After I said good-bye to the *principales,* we carried the image of San Juan to the church. The truth is that I felt sad, with tears in my eyes. On the main day of San Juan, 24 June, at 3:00 A.M. the explosion of *bombas* and firecrackers joyfully announced another anniversary of the birth of San Juan Bautista. At 4:30 A.M. we carried our large candles and the incense holder and put them at the foot of San Juan Bautista in the church. We stayed until 6:00 A.M. Also on this day we prepared food in the house to give to those who wanted to visit the *cofradía.* They had to be given some breakfast or lunch, depending on the hour.

At 8:30 A.M. we *principales,* Catholic Actionists, and others went to the beach to welcome the bishop of Sololá, Benando Gálvez. At 9:00 A.M. the celebration of the holy mass began. After mass we took out in procession the images of María and Santo Domingo Guzmán to accompany San Juan Bautista on his day.

While I was walking in the procession, I saw the anthropologist, James D. Sexton. After the procession we went to the *cofradía,* and not until then did I chat with my good North American friend, Jaime. Some *compadres* from Sololá had come to visit us, and I drank some *tragos* with them.[69]

The final drama of my service in the *cofradía* was on 29 June. During the night while my wife was preparing the food and the *tamalitos,* she and I drank two *tragos.* She continued to work, but I continued to drink.

19. *Parading the image of San Juan Bautista through the main streets of the town.*

On the morning of the thirtieth, we said good-bye to the *cofrades* of Santo Domingo, María Concepción, and San José, to a group of singers who had been participating with us for six months on Saturdays, and to the catechists who were with us. We served all of them breakfast.

At 3:00 P.M. my soul began to get sadder when all the *principales* of the town and the members of the organizations of the Catholic Church arrived to drink the *atol* of farewell. My friend, Jaime Sexton, was participating with the *principales* of the town. He drank *atol* in the *cofradía* with us. After drinking *atol,* I said good-bye, asking forgiveness for everything because I felt a little drunk. Then we carried the images of San Juan Bautista and San Juan Evangelista to the church.

The first of July is the day we took the images to the new *cofradía,* in the house of Señor Velásquez Cholotío, whose *juez* is Señor Teodoro Vicente García. During this night our hearts were full of sadness and our eyes were full of tears with the saddest sounds of the flute and drum. The *mayordomos* carried the load of the clothes chest and all the materials to bury the dead. My wife positioned herself in front of the *mayordomos* with a big incense holder. Also, friends and family and the other *cofrades* accompanied us.

After delivering all that we had in the inventory, we said good-bye to everyone and went home. My wife and I were almost crying, but the outgoing *mayordomos* and their families were still with us. When we arrived home, we drank some more *tragos*. The *mayordomos* left for home, and we went to sleep because we still had another day left.

On 1 July my wife, Josefa, made the preparations. Since I felt a little drunk, she was in charge of everything. She bought meat and fish. The ex-*mayordomos* and their wives arrived. They prepared the food and tortillas, and we ate lunch together. Also, kin and friends came, and this is the way we said good-bye to the *cofradía*. The ex-*cofrades* and their wives bought *aguardiente* and sodas, but we provided the food.

I ask forgiveness from God and San Juan Bautista. Now the people of my pueblo designate me as a *principal*, and I have to accept it.

In 1958 I served as the last *mayordomo* of the Virgen María, when the *alcalde* was Franco Coj Vásquez and the *juez* was Santiago Vásquez Bizarro. In 1960 I was *alguacil* of the municipality when Juan Bizarro Gómez was mayor. In 1964 and 1965 I was second *mayordomo* of San Juan Bautista when the *alcalde* was Humberto Bizarro Mendosa and the *juez* was Don Ernesto Ujpán Canajay, may he rest in peace. From 1974 to 1975 I was the first *mayordomo* of Santo Domingo Guzmán. At that time the *alcalde* was Santiago López García and the *juez* was Bernardino Ujpán Flores. From 1981 to 1982 I was the *alcalde* of the *cofradía* of María Concepción and the *juez* was Ignacio Oliva y Oliva.

All these services are without pay in my community. They require time and money, but they can be done. It only takes willpower and a little love to maintain the traditions of our ancestors.[70]

At this point in Ignacio's diary, almost two and one-half years lapse before he records a significant event. My presence in Guatemala had always stimulated him to polish episodes he had recorded periodically in his notebooks. In 1996 I was unable to return to Guatemala, however, and in 1997, instead of going to Guatemala, I went with my wife to Venezuela, Barbados, and Puerto Rico. During this period, Ignacio sent me some folktales that were later published in Heart of Heaven, Heart of Earth. *Thinking that perhaps Ignacio had been more interested in the folktales than in his diary, in summer 1998 I asked him about the gap. He said what had happened from August 1994 to December 1996 was not as important as what had happened more recently. Because we already had more*

*than enough relevant material for this last volume, I did not press
him for more information.*

Peace Accords
30 December 1996 to July 1997
I need to say something about the signing of the peace document in
Guatemala. Signing the peace agreement is of vital importance to my dear
Guatemala. It has a lot of merit. Thanks go to the big private sectors, the
government of President Alvaro Arzú Irigoyen, the bishops and priests
of the Catholic Church, the procurator's office of human rights, and
the international organizations. They struggled to get the two groups
to understand each other. The army and the guerrilla organizations
have spilled a lot of blood; they have massacred thousands and thousands of innocent Indians who did not know or understand the goals
of these two powerful groups. The army is the more responsible of the
two groups for the massacres in the provinces of this land.

We have listened on the national and international level [news] about
the common graves where many cadavers have been exhumed, without mentioning the thousands whose bodies have not been found. This
was an injustice; the blood of our brothers and sisters cries out now to
the All Powerful for justice.

As it is written in the Bible in Genesis when Cain killed his brother,
God asked him, "Cain, where is your brother Abel?" Cain answered,
"I don't know; by any chance am I my brother's keeper?" God in turn
said to Cain, "You have killed your brother Abel; his blood cries out
from the ground."

That is how it is now—many lives have been lost because of these
two armed groups. [Their] weapons are the number one enemy of the
Guatemalan people. The true Guatemalan people never take up weapons, because the Guatemalans who really love their homeland never
think about causing the death of another person. We know that human
beings are children of the same God who is the heart of heaven; that we
are children of mother earth who is the heart of the earth.

Neither the army, ORPA, URNG, nor other groups thought about
the love of our homeland, about the love of this earth. They thought
only about earning good money and obtaining better positions with
the government. They said that they were doing it for their people, but
it was not true. The people, for them, are just in the middle of the white

target so that they can tell who has the best aim.⁷¹ It seems that all the people realized that when the negotiations took place the representatives [for] the army as well as [for] the guerrillas were all Ladinos. There was not one Indian, and they said they were doing it for the people. It was all false. The truth was they fought for the same potato—power—each group wanted to eat it. These negotiations should have been reached much earlier, and there should not have been so many lives lost. Now, how many mothers have lost their children? How many wives have lost their husbands? How many children have been orphaned? It appears to me that it is better to give medicine to the sick person, not the dead one.

When they signed the peace [treaty] in Guatemala, a big party was celebrated on the national level. The [national] government sent money to the departmental governments, which in turn sent money to the municipalities for the celebration of the signing of the peace accords. In each town an act was drawn up for the signing of the peace accords.

So it also was in my town. The municipality set up a marimba and bought strong drinks and a lot of food to give to the people of the town. But they didn't reach beyond the corporation and their comrades. They celebrated among themselves. The entire town did not sign the act. [Anyway] those who needed to sign that agreement were the members of the army and the guerrillas so that they would no longer continue to kill the working people and the innocent.

It had already happened. Guatemala had already been bathed with the blood of its children. That the people know. There was a lot [of bloodshed] in Guatemala. And why not mention my small town and Tzutuhil territory. Those of us who thought of God and love of our fellow men are of flesh and bone. We didn't [think we] had the right to take the life of another person. We were neither on the side of the army nor on the side of the guerrillas. We only thought about God and our families, about working honorably, grasping the hoe and the pickax from sunup to sundown, eating tortillas and salt, and drinking a gourd of water. But we never considered being servants or supporters of either the army or the guerrillas. We had to maintain our spirit of being *Joseños*. We have had problems in our community, but we never went to the army or to the guerrillas to denounce somebody.

When the Catholic church was divided in two groups in the year 1987, there was an intense religious conflict. One group sided with

20. *A large flag and an eternal flame in the plaza in front of the National Palace in Guatemala City serve as a monument to the signing of the peace accords in December 1996.*

Father José McCall and the other group against the same priest. The army wanted to intervene to end this conflict with the intent of kidnapping the leaders of both groups. But never did either group give the army names. Members of the intelligence section of Zone 14 of Sololá arrived three times in San José at night to interrogate the mayor. The last time [they came], they carried off the mayor to an unknown place where there was no light; that is to say, they took him to a mountain outside of San José in a car to interrogate him to obtain the names of the leaders of the two groups. The army's intent was to stop the religious conflict by eliminating the leaders of the two groups. Benjamín Peña Cholotío was the mayor then, and they told him that he had the final say in providing the names.

Although Benjamín also was involved with the group that supported Father José, he did not want to give the army the names of the leaders of the other group. Three times the soldiers interrogated him! And the last time when they saw they were gaining nothing, they beat him in the middle of the night and left him near the town. For that reason, I say we have maintained the spirit of being *Joseños,* unlike what has happened in other towns, where they accused each other for debts, for women, and perhaps for business.

It has been a year and seven months since the peace treaty was signed by those in power, but we poor people and Indians are the same as before—marginalized, forgotten, and despised. Every day prices go up; fertilizers cost more. There is no way the poor can help themselves. The big millionaires get richer, while the poor continue in extreme poverty. In the peace negotiations, they talked about equality for all Guatemalans and the distribution of land. All of this was a lie. The lands that truly belong to the Guatemalans are in the hands of the big landowners, who are aligned with the government. The poor people still end up in extreme poverty.

Peace now is signed. The army is happy because it enhanced its budget. The URNG is even happier because it reached its zenith of becoming a political party. Now there is talk that it is looking for an alliance with the official party or with another party of grand scale. I am sufficiently sure that in the coming campaign the URNG will not be able to say anything about the army, much less the big landowners, because they will then damage their image and there will not be support for their party.

It was heard that after the peace accords were signed, the developed countries gave a lot of money to change the image of the country. The truth is that this money ended up in the pockets of the wolves, [because there is] much corruption in Guatemala. They spend a little of the money on the infrastructure of the towns and the rest [goes] in their pockets.

What has happened in my town is clear. The municipality has stolen a lot of money. It can be seen that the salary of the mayor is not more than Q1,500 a month. But now the mayor has a car valued at Q32,000; [he is] happy with two of his own computers, and he has bought about fifty *cuerdas* of *cafetal* [coffee grove], which now costs Q3,000 per *cuerda.* And he has more money in the banks.

There is a lot of waste of money, but this is also the government's fault because it does not supervise the use of the money. They [members of the municipal government] administer to their own tastes and whims, but the [municipal] treasurer is the originator of these robberies. The people don't say anything; they are only seeing how far they [the municipal officials] will go with this corruption. This is not just in San José; it is worst in the big towns. For them the signed peace is a blessing. Now for the people *nel pastel* [no cake; that is, there is not anything good].

The Death of My Uncle José
5 to 18 April 1997

What is life? It seems to me that life is like a dream. Life is like the mist—it falls and then it disappears. When a person least expects it is when death comes like a thief. We all know that we are going to die, but it's a pity that none of us mortals knows when and how we are going to die.

There are people who work and eat well during the day, and after the course of the night, at dawn the next day, are dead or seriously ill. Death is the most powerful thing there is in the world. It doesn't ask if one is white or brown; it doesn't ask if one is tall or [short], chubby [or thin], or muscular or flabby. Death doesn't ask if one is rich or poor or if one is young or old.

Death doesn't use a weapon or a knife; but indeed it tortures [people] a lot. It happened to us. We in my family were not thinking about what would happen. I was not really happy, but I surely was content with my work in the field. The truth is we didn't have money, because Holy Week had just passed, and we had spent the little money that we had. Well, we had enough corn, beans, and firewood. We only had a few quetzales with which to buy the most necessary things for the kitchen.

On Sunday, 5 April 1997, the youngster, son of Samuel Teodoro Ujpán and of Melina Ramos Temó, disappeared. The news spread throughout the town. The people struggled to find him, but it was impossible because it was then late at night. Not until the next day between 7:00 and 8:00 A.M. did they find the cadaver of the boy who had drowned in Lake Atitlán in the place named Panoxtín. He had fallen from a canoe. Then, having recovered the body, they sent for the justice of the peace of San Martín la Laguna. The justice carried out the law, ordering the transfer of the cadaver to the national hospital of Sololá.

Seeing the necessity, [since] the parents of the deceased were poor people, I begged the señor justice of the peace:

> Have consideration. Don't send the remains to Sololá, [because] the boy only drowned and there was no foul play. The parents live in extreme poverty, and they don't have the money to pay for the boat and other expenses to take the dead one released from the hospital.

The señor justice of the peace replied, "Who are you to the deceased?"

I said that I am not anything, only a citizen of the town who sees the circumstances and the poverty of the parents of the dead.

Then the judge called the papá of the dead one and asked if it was true that they did not have the money to pay for the expenses. Samuel Teodoro said to the judge that it was certainly true that he was a poor person who works in the field, living on what he can make daily. The señor judge understood the request and said in effect not to send the cadaver.

We carried the remains to the house of his parents. Seeing the need that confronted that family, I spoke aloud, requesting the generosity of each one of those who was present in order to help to the family.

The people understood. Indeed, they helped with money and provisions. The burial of the drowned youth was in the afternoon on Monday. There was much sadness. They say that on Sunday the boy had eaten lunch happily without knowing what would happen later.

It is a custom among us Indians that nine days after the burial the parents, relatives, and friends go for a visit to the cemetery to deposit flowers and leave a cross on the tomb of the dead.

Thus the parents of the deceased did the prayer of the *novenario* during the nights. These nine days concluded on Tuesday, 15 April. The relatives ordered a mass, but because the priest was really busy, he said he could not do it until Wednesday, 16 April.

On Tuesday, 15 April 1997, my son Erasmo Ignacio and I had to plant corn in the place named Patzunoj. In the afternoon I had to bring firewood with the beast [horse]. When we arrived at the house, I put the load of firewood in the homesite, and my uncle José untied the knots and put the lassos in the place where we always keep them.

My uncle didn't eat tortillas; he only ate a piece of bread and drank a little coffee, and he went to bed. After dinner we planned our work for the next day. Then my wife and I went to the house that we have in the Chibax Canton without knowing what would happen the next day.

At dawn on Wednesday, 16 April, we got up, as always giving thanks to God for another day more [of life]. Then we went to the house of Samuel Teodoro Ujpán for the visit to the cemetery that marked the end of the nine days since the death of their son. About one hundred people arrived, including relatives, neighbors, and friends. After all the rites of the days, we arrived again at the house of the father of the fallen. It was the custom that they serve breakfast to all of us. After having breakfast, group by group, family by family, we said good-bye to the parents of the deceased, offering words of consolation.

At 8:00 A.M. we arrived home. My children were waiting for us in order to eat, but we told them that we had already eaten. Then I began to arrange the things I needed to take to work. Ramón and Ignacio had already gone ahead because the previous day we agreed to sow two *cuerdas* of milpa at another site. I began to catch up to the horse because I planned to bring firewood back in the afternoon, but everything turned out bad.

I grabbed my ax and my machete, and I was ready to leave when my daughter Susana said, "Papá, uncle has not gotten up, and now it is late."

He always got up early. I ran to where my uncle always slept. I spoke to him in a loud voice, but now he could not speak. I spoke to him again, but he did not respond, even with signs.

My uncle had physical impairments: he could only hear with one ear, and he didn't speak well. He could speak a few words, however. I thought that he was sleeping, but when I realized he was dying, I held him tight. I wanted to lift him up, but I was not able. I shouted like a lunatic, calling to my wife and daughter Susana Julia to come to help me lift him up. We were able to raise him up, but he was unconscious. We gave him hot water. In his agony he requested some juice. We gave him the juice, but he no longer was able to drink. We saw that his situation was serious, and we took him out of the little house where he slept and put him in the big house.

It was a Wednesday, 16 April, the worst of the worst. We didn't have money; we only had seven quetzales with which we had planned to buy a few pounds of sugar. We had a little ripe coffee, but we had not been able to pick it. Even with this [coffee], however, we would be unable to pay for the funeral expenses. I was in a dead-end alley; I had no money in the bank, and my wife didn't have any money.

I thought a lot about my uncle. He had three *cuerdas* of land in Joyabaj. Moreover, he had a small piece of homesite where he had lived with my grandmother Isabel. There was no one else living in that homesite who could take care of him. Then I ran to the house of my son José to tell him what was happening to us. José had been sick in bed for several days, but when he heard this news he got up and put on his *caites*. He went with me back to my house. On the way, I said that I didn't have any money and that I was thinking about taking out a loan to buy material to build a *panteón* for the body of my uncle. José told me that he could help me with a loan of Q1,000 for a month. Then I felt some relief.

At 11:00 A.M. I went to the municipality to ask for land in the cemetery. Then I went to the cemetery with Santiago Eric Chávez, the syndic. We measured [a plot] three meters long and one meter and twenty centimeters wide. I paid for the right [to the plot] and for the taxes. I didn't wait for a legal document. We agreed to do that later because it was an emergency.

We began the construction of the *panteón*. We carried stones from the homesite for the foundation. I had to buy [cement] blocks, iron, cement, and sand. I contracted a mason, Señor Benjamín Peña Letona. He hired his own assistants, although we helped to carry the material to the cemetery.

We were unloading the material when, at 2:00 P.M. on 16 April 1997, my niece Elena arrived to tell us that my uncle José had died. When they told me that José had died, I had another problem. I did not have a box [coffin] for the body. With a thousand quetzales, one could not do much. Then I went to the house of Señor Santiago Juan Puzul to ask him to give me a box on credit for fifteen days. This señor didn't deny me. The box was not expensive, only Q400, and that is where we put the body of the dead.[72]

There are things that [people do to] help the spirit of the sick. They say that seeing the agony of the sick person, Agustín María, the husband of my sister-in-law Esmeralda, ran to his house to fetch a book used to recommend the souls of the sick person. Then everyone present kneeled down and began to recommend his soul with sacred prayers. They had been doing this when he passed away.

Fifteen days earlier at about 3:00 A.M. I had a bad dream. I had a foreboding that something bad was going to happen. I was overcome with a bad feeling, but I didn't know what was going to happen. In the dream an old kitchen appeared to me that we had from 1955 to 1960. That kitchen had cane walls and a tile roof. In the kitchen were three people who had already died. They were Martín Coj, María Bizarro, and Señora Clara Tuc. When I opened the door of the old kitchen, there they were, the three dead persons, and with them was my uncle José. The four of them were eating fish. In the dream I spoke to them in a strong voice, saying: "Well, what are you doing here? You have already died. You can no longer be here."

In the dream the deceased Martín spoke to me: "Let's eat a little inside your house; we're going to retire soon. We will be only a moment. As soon as we finish eating, we will leave."

In the dream I remained still; I was no longer able to move. When the dead ones finished eating, they left one by one. The last to leave was my uncle José, and he disappeared.

Then the dream ended. It bothered me a lot.

Many Catholics and evangelicals arrived. They stayed the rest of the afternoon and all of the night. The custom is that when a person dies, the women help with sugar, coffee, rice, and beans. The men help with a little money—one or two quetzales, depending on their ability. They did so with us. Also, there were many who didn't have money, but they helped us psychologically. The truth is that many people came; only a few did not. At that time, I fully understood the importance of accompanying and helping people when they are suffering from such a distress in life. The warmth of sharing the pain is needed. We human beings need to share in sadness as well as in happiness because there is no telling when a person is going to die.

The burial of my uncle José was on Thursday, 17 April 1997, at 3:30 P.M. After the celebration of a holy mass in the Catholic church, we placed his body in the *panteón*. After the funeral, I said good-bye to all the people, thanking them for all they had done for us. I also asked for forgiveness if we had committed any error.

When the burial was over, my uncles and cousins accompanied me to the house. They bought a little *aguardiente*. We drank with them and became intoxicated. The previous night we also drank some drinks, but not to get drunk, just to warm up from the cold. I had to restrain myself because I had a lot of commitments and I was the one responsible for anything that needed to be done.

So it was also with my wife; she had the responsibility of the kitchen. All the kitchen work was done on the patio of the house because they were big jobs. Not many women worked preparing the food for those [coming] to the wake. Meat was not bought; the guests were only given *tamalitos* and beans to eat.

Friday, the eighteenth, we awoke somewhat numbed from everything that had happened. It is sad to lose a loved one.

We asked Señor Fernando Vásquez, a responsible person, to look after the money that the people donated for the deceased. He counted Q386. He saved it for the end of the nine days [of mourning] because there also is an expense for that day.

Also, there is a wake for the nine days. This wake is called the wake of the cross. All night until dawn food is given to everyone. During that night, with us were neighbors, relatives, catechists, and a choir from the church. After the midnight prayer, they all were served food. At five o'clock in the morning, we went to the cemetery to end the nine days of bereavement. When we returned from the cemetery, we all went again to my house to have coffee and bread.

Although my uncle José was physically impaired, he worked hard. He was a man who was appreciated by the farm managers. He didn't like to waste time. He worked many years on the southern coast in Caoba, Totonicapán, Esquipulas, Los Alamos, Santa Candelaria, Santanderina, and Coyolate Pangolita.

Also, I was with him sowing milpa for two years in Santa Elena Río Bravo. Regularly, we had to cross the Río Bravo, and once he was swept away by the current. I had to help him. His *caites* were lost. They were carried away by the current. Earlier he worked a lot, but after my grandmother Isabel died, my uncle José no longer went to the coast. My grandmother had told me that I would have to look after my uncle. She recommended that I take care of him and give him food because he didn't have a family. There was no one else to look after him. Thus my uncle lived with me. He and my granny lived with me for many years. My wife gave them their meals, since my grandmother no longer could work to make the tortillas and she could no longer prepare their food because of her advanced age. They always were in their little house; they always had a fire but only to warm themselves. My uncle was the one in charge of taking the food [to her], and they ate together inside the house.

When my grandmother died, my mom, Elena, and my uncle Bonifacio requested that my uncle José live with one of the two of them. My uncle told them that he would remain with us. They asked him so many times that he finally became mad at them. After the death of my grandmother Isabel, my uncle stayed with us for fourteen years.

I am not going to say that he rested for fourteen years. He still worked part-time. I told him to rest more, but he didn't want to do so. He became angry with us if we did not let him go to work. He was used to doing the work of the field. But during those fourteen years, he didn't carry a single load of firewood on his back. He was highly esteemed, and he didn't have a family to support. But he hardly had the need to work. Ultimately, his job was to thresh corn for the *nixtamal* [kernels of corn softened and hulled by boiling in limewater to make hominy, which is easy to grind into dough for tortillas] and to sweep the patio of the house. Later he looked sick, but he wasn't bedridden. He walked around and ate. He told us that he had an ache in his stomach. I told him that I would take him to a doctor in Sololá, but he told me that he didn't want any medicine or to go to a hospital. He also refused home remedies. I thought that he still had some life left in him, but I was wrong. We only suffered one day with him.

My uncle José collaborated a lot with the *cofrades* during the fiestas of María Concepción, Santo Domingo Guzmán, San Juan Bautista, Christmas, All Saints' Day, Ascension Day, Day of San José, and the weeks of Lent. He was the one in charge of playing the *tun* (big drum) in the processions. They didn't pay him; they just gave him drinks. Many times he became drunk, and he was not able to go home because he was advanced in age and he lost consciousness. Finally, I told the *cofrades* to find someone else to collaborate with them because he was too old. The last year that he played the *tun* was when I was the *alcalde* of the *cofradía* of San Juan. Not participating anymore bothered him a lot, to the point of becoming angry with me, but I only wanted his well-being.

The Man Who Was Eaten by Coyotes
2 to 22 August 1997

It's incredible but true. It is not God who punishes us. A man suffers from his own evil deeds.

Many times a man says, "God has punished me." But God punishes no one; he is great in his mercy. Man is punished by his own nonsense. A really strange case happened in my dear town of San José. There was a man who was called Leonel Bizarro Oliva. He had a wife, and they had three children. He bought ripe coffee and avocados as a middleman and sold them.

The people said that the jefe of those who stole coffee at night lived in the *caserío* of San Joseñita. The thieves left between 8:00 and 9:00 P.M. and returned between 3:00 and 4:00 A.M. The boss had to open the door of his house to receive the stolen coffee. The truth is that indeed a lot of coffee was lost during the harvest. Jorge bought it for half the price, and he earned good money. I do not know why he allowed himself to be dragged down by the vice of women. He had mistresses for whom he bought dresses, shoes, and even television sets. He got involved in taking out loans in order to live a little better. Under the auspices of Visión Mundial, a project of Chimaltenango, the last loan that he received was on 10 July 1996.

I was one of those [who received a loan] in that project. The name of the group is called Amigos del Campo [Friends of the Field], and it still exists. The loan that was given to him was from Asies Kas [a self-help organization] whose headquarters are in Santiago Atitlán. It was for purchasing fertilizer and maintaining the coffee crop. We were eleven in the group, and to each they gave Q2,500 for the period of one year with interest of 22 percent. They say that our companion Leonel told his wife that the amount of the loan was only Q1,000, and the remaining Q1,500 he gave to a mistress by the name of Paulina. That woman has a husband. Within a few days of Leonel's giving the money to the mistress, his wife had found out what had happened. They say that Leonel's woman had talked to a neighbor who agreed to tell her when Leonel went into a house with the mistress.

A certain day came when Leonel went into the house, and the neighbor ran to advise his wife. The wife left running, opened the door to the rustic cane house, and found them in the middle of a sexual act. The woman shouted, calling for the neighbors to come see what was happening. They say that Leonel began to tremble inside the house, but he could not leave because the people already had surrounded it. When Leonel came out, they say that he now was not in his normal state of mind. He was like a demented person, taking to the coffee groves. He didn't arrive home until night.

He no longer ate or slept. They said one thing to him and, like a fool, he took it to be something else. On 2 August he went out to work for half a day. About one o'clock in the afternoon, he arrived home, but he didn't eat lunch. He said he had to leave on a journey to Quezaltenango. He took a machete and a lasso and said that he was going to Quezaltenango, but the woman didn't believe him because Leonel didn't have any money. In a half hour he returned and said to his wife: "I'm going to look at the land there, up above where we have the coffee."

He left again about 3:00 P.M. and returned no more. In the night a public announcement went out through the streets that said Señor Leonel Bizarro Oliva had disappeared and that if somebody had seen him to tell the commissary. All day Saturday, 3 August, there was a great deal of alarm in all the town. In the afternoon we left to search among the coffee groves, but we could not find him.

When night fell, we arrived home and told his wife that we didn't find anything, not a sign. That same night, together with other friends, I went to the office of Catholic Action to tell the president to ask the whole town for help the next morning to look for the man who had disappeared.

The gentlemen of the Catholic Church made the announcement. When Sunday dawned, about four hundred of us, including men and women, went searching among the coffee groves. Since the husband had told his wife that he had to die during these days, we thought he might already be dead. We climbed up the steeper hills where the people had not gone. We suffered a lot, but we did not find anything. Wherever the vultures where flying, we went to see if they were eating the dead one, but we found nothing.

Others went to the *aldeas* and still others to the coast to see if they would find him drunk, but again they found nothing. We got tired and returned in the afternoon; others returned in the night.

So it was. Some said that he had been kidnapped. There was much alarm in the town. On Monday, 4 August, other people went to search in other places, but they found nothing. Like that it remained.

It wasn't until 22 August that some youngsters were looking for firewood on the Chaj Hill, about a kilometer and a half from the town, and saw the cranium and two other bones of the dead one. They ran to give the news. I remember well that we were listening to mass when a youngster ran into the church to tell some of his relatives that they had found the place where Leonel had died. Finishing the mass, the people ran to the place.

It is certain they found the machete, the lasso, and the shirt that he had been wearing before he died. They also found his watch.

That afternoon they found only the skull and two pieces of the bones of the hand. They also found an empty container of an insecticide called Tamaron. With this poison Leonel took his life, and he was eaten by the coyotes.

They called the justice of the peace from San Martín to conform with the law. In the coffin they only put the skull and two pieces of the bones of the hand. The coyotes had carried off the rest of the bones. They had to take the coffin to Sololá where the forensic doctor said in his report that the dead one had ingested insecticide and that he had been eaten by the coyotes.

Then the townspeople buried the remains of the man in the local cemetery. Fifteen days later, two kilometers from the place where he died, they found more of his bones. All the people said it was the first case like this that had happened in San José. Never before had anyone seen a death like the death of Leonel Bizarro Oliva. The wife says that her husband had made the decision to take his own life because he owed a lot of money, that he no longer could pay the quantity of Q35,000. But he killed himself because of the women.

My Half Sister María Catarina and My Former Son-in-law
11 March 1998

A lot of things happen in life, some good but many times bad. I have written previously about my daughter María. She had a husband who is called José Mario Ramos García, but this man fell in love with one of my sisters who is called Juana Rubenia Ujpán Ramos. My sister was old; she already had grown children, about the same age as José Mario.

I don't know why she separated from her first husband, named Mariano Gonzales. Juana Rubenia surrendered to perdition; she had a son by a man who was a commissary from San Martín. At the end of her story [earlier in the book] she had joined my son-in-law José Mario, who then became my brother-in-law. I didn't want to say anything. I only pleaded to God that my daughter María would continue her studies in Quezaltenango. Her baby, Rose Josefa, she left with us. My wife and I had to make the effort to buy its milk and [to raise] the money for María's studies.

Many times my wife thought about filing a complaint against José Mario to make him give us a little money to buy milk. I told her not to do so. I did not want to make a demand against anyone. I told my wife that we would wait for the law of compensation, that God may be late but he does not forget.

We tolerated and suffered a lot from the mouth of my sister, who spoke gross, terrible words. Many times she attacked us with abuse, but I told my family not to respond. Thus it was.

José Mario and Juana Rubenia had two children, but none of their business ventures turned out well. Their luck turned bad. Two years later Juana Rubenia took sick with a terrible illness. They say she had cancer of the vagina. She went to many doctors, but they were unable to cure her.

She struggled with many sorcerers, but neither were they able to help her. They called many evangelicals who were supposed to be able to perform miracles, but nothing worked.

They criticized me, saying that I was a sorcerer, that I had witchcraft performed with San Simón [Maximón] in Santiago Atitlán, and that I was the father of the sorcerers and of the *characoteles*.

Her relatives joined together and took up a collection to pay for an operation on the vagina. A specialist said that the cancer was very advanced, and he did not want to operate. Again they went to Quezaltenango to a parapsychologist who practiced under the pseudonym Luzfander.[73] They gave Q3,000 to this man so that he would cure the cancer. Three days after receiving the money, this man had an accident and died.

When Luzfander died, criticism was aimed at me, saying that I was the number one enemy. Juana's relatives said that I had bewitched the parapsychologist so that he could not cure the patient.

They struggled a lot to cure the patient, but they achieved nothing. In December of last year she recovered a little and spent Christmas and New Year's Day a little happier, but in the middle of the month of January, she was bedfast again. The medicine did not help. Juana Rubenia died on Wednesday, 11 March 1998.

We are siblings of the same parent [father], but when she died I did not go to the wake or to the burial. We are neighbors, but I could not go lest I provoke a big problem. Only God [knows what's best] for her, and God [knows what's best] for myself. I want to clarify what they are saying—that I am the father of the sorcerers and *characoteles*. I am no such thing; I'm only a man like any other man. What right would I have to take the life of another person? What can I do to send some witchcraft to inject into the body of a person. Nor am I a *characotel*. I am not anything. The only thing I know how to do is to invoke the name of the living God and to respect and invoke mother earth because I also have my sins. I can't wish evil on another person, because if you bring about evil your own conscience will multiply your pains.

The relatives of Juana Rubenia criticized me wrongly for the death of that woman, even to the point of saying that they were going to kill my children. The people friendly to me said that I should present an accusation before the Public Ministry.[74]

I told my friends, "No, I don't want to make a demand on anybody. I know that my conscience is clean and that he who is clean doesn't need much soap with which to take a bath."

Anger passes like the air and the rain. When there is a strong hurricane and it rains heavily, a man must take a little care. When the storm has passed, he will see peaceful times again. That's the way people are when they are angry or resentful. There is no reason to bother them. Once their anger or resentfulness ends, they become calm again.[75]

The First Anniversary of My Uncle José's Death
16 to 17 April 1998

A year passes quickly, but when someone in the family dies the sadness is still felt because of the void left by the one who has gone to rest with our forebears. Such is the case of my uncle José who, on 16 April, has been dead for a year. Then we, the family, felt sad for him. A great void was left inside of us, but what can you do about death? Every time we eat, especially fruit, we always think about Uncle José.

Before the end of the year [1997] my family and I agreed to remember this date. My boys went to the office of Catholic Action to ask for a mass for 16 April of this year of 1998. Some days later they gave them the answer that there would be a mass celebrated on 16 April at 5:00 P.M. Then we arranged for spending a little money on this day. Before the indicated date, we invited all the relatives, *compadres*, and friends, that is to say, all the people who had participated with us in the bereavement of last year.

When the time was near, we decided that after the mass we would visit the cemetery. After everything, we would serve a dinner to everyone. My wife and our daughters worked hard preparing the food and making the little tamales. Meanwhile we prepared the wreath and the flowers. When we were about to go the church, my neighbor Diego told me: "Ignacio, they say the priest is not going to celebrate mass because he is angry."

I told Diego, "They are lies. He has to do what is sacred even if he's mad."

So it was. I sent my son Ramón to ask whether what my neighbor had said was true. It was. The president of Catholic Action told Ramón that there would not be a mass today. And our preparation was already done. We had told all the guests that we would meet in the Catholic church to witness the holy mass.

When they told us that there would be no mass, it upset us, but we calmed down and had patience. My children and I ran to the houses of the guests to tell them that our meeting is going to take place in our house and not in the church as we had said before.

Well, the hour arrived, and everyone came to our house. Then we went to the cemetery for the visit. There we celebrated the prayer for the dead, and we left the wreath and the flowers. We were there for a good while, each one praying conscientiously. Then we returned to the house, where we served dinner to everyone. After dinner I gave them my words of gratitude for sharing with me a year ago, and I [said], "May the Heart of Heaven and the Heart of Earth illuminate each one of you and your families." Then they said good-bye to me, and each one went home.

They say the priest was angry because during Holy Week some other priests of the Carmelitana congregation came to officiate the masses. When the priests were ready to return to Guatemala City, each one of them was given his money, but none was given to the priest of San Martín. He had not done any work here in San José. That is when I came to the conclusion that no person is good, only God is.

A Bishop Is Murdered
Sunday, 26 April 1998
Guatemala is a such a beautiful country, so good that God has placed

its green countryside in the center of America, where the little birds sing their songs in praise of God All-Powerful. But it's a pity that my beautiful country is going every day from bad to worse. Every day they are bathing it with the blood of their children who loved so much this beautiful land of the quetzal.

The unforgettable date was Sunday, 26 April 1998. It was when they killed the auxiliary bishop of the San Sebastián Church in Zone 1 [in Guatemala City]. It is not far from the city center. It is not known why the authorities could not police the middle of the city.

They say that Monsignor Juan José Gerardi Conedera, after having returned from dinner at his relatives' house, parked the car in the parking space. He left the car in which he had traveled and entered the corridor of the house, where a *desconocido* was waiting to kill him.

The first report said that his head was smashed with a stone or a piece of iron. Some shoeshiners who slept in the area saw a man leaving, shirtless, with his hair cut in military style and wearing boots. One of the shoeshiners said he had forgotten to buy cigarettes, and at about 10:30 P.M. he had left to go to a *tienda* to buy some. The man who wasn't wearing a shirt asked to buy a cigarette from the shoeshiner for a quetzal, and the shoeshiner said that for a quetzal he gave the shirtless man two cigarettes, not one. It is suspected that the man was the one who killed Monsignor Juan José Gerandi Condera, but there is no eyewitness to the crime.

Those who lived in the parish said that they realized the light was on in the garage. Then they found the body of the monsignor stretched out near his room. They sounded the alarm, but it was impossible to capture the murderer.

This is how everything remained. In a few days members of the FBI from the United States wanted their jefes to say that they had done their job well so they captured a drunk by the surname of Vielman, took him to jail, and indicated that he was the murderer of the bishop. But the owner of a bar in Zone 4 told the authorities and the press that Vielman, the drunkard, had been sleeping on the sidewalk in front of his business from 9:00 P.M. until the early morning of Monday the twenty-seventh. Furthermore, Vielman declared that he didn't know Monsignor Gerardi, that he didn't go to Zone 1, and that he was only familiar with Zone 4 and the bus terminal. In the last days of July, they took this man out of jail and delivered him into the custody of his mother.

The case of Monsignor Juan José Gerardi Conedera is very delicate. He was murdered two days after having delivered a manuscript of historic enlightenment titled *Guatemala Never Again*. This work reveals everything that happened in the time of the massacres. It is said that the book has the name of twenty-six persons responsible for the violation of human rights. My only thoughts are that the twenty-six people who are named in the book were those who paid to have Monsignor Gerardi Conedera killed, so that the truth of these deeds would not come to light.

They captured a priest named Mario Orantes Vájera, saying that he was the one who murdered Gerardi Conedera. The Ministerio Público had given the order to apprehend Father Mario Orantes Vájera.

The situation is critical. They even involved a dog named Balú (in another language Baloo, a German shepherd). They say that the monsignor was attacked and bitten by the dog, Balú, who is owned by Father Orantes. The Catholic people of Guatemala say that it is not Father Orantes who killed the bishop. More [of them] say that members of the right wing are the cause of this bloody deed.

Then the Ministerio Públic gave the order for three or four search warrants at the house of the priest Mario Orantes Vájera where they say they found proof [of the crime]. They used a chemical called Luminol to check where there had been a pattern of blood after it had been cleaned.

They say that when they used the Luminol, they could tell that the murderer had been walking around the furniture in the house and that he had been walking in the kitchen, the bathroom, and the hallways. After the murder, the assassin had blood on his shoes, and the chemical revealed that he had been walking around in all these places. There was no evidence in Father Orantes's bedroom because he could have removed or changed his shoes before entering it.

When the monsignor had been killed, the dog Balú had not been mentioned either in the newspapers or on the radio or television. Now the dog is involved in the murder. There are many comments that they are going to exhume the body, and the Public Ministry has confirmed it. The Catholic Church doesn't want the exhumation, but a sister declared that an exhumation of their brother would be beneficial for Father Orantes's liberty.

Also, a cook went to jail because it is said that she helped Father Orantes clean up the blood with a floor mop, but this lady has already been set free. Father Orantes continues to be imprisoned in the jail in Zone 18 in the capital city. He is in poor health, although three forensic doctors of the Public Ministry examined him and declared him to be in good health. Who knows what kind of doctors they are, because Father Orantes continues to complain about an ache in his head. Some days ago they transferred him to the national hospital, San Juan de Dios, for treatment, but also he is under custody.

This matter is not clearly understood.[76]

Reflections on Aging
11 August 1998

Many things happen in a man's life, and mine is no exception. I have experienced slander, gossip, sickness, poverty, and other unsavory things. But I have endured them with a lot of patience.

Many people say that it is better not to have children. Well, for them it is better not to have kids. But for others it is good to have them. The truth is that my wife and I have had many children—four sons and four daughters—and it has been a great sacrifice to rear them. They've needed food, clothes, education, and medicine. These things are expensive, and we are poor. Neither my wife nor I had much inheritance. My [real] father, Jesús, had a lot of land, but he lost all of it by selling it to spend on *aguardiente* and women.

[Because he had abandoned me at birth] I didn't want to bother my father. I only gave thanks to God and to my father for having begotten me and my mother for having given me birth. The best inheritance is a body and life.

My wife's father is a man of many goods, but we didn't wish to bother him either. We are struggling alone. God has helped us a lot, and I am appreciative for the noble heart of Dr. Jaime D. Sexton for everything he has done with my pages of the books. He has helped me financially, and without his help who knows how it would be. I want to write and say that it is true that with the aid of Dr. Sexton I was able to provide my children with a little education.

There are many changes in life. Everything changes with age, and all of our lives will end. We just don't know when. When I was young, I liked soccer. I also liked the fiestas. My sport was to leave at night for the hills to hunt animals together with friends who had hunting dogs.

But now my physical condition has changed. When I was 55 years old, I worked like a young man of 20 to 25. During the last two years, however, I have felt a fatigue. When I arrive home [from the field], I am very tired. The other day my muscles ached, although when I began working them again, the blood in them warmed up. Nevertheless, I no longer can tolerate working twelve to fourteen hours a day as I did before.

There was a time when I was traveling to the *fincas* to sell typical food, especially what we call *patín* [tomato paste]. The load I carried was light, about thirty-five pounds. I left my house at 3:00 A.M. and went to several *fincas* until reaching the *finca* Abundancia. On my return trip, I went back by another route and passed through other *fincas*. I walked a distance of nine leagues going and nine leagues returning, a total of eighteen leagues in one day. I didn't arrive home until 9:00 P.M. I did this not every day but one or two times a week. Now it takes all my energy to just walk from my village to my milpa. I have certainly changed with age. I, though, am really thankful to the Heart of Heaven and the Heart of Earth for the respect that my townspeople give me. I am a simple person, friend to everyone. I say hello and chat with all. I don't make distinctions according to religion. It is true that I am Catholic, but I also love members of other churches, because my thought is, God is for all and all are for God. It is not religion that saves a man. His salvation comes from the fear of God and the love of his fellow man, which is the beginning of wisdom. And I don't say to a person, I am of such a religion and I can avoid death. No, that is not true. Religion helps one to behave well toward his family and toward the other people. Everything depends on one's attitude. We people are exposed to the sufferings of life, and we have to bear them. We cannot escape from them.

Notes

1. Except for Sololá, Panajachel, Santiago Atitlán, Cerro de Oro, and San Lucas Tolimán, I have changed all place-names. I have also changed the names of individuals, except for those of public figures and individuals who have received wide media coverage, such as the people who were massacred in El Aguacate and Santiago Atitlán. For consistency with my previous publications and the vast majority of the literature on Guatemala, I have retained the traditional spelling of Indian proper names. As Dennis Tedlock (1996:202) mentions, these are the spellings that are generally used in Spanish and English publications.

2. Other subjects have kept diaries, but I am unaware of anyone else who has kept such a personal, chronological record for this length of time. With the episodes that I collected in summer 1998, the present volume completes twenty-eight years of Ignacio's autobiography and diary.

3. Ly-qui-Chung (1970) points out that during the Vietnam war peasants were caught in the middle of two fires (armies). David Stoll (1993) discusses the same theme for the Ixil, Richard Wilson (1995) for the Q'eqchi' Maya.

4. For research results of this earlier project from which Ignacio's life history emerged, see Sexton (1972, 1978, 1979a, 1979b), Woods and Graves (1973), Woods (1975), and Sexton and Woods (1977, 1982). For a comparison of folklore in two towns, see Sexton (2000).

5. While Ignacio and I were collaborating on *Campesino,* I told him how much I liked the folktales that appeared in the text, and he recommended that we do a separate book of folktales. In 1992 we published *Mayan Folktales.* It was so well received that we published *Heart of Heaven, Heart of Earth and Other Mayan Folktales* in 1999.

6. An example of judicial corruption and inefficiency is the sentencing of twenty-five soldiers who were found guilty of manslaughter in the 1995 massacre of eleven people in the Xamán community of returned refugees in the municipality of Chisec in the northern department of Alta Verapaz. The defense argued that the military patrol was provoked by the villagers, and the killers were sentenced to four to five years in prison but may pay off the penalty at Q5 (U.S. $.067) per day (*Central America Report* 1999b:1)

Crime is becoming so commonplace and the justice system so inept that many Guatemalans are taking the law into their own hands through lynchings and other summary executions. A United Nations monitoring mission, Minugua, reported forty-seven such cases from April to December 1998. Also, on 17 March 1999, narcotics police made a record haul when they found three tons of cocaine in two trucks on a country road in southeastern Guatemala (*Latin American Caribbean & Central America Report* 1999b:4).

7. An extraordinary interview of Arturo Taracena by Luis Aceituno (1999) is posted on the Rigoberta Menchú Tum Web site. Taracena, who was the EGP representative in France, talked about his role in editing Menchú's story in 1982. He said that by mutual consent he and Burgos-Debray decided to suppress any mention of his work because he was afraid that readers would consider Menchú's story EGP propaganda and fail to value it for its literary merit. Burgos-Debray and Taracena taped twenty-six hours of Menchú's testimony, and from this material they realized that they could produce a book narrated in a first-person voice so strong that it sang. He said that the last cassette of this interview was taped by Rigoberta and himself alone. Furthermore, he said that Burgos-Debray insisted that she had done the transcription but that was totally false. She had tried but failed. So, according to Taracena, he found money to hire a Cuban woman named Paquita Rivas, who was the secretary of Gonzalo Arroyo, a Chilean Jesuit exiled in France. They gave the complete transcription to Rivas. After Rivas cleaned up the material, Taracena and Burgos-Debray edited it, but Taracena said that he had done the most difficult editing. He insisted that, contrary to claims in the Guatemalan press, no part of the book was written by Burgos-Debray; she edited the book, with his approval. "That is, it is a narrative done completely by Rigoberta, with her own rhythm, with her own inventions, if there are any, with her own truths" (Aceituno 1992:2). According to Taracena, his role was to correct Rigoberta's grammar, because she did not have a good command of Spanish. At that time, Taracena said, he was working on his dissertation on the labor movement in Guatemala at a French university. Contrary to popular belief in Guatemala, Menchú did not have a bachelor's degree and spoke very poor Spanish. Taracena said that he deleted repetition and the interviewers' questions, that he grouped all the Guatemalan expressions in a glossary, and that he presented Burgos-Debray with a document reorganized according to major themes, for example, father, mother, death. Once he had done this, Burgos-Debray organized the material in chapters. When she had completed the narrative, she gave the manuscript back to Rivas, who further polished it.

According to Taracena, when they had a fairly clean version, the manuscript was sent to comrades in Nicaragua for proofreading, not to Mexico as Burgos-Debray had told Stoll (1997, 1999a). Mario Payeras did read the manuscript, but it was Gustavo Meoño, now president of the Rigoberta Menchú Tum Foundation, who argued that three passages should be deleted. One of these passages referred to children being used to collect unexploded bombs. Taracena said that the passage was really about the children serving as messengers between the people and the guerrillas. When the editors at Gallinard wanted to further polish Menchú's words into what they considered better French, Burgos-Debray defended Menchú's syntax and narrative voice. Taracena said that, contrary to rumor, he did not correct the page proofs for the simple reason that he did not have a sufficient command of French to do so.

With regard to Stoll's concern about the nature of the death of Patrocinio, Menchú's brother, whom she said she saw burned alive, Taracena replied that in 1982, when they were putting the book together, no one knew how Patrocinio had died. Rhetorically, Taracena asked who invented the version that Rigoberta gave? Was it Rigoberta, her companions in the CUC, or members of her family? Without really answering his own question, Taracena said that Stoll did not understand the narrative voice of the book, in which an Indian intermixes both an individual and a collective voice. Furthermore, he thought that, like a reporter, Stoll was more interested in the truth than in anthropological analysis.

Finally, Taracena said in the interview that he coordinated Menchú's campaign for the Nobel Peace Prize. After she received it, he dedicated himself mainly to his profession. While he disagrees with some of the things she is doing now, he agrees with many other things she is doing, although he did not elaborate.

Unfortunately, Taracena did not keep the first draft of *I Rigoberta Menchú*. He did not say whether he had a copy of the last tape that he said Rigoberta and he recorded. Without such evidence it is difficult to assess whether he is taking more credit for producing the book than he deserves. As Stoll (1999b) points out, commentators in the Guatemalan press have been quick to accept his claims, as if to repatriate a book that came into existence only through Burgos-Debray, a foreigner.

8. According to information posted on Glenn Welker's Web site (1998), the Rigoberta Menchú Tum Foundation, which has branches in Mexico City and New York, receives financial and technical support from governmental and nongovernmental entities in Germany, Australia, Belgium, Canada, Spain, the United States, France, Greenland, Holland, Italy, England, Japan, Mexico, Norway, Sweden, and Switzerland.

9. In *Son of Tecún Umán* (Sexton [1981] 1990:229–30), the first volume in this series, I tried to say something about the extent to which Ignacio was alike and different from his fellow countrymen. Since Burgos-Debray had not done fieldwork in Guatemala, she could not systematically compare Rigoberta on a number of variables with other Maya Indians. Fortunately, I was able to use our extensive quantitative data to make such a comparison. What follows is a comparison based on that quantitative data and on qualitative data I have collected over the last three decades.

Like numerous other Latin American Indians, Ignacio is partially assimilated to a Hispanic culture, but he is not necessarily representative of everyone in his community or culture in every respect in a statistical sense. Unlike central figures of other life histories, Ignacio is neither famous nor psychotic; he is an ordinary workingman. Abandoned at birth on 13 August 1941 by his parents, his childhood was hard. Despite his third-grade education, Ignacio is exceptionally perceptive, and he gives a keenly insightful account of his eventful life.

Between 1971 and 1975 members of our field school collected random samples of *Joseños* and Maya Indians in thirteen other towns (919 household heads). These data clearly showed that Ignacio is both alike and different from his countrymen with regard to socioeconomic and psychological characteristics. Like his Indian countrymen, Ignacio speaks a Mayan language and shares a cultural tradition that is mixed with both Mayan and Spanish elements. Like numerous other countrymen, he is socially and economically oppressed compared to richer Ladinos and Spaniards in Guatemala and compared to citizens of more economically developed countries.

Compared to the average *Joseño* of his generation, Ignacio has been more exposed to the outside world through formal education, travel, and military service. Although he served in the Guatemalan army from 1961 to 1962 (Sexton [1981] 1990:35–46), his unit was put on alert just once, when students from the University of San Carlos were demonstrating in Retalhuleu against a state of siege. Fortunately, his unit was not involved in any violence during this period.

Ignacio writes and speaks Spanish fluently, and he has taught himself to type. Also, compared to his peers, he has been more exposed to radio, films, and television and to newspapers, magazines, and books. His superior literacy and greater political knowledge are because of his greater exposure.

As a young man, Ignacio seemed somewhat more oriented toward change than most other *Joseños*. He appeared dissatisfied with his life condition and had high occupational aspirations for himself and his children. Ignacio would have preferred to have been a teacher rather than a farmer and a labor contractor. Although he still grows corn, beans, squash, and coffee, he has not taken crews to the coast to work on the cotton farms since 1984 because the guerrillas made it dangerous for him and his crews and because the *finqueros* exploited the laborers. Despite the low pay and poor working conditions, he and his crews saved enough from their wages to buy their own modest tracts of coffee land at home. Ignacio wanted his eldest son to become a pharmacist, but he was realistic and understood that he would have to settle for a less prestigious job such as a chauffeur. In fact, his eldest son became a farmer, like Ignacio, but two of his siblings are among the few children of *Sanjoseños* to earn their teaching credentials. Ignacio's wife, who did not have the opportunity to attend school and who felt deprived because she did not learn Spanish, also encouraged their children. Whenever it was possible financially, Ignacio believed in putting off his rewards to a later date, which helps to explain the considerable patience he exercised in producing six books, including this one. It also explains why he completed the technical training necessary to become a baker and why he encouraged his sons to apprentice as operators of foot looms.

Like other *Joseños*, Ignacio has elements of a traditional worldview. He believes that a person's life is relatively fixed at birth, that it is better to accept things as they happen because one cannot shape one's future, and that whether one has good or bad luck depends on one's heritage. But this fatalism appears to be the result of realistically assessing his limited environment rather than resistance to change.

Ignacio believes that one should perform ceremonies before harvesting and planting, that there are spirits who may taunt people during the night, and that some people, particularly shamans, can change into their animal form, or *nagual*. Thus elements of Ignacio's nonmaterial culture are changing more slowly than aspects of his material culture. In the latter stages of his life, as documented in the present volume, Ignacio's deep religious convictions are reflected in his role as a *principal*.

10. In early 1995 Silvia González-Martínez, a doctoral student from Mexico who was studying literary criticism at the University of Nebraska, Lincoln, asked if she could interview Ignacio and me for her thesis. Her goal was to compare the testimony of Ignacio and Rigoberta Menchú. I agreed to answer her questions and to take a brief questionnaire with me to Guatemala in summer 1995 to give to Ignacio on the condition that I might use some of the information in the introduction to the next volume of his life story. In June 1999 I contacted Silvia, who had completed her dissertation in

May 1997 and accepted a position at Southern Oregon State University in the department of foreign languages. She told me that on the advice of her adviser, she had changed the emphasis of her thesis and had not used any of the information that Ignacio and I had provided to her. I have used some of that information in the remainder of this section.

11. As Stoll (1999b) pointed out, Ignacio's personal philosophy may reflect more of a local Mayan perspective that has proved remarkably resilient in the face of external political ideologies than it does external ideologies.

12. During my trip to Guatemala in 1987, I bought a copy of *Me llamo Rigoberta Menchú y así me nació la conciencia* in Guatemala City and gave it to Ignacio. Menchú has received considerable attention in the Guatemalan media. Ignacio told me that he had found some contradictions in her story but that overall it was a good book. He was reluctant to say anything negative about it then.

13. For more information on *el santo mundo*, see *Heart of Heaven, Heart of Earth* (Sexton and Bizarro 1999).

14. There is the belief among the Maya that, as with corn, a person's life essence is transformed and regenerated after death in his or her own descendants, which explains the practice of naming a grandchild after a grandparent (Sexton and Bizarro 1999:12).

15. *Colegio,* depending on the context, may refer to primary school, secondary school, or college.

16. In March 1986 Father Andrés Girón and his landless followers formed the National Association of Peasants for Land, which seeks to purchase land on concessionary terms and to find credit to work the land as cooperatives. Girón advocates the need for basic land reform by converting large *fincas* owned by families into cooperative farms owned by campesinos who actually work the land. He has acquired a few farms with loans from the Guatemalan National Development Bank.

Some landowners have made a number of attempts to discredit the movement of poor campesinos to gain rights to land, warning that it is a prelude to calls for expropriations and invasions of land. Girón's hinting at squatter tactics has reinforced this fear. And some peasants have resorted to moving onto lands without permission. These "invasions" have taken place in Retalhuleu, Palín (Escuintla), Alta Verapaz, the Petén, and Izabal.

Other landowners may view such acquisitions as a bailout for Guatemala's crash of cotton exports and as a vehicle to sell their land at inflated prices. At least this is the view of some members of labor unions.

Girón admitted that he was considering running for president in the elections of 1990, stating that if there were no other land reform candidate, he didn't want to sin by omission. He and his followers believe the fight is for Guatemala, not to gain a little bit of a plantation, but to change the whole country.

Girón has received numerous letters and phone calls threatening him with death. His father and four other relatives were assassinated in the late 1970s, and he spent two years in exile in the United States. His aunt was murdered in Guatemala City. There have been several abductions and assassinations of farmers involved in the efforts to redistribute land. Thus the priest is always accompanied by a four-man, submachine-gun-toting bodyguard that the president assigned to him.

As Ignacio stated, Girón was wearing a pistol in his belt when he appeared in San José la Laguna. An armed priest shocks some parishioners, and conservatives in the Catholic Church resent his militant tactics. Others fear that radicalization of the land reform movement will bring bloody reprisals and that instead of Father Girón obtaining land for the campesinos to cultivate, he may only be getting land for their graves (Dewart and Eckersely 1988:6–8, 11; Katel 1988:AA12–13).

17. This thread is used to tie strands around the weaving thread to keep the dye from penetrating, thus leaving portions of the tied thread the same color to make patterns or figures. When the threads are untied they are called *labores* (figures or patterns) de *jaspe*. The *guindana* comes in three sizes: six strands per thread, nine strands per thread, or eleven strands per thread. The strands are twisted together to make one piece of thread, as a rope is twisted from several strands to make a single rope. The six-strand size weighs one-half pound, the nine- and the eleven-strand sizes weigh one pound each. The six-strand size is used to make small figures; the nine- and eleven-pound sizes are used to make large patterns or figures, such as those in jackets or blouses, depending on the style. Nothing has to be done to crude thread to keep the dye from penetrating the wrappings. However, bleached (cooked) thread, which is finer, has to be treated with candle wax or paraffin to keep the dye from penetrating the *guindana* thread.

18. The son will go to the house of the person who is being called and bring him or her back to take the call.

19. In the past on the afternoon of Holy Wednesday, the *mayordomos* would put together Maximón and place him high in the window of the church. They would place a cigar in his mouth and a whip in his hand and dress him in old clothes, such as battered *caites* (typical, Indian-style sandals), as if to ridicule him for having betrayed Jesus. But the same *cofrades* prohibited the children from bothering Maximón, because he could cause their death. They said that Maximón was the judge of the earth and Jesus was the judge of the heavens and clouds.

20. Protestants believe that worshiping the images of Maximón and the Catholic saints is idolatry.

21. Several military commissioners in San Martín were sent to prison for their mistreatment of the people during the height of the insurgency and counterinsurgency. For more details, see Sexton (1985, 1992).

22. Tomuschat, Lux de Cotí, and Balsells Tojo (1999c:1–9) documented this massacre as "Illustrative Case Number 86" and attributed it to the ORPA. At the end of the report they listed the names of the victims.

A guerrilla patrol of ten combatants, commanded by Second Lieutenant David, set up operations in the area. On 22 November 1988 at about 5:00 A.M., Carlos Humberto Guerra Callejas, who was an epileptic, went looking for his cattle that were pasturing at a place called Astillero de San Isidro. He ran into the guerrilla position, and the guerrillas captured him. The following day, 23 November 1988, twenty-six townspeople went looking for him. They split up into groups, and when they couldn't find him, they concluded that unknown people had kidnapped him. They decided that they would search for him the following day, and if they did not find him, they would notify the army.

On 24 November they continued the search, but this time they divided into three groups of ten persons each and looked in other areas of the mountain known as Filón de la Minas and Filón del Sojo. Suspecting a kidnapping, they brought along a mediator, an evangelical pastor named Antonio Olivares Blanco. The campesinos in the first two groups encountered guerrillas dressed in olive green and carrying arms.

When the third group realized that the first two groups and the evangelist had been captured, they went to the military Zone 302 to inform the army. The Callejas Tobar brothers led two army patrols back to the vicinity of the disappearances. Because they arrived late in the day, they decided to postpone looking for the villagers until the next day.

Some of the prisoners recognized members of the guerrilla patrol who had captured them. The guerrillas claimed that these men were army collaborators. They also thought that two of the people they had captured were military commissioners. Coincidentally, a guerrilla contact named Mijangos arrived at the same time that the captured campesinos arrived. Since only David, the commander, knew the true identity of Mijangos, his men captured him too, as if he were just another villager. David explained to his fellow guerrillas that their mission was more important than the lives of their prisoners, and he ordered that they be executed. His order included Mijangos, whom he now suspected was an army informant. In any case, if the guerrillas didn't kill him too, he later could be a witness to the premeditated murders. One by one, the prisoners were brought forth and strangled. The guerrillas did not shoot them because they were afraid the sound of arms would give their position away to the army. After the insurgents strangled their captives, they buried them at the same place in trenches they had dug. Altogether they executed twenty-two people.

In the middle of the morning of the next day, the guerrillas attacked an army patrol that was advancing from the north. At noon, near Plan Canaqué, a solider noticed disturbed dirt and found the bodies of Carlos Humberto Guerra Callejas and his three dogs. At about 1:30 P.M. there was another confrontation with the guerrillas that resulted in the wounding of a second lieutenant and a soldier.

On 26 November the same military patrol was attacked again by the guerrillas. Another military patrol that was advancing from the south found four graves with cadavers near El Chiquero. They waited for the authorities and the press to arrive by helicopter. They were not able to move all twenty-one bodies until 28 November. The bodies were taken to San Andrés Itzapa, where they were buried the next day. The only body that was not identified by anyone from El Aguacate was that of Mijangos, whom they buried as XX. Forensic analysis for all but two of the bodies, which were too decomposed, concluded that they had died of asphyxiation by strangulation.

The URNG released two communiqués, on 28 and 29 November 1998, regarding what had happened. The first claimed responsibility for inflicting twenty-five casualties, including dead and wounded, in the ranks of the army but said that they were the result of acts of war. In the second communiqué, the URNG categorically denied their participation in the kidnapping and subsequent executions of the campesinos of El

Aguacate, and it accused the army and the government of being responsible, adding that they were party to a new wave of terrorism, repression, and intimidation.

The massacre of the campesinos from El Aguacate was under study for two years by the Office of Human Rights in Guatemala. On 15 November 1990 the *licenciado* Ramiro de León Carpio said that the victims' human rights had been violated but that it was impossible to determine who had been responsible.

23. Ignacio told me that the Tzutuhiles believe both are gods of corn, since without Toj, the god of rain, there is no corn. Although Ka'nel means "rabbit," it is the god to whom one petitions for good harvests of corn, beans, and other crops. Ka'nel is a powerful and strong *dueño* of the enchanted hills. Ignacio also said that in Santiago, San Jorge, San Martín, and San José, Ka'nel is pronounced "ka'nel, not "Kjánel," as it has been spelled elsewhere.

24. Ignacio explained that Eduardo was referring to the law of compensation. If the parents do something bad, a curse may be put on their family to the third and fourth generations, as the Old Testament version of the Bible says. In a later episode, dated 10 July 1990, Ignacio elaborates on what he thinks Antonio's father, Juan Bizarro Gómez, might have done to experience such karma.

25. Anica, Ignacio's wife, was still nursing her own infant, Dominga Marta Bizarro Ramos, who would be three years old the following month, on 22 February. Her breasts weren't completely dry; her own infant was eating food and not nursing much.

26. When Ignacio wrote this episode, he included a clipping of a piece in *Prensa Libre* (23 April 1989:1, 4, 38) on Juan Sisay.

27. Ignacio explained that if a person asks for forgiveness and the person (or god) petitioned gives it, then it is a benediction to the offender, not to the one giving forgiveness, which is like saying, "Bless me, Lord, for I have sinned."

28. Free elections also actually took place locally and nationally in 1985 when Marco Vinicio Cerezo Arévalo was elected to the presidency and took office. Because all those mentioned in this episode are public figures, their real names have been used.

29. Amy Sherman (1997:141) states that as of 1992 evangelicals had established more than 210 private schools in Guatemala.

30. There are two beaches called Chuitinamit. One is in San José, and one is in San Jorge. Both of the beaches are close to the hill of Chuitinamit, but the hill is in the jurisdiction of San José.

31. It could be the volcano of San Martín, Santiago Atitlán, or San Lucas. But Ignacio says the people believe Santiago Atitlán has a stronger current. The Tzutuhil people believe that during the earthquake, there was a rupture in the crater, and for that reason the water is draining out of the lake. Even when it rains hard, the water level does not rise.

32. The technical director, a *Joseño* who already had a *colegio* in Panajachel, was taking steps to establish the school in San José. He spoke at the inauguration. The departmental supervisor, a government employee, is responsible for supervising all the primary and secondary schools in the department. The *supervisor nucleo,* or central supervisor, is under the departmental supervisor. His area includes San Martín, San José, San Jorge, and San Benito.

33. The list of one hundred had already been sent to the jefes, and the committee could not adjust it. So, the total was 125, but the new families still had to pay Q5 because the mission would not pay for the extra students.

34. The term "4-S" stands for *servicio* (service), *salúd* (health), *superación* (self-improvement), and *seguridad* (security).

35. Here Ignacio's informant is referring to Heart of Heaven, Heart of Earth. See *Heart of Heaven, Heart of Earth* (Sexton and Bizarro 1999) for a folktale about this concept.

36. This is the last grade necessary to teach primary school. After teaching three years in primary school, one can teach *básico,* although exceptions may be made if there are not enough teachers.

37. Ignacio said this organization has no formal name or abbreviation.

38. This organization seems to be a predecessor to two similar organizations mentioned in *Guatemala: los contrastes del desarrollo humano* (United Nations 1998:139). They are the Consejo de Organizaciones Mayas de Guatemala (COMG) and the Coordinadora de Organizaciones del Pueblo Maya de Guatemala, Saqb'illchil (COPMAGUA). *Cholb'al Q'ij Agenda Maya* (1998:14) refers to the latter organization as "SAQB'ICHIL, the Coordinación de Organizaciones del Pueblo Maya de Guatemala, COPMAGUA."

39. The patrolmen in Santiago Atitlán quit calling themselves *patrulleros de autodefensa civil* (civil defense patrolmen).

40. He is the nephew of Jorge Carpio, twice a candidate for the presidency of the republic, and a right-wing millionaire.

41. In the past *papel sellado,* or official paper, could be purchased in stores for 15 or 25 centavos a page. Now it is available only to lawyers, and it costs 10, 15, 50, or 100 quetzales, depending on the value of whatever is being certified. It is used for birth certificates, proof of purchase of property, and the like. The letterhead is stamped "Ministry of Finance," and the upper right-hand corner of the stamp bears the value of the paper.

42. Rodrigo said he was Miguel's brother to confuse his enemies. Thus Ignacio and others first thought that Rodrigo was Miguel's brother, but it has come to light that he is actually his son. By 1998 he was a jefe of the political party Unión Revolucionario Nacional Guatemalteca.

43. There is a small metal deer in the transmission tower. In Nahuatl *mazatl* (*mazate* in Spanish) means "deer." Thus Mazatenango is "the place of the deer."

44. In other words, no one knows when he or she is going to die. This is similar to the saying that Ignacio uses: "We all know where we were born, but none of us knows where we will die."

45. For a folktale about the Lord of Esquipulas, see *Heart of Heaven, Heart of Earth* (Sexton and Bizarro 1999).

46. At this time he was in *quinto año magisterio* (fifth year of teacher training), and his next year of study was *sexto año magisterio.* After completing this sixth year, he will be a teacher.

47. He had malaria, but blood tests show that he doesn't have it anymore. He, however, was warned not to get overheated and not to overwork lest he have a relapse.

48. Juan Benando and Roderico are sons of Ignacio Tuc González, who is the brother of Víctor Tuc González, Ignacio's friend. Víctor's sons, Eduardo, Hugo Zamora, and José de León Tuc, gave Ignacio no trouble.

49. This is communal land. A person has the right to use the land and to hand it down to his offspring but not to sell it. This provides a kind of security to the community, because the people will not lose their land.

50. When Ignacio's grandfather Ignacio Bizarro Ramos (married to his grandmother Isabel) was working the land, he had a private, rather than a communal, title to it. This title burned in the fire. In 1983, when Ignacio Bizarro Ujpán asked for the communal land, the mayor was Andrés, the son of Diego Bizarro Ramos, Ignacio Bizarro Ramos's brother. Thus, through his father, Andrés knew that Ignacio's grandfather had owned the land and lost his title. In those days the municipality did not keep records of who owned what, and if you lost your title, you were out of luck. When Ignacio Bizarro Ujpán asked for the communal land, he asked for the same land that his grandfather had worked, and Andrés gave it to him. Now Ignacio has an *acta* that says he is entitled to work the land as an usufructuary. Thus he can work the land and pass it down to his children, but he cannot sell it. Ignacio's grandmother showed him where his grandfather had planted poles of *izote* (a plant with multiple erect stems that has a white flower that is edible and tasty) as boundary markers. Ignacio also said that Mario, Cristóbal, and Luciano all claimed that the land was theirs, but Ignacio was clever and hired a lawyer who argued that Andrés would not have signed the *acta* of communal land if the land had belonged to his brothers. If this was the case, then Andrés would have to go to jail. Andrés is the same man who in *Campesino* (Sexton 1985:74–94) was accused along with Ignacio of killing the lad from San Martín and had to hide out in Sololá with Ignacio.

51. The holdings are scattered throughout the jurisdiction of San José. Ignacio's thirty *cuerdas* are in Patzunoj; others have their land in other places. But the entire fifty residents are listed in the same document, which says who has the holdings and where they are located.

52. There are earlier episodes about the Tuc brothers in *Son of Tecún Umán* (1990) and *Campesino* (1985). Tuc is an Indian surname, but Ignacio says that the members of this family are blond and that they are Ladinos. He thinks that a Spaniard might have married an Indian woman and taken her name.

53. Ignacio further explained that *tarea* means "a task," or a job one has to do. Hunajpú means "a daylord who is a hunter." Thus the meaning of their name, Tarea Hunajpú, is something like "a job that a hunter has to do." The name is also intended to make the people think they are identified with this god of the Mayan calendar, but they are not. And it is supposed to imply something strong so that the people will fear them.

54. I went out on one of these boats on 24 June 1994. It was simply packed. Off San José and San Martín, three boats of the same line rendezvoused, but instead of dividing the people up into two boats for the return trip, they crowded even more onto the obviously overcrowded boat. A smaller boat came to pick us up at San José to take us to San Martín, and the pilot, a mute, wanted to pull away because it too was obviously overloaded, but one of the passengers from San Jorge yelled, "Stop," with arm

gestures. The pilot reluctantly stopped and crowded even more people onto the boat. This was immediately after a hurricane had blown the sheet metal roof off one house and completely destroyed another. The assistants cram passengers on the boats the same way they cram them on the buses, getting three people per seat when there is only room to seat two per seat comfortably.

55. The most important day is 10 May, but the whole month is for mothers, and it is the month of Mary, mother of Jesus.

56. A week after Ignacio ended his year's service in summer 1994, he wrote this episode and gave it the title, "My Life in the *Cofradía, Costumbres* and Traditions of my Ancestors, the Heritage That One Cannot Lose."

57. Ignacio said that during each procession, the wife of the *alcalde* of a *cofradía* is expected to participate.

58. When *atol* is prepared in the *cofradía*, corn is cooked with ash from the wood fires (just as corn for tortillas is cooked with lime). Then the *masa* (corn dough) is cooked in large earthenware bowls. A condiment is made separately. Yellow corn is toasted, and it is ground with the *piedra de moler* (grinding stone). *Aniz* (anise), *chan* (*salvia chio,* an herb whose seeds are small black grains), and a little chile also are ground and then mixed in a clay bowl with the toasted yellow corn. Then this condiment is put into the plain corn to give it its spicy flavor. When the product is consumed, it is called *atol*.

59. The aroma of the incense calls their spirits to come to be with the person or persons burning it.

60. Ignacio explained that reaching old age is a gift of God, and you can't buy white (gray hair), which makes those of us who have it feel better.

61. For the mass, Ignacio had to give another offering to the church for the flowers and the incense.

62. The gate to the cemetery usually is closed and locked so that the *brujos* will not enter to use it.

63. The celebration described for 29 October is separate from the celebration for 1 and 2 November. The first is a private ceremony for the *cofrades,* and the *alcalde* of the *cofradía* of San José is responsible. The second is a public ceremony, and the *alcalde* of San Juan is responsible. Thus Ignacio's wife directed the preparations for the second but not the first. The ceremony held on 1 and 2 November is a big one, and it is for the whole town, not just the *cofrades.*

64. The custom is for the *mayordomos* to cook this food without the help of their wives.

65. For *las posadas* the *cofrades* make the *ranchitos* of cane and straw, similar to the ancient rustic structures of biblical times. They put them on *andas* (litters, or portable platforms for carrying the images) and take them to a different house on each of the nine days before Christmas. They reenact Mary and Joseph's search for shelter before Mary gave birth to Jesus.

66. Although Ignacio was in the *cofradía* of San José, as head of the highest-ranked *cofradía,* San Juan, he was the senior religious person there and he initiated the breaking up of the meeting. In a short, formal speech he said that it was time to go, that those who

wanted to stay could do so and those who wanted to leave for home could do so.

67. Flowers of the cohune palm that are like perfume. The flowers bear fruit, but the people don't eat it. They just use the flowers for the scent and decoration.

68. The image is an image of Jesus that is upright with holes in its hands and red painted over its heart to indicate where Jesus had been wounded. The image of Jesus of Nazareth has a living but sad color, with spots of blood on his face and a crown of thorns. The color of the image of Jesus Entombed is the pale color of death. The color of Jesus Resurrected is a resplendent, white color. He still has holes in his hands and feet and a wound on his side.

69. The *Sololatecos* were the parents of the husband of Ignacio's daughter María, who had married a man who was a Cakchiquel Maya from Sololá.

70. Ignacio didn't want to report the costs of the *cofradía* because he was afraid that San Juan Bautista might punish him.

71. On my query, Ignacio explained that these forces simply use the people for target practice.

72. Ignacio called me to tell me about his predicament, and I sent him the money to cover his expenses.

73. In response to my query, Ignacio said it is common in Guatemala for parapsychologists to use false names because they deceive people to get their money and therefore need to remain anonymous.

74. This is a court for people who cannot afford lawyers.

75. His critics are not on speaking terms with Ignacio. He said this was just ignorance. His enemies said he was the father of the *brujos* because the *brujos* that they consulted could not do anything to help her. They thought that his bewitching was stronger than that of the *brujos* they consulted and as a figure of speech said *Padre de los brujos,* or "Father of the *brujos.*"

76. A prosecutor, Celvin Galindo, who was probing possible military involvement in his murder resigned and fled Guatemala after he and his family were threatened. Father Orantes had already been released because of lack of evidence that he had committed the crime. The first judge and prosecutor overseeing the case were forced to resign after international complaints that they had ignored the evidence that the army might have been involved. The second judge, Henry Monroy, quit in March after only a month on the job and fled to Canada after receiving death threats (Anzueto 1999).

Glossary

Abbreviations

ANN: Alianza Nueva Nación (New Nation Alliance)

BANDESA: Banco Nacional de Desarrollo Agrícola
(National Bank of Agricultural Development)

CACIF: Comité Coordinador de Asociaciones Agrícolas,
Comerciales, Industriales y Finacieras (Coordinating
Committee of Agricultural, Commercial, Industrial,
and Financial Associations)

CCCAAS: Comité Campesino Contra Abusos de las Autoridades
(Campesino Committee against Abuses by the Authorities)

CEH: Comisión para el Esclarecimiento Histórico
(Commission for Historical Clarification)

CONACPUMAGUA: Coordinadora Nacional del Consejo de Pueblos Maya
de Guatemala (National Coordinator of the Council of
Mayan Peoples of Guatemala)

CONALFA: Comité Nacional de Alfabetización
(National Committee of Literacy)

CONFECOP: Confederacíon Guatemalteca de Federaciones de
Cooperativas (Guatemalan Confederation of Federated
Cooperatives)

CUC: Comité de Unidad Campesina (Committee of Peasant Unity)

DCG: Democracia Cristiana Guatemalteca
(Guatemalan Christian Democracy, or Christian Democrats)

DIGESA: Dirección General de Servicios Agrícola
(Office of Agricultural Services)

DIGESEPE: Dirección General de Servicios Pecuario
(Office of Livestock Services)

EGP: Ejército Guerrillero de los Pobres
(Guerrilla Army of the Poor)

FRG: Frente Republicano Guatemalteco
(Guatemalan Republican Front)

FAR: Fuerzas Armadas Rebelde (Rebel Armed Forces)

GUATEL: Empresa Guatemalteca de Telecomunicaciones
(Guatemalan Telecommunications Company)

IMAGUAC: Instituto Maya Guatemalteco de Ciencias
(Guatemalan Maya Institute of Science)

INDE: Instituto Nacional de Electrificación
(National Institute of Electrification)

INSO: Instituto Nacional para Señoritas de Occidente
(Teachers' Training Institute for Señoritas of the West)

INTECAP: Instituto Técnico de Capacitación
(Institute of Technical Training)

INVO: Instituto Normal para Varones de Occidente
(Teachers' Training Institute for Young Men of the West)

MAS: Movimiento de Acción Solidaria
(Movement of Solidarity Action)

MLN: Movimiento de Liberación Nacional
(Movement of National Liberation)

ORPA: Organización del Pueblo en Armas
(Organization of the People in Arms)

PAN: Partido de Avanzada Nacional (National Advancement Party)

PDCN: Partido Democrático de Cooperación Nacional
(Democratic Party of National Cooperation)

PID: Partido Institucional Democrático
(Institutional Democratic Party)

PGT: Partido Guatemalteco de Trabajo (Guatemalan Labor Party)

PRG: Partido Revolucionario Guatemalteco
(Guatemalan Revolutionary Party)

PSD: Partido Socialista Democrático (Social Democratic Party)

UCN: Unión del Centro Nacional (Union of the National Center)

URNG: Unidad Revolucionaria Nacional Guatemalteca
(Guatemalan National Revolutionary Unity)

Spanish and Indian Words

achiote: a shrub whose reddish seed is used for food coloring.
acta: a record of all the steps in establishing a school; memorandum,
   official document.
aguardiente: firewater, sugarcane rum.
aquila: assembly operations.
alcalde: mayor, head of a town or of a *cofradía.*
aldea(s): village(s).

alguaciles: municipal policemen, aides, and runners.

aliados de la paz: allied patrolmen of peace.

anda: litter, or portable platform for carrying an image.

aniz: anise.

apazote: herb used to flavor food, such as beans, or used in medicine.

arco: arch, special decoration made of fruit or flowers.

artesanos: artisans, craftsmen.

asofate: round gold platter with a gold cross in the middle.

Atitecan: of Santiago Atitlán.

Atiteco(s): person (people) of Atitlán.

Atitlanecos: see *Atitecos.*

atol: ritual drink of cornmeal or of rice, wheat, or corn flour, boiled and served hot.

atrio: atrium; the front part of a *sitio* or courtyard.

bachiller(es): secondary school graduate(s).

bandeja: platter.

beneficio(s): processing plant(s).

Beniteño(s): person (people) of San Benito.

boca abajo: lying face down.

bolos (ebrios): drunks.

bombas: bombs, fireworks shot from mortars.

borrachos: drunken; drunks.

bravo: irritable, bossy, rude.

brujo: witch, sorcerer, wizard, magician.

bulto: bulky load.

cabecera: departmental capital.

cacaste: wooden frame usually with four legs and shelves sustained by a tumpline
   that traveling salesmen use to carry goods on their backs.

café pergamino: second-class coffee, hulled once, pulped but unshelled
   or with the parchment still intact.

cafetal: coffee grove.

caites: typical (Indian-style) sandals.

caja rural: rural cash desk; small agency where loans can be paid but not taken out.

Candelaria: Candlemas.

caliente: a cooked drink made of minced pineapples, apples, plantains and peaches.

campo: field, countryside.

canícula: relatively dry period from July to August (dog days) between the two
   periods of maximum rainfall (June and September).

cargado: carried on the shoulders or back as cargo.

cargo: yearlong burden; office.

carnet de indentificación: identification card.

casa de duelo: house of mourning.

caserío(s): hamlet(s), small village(s).

católicas antiguas: folk Catholics.

Castellanización: preceding first grade; learning Spanish.

cayaques: canoes.

cédula: national identification card.

cerro: hill.

chan: a plant, or herb whose seeds are small black grains.

characotel(es): nagual(es), or spirit(s), that turn(s) into an animal form at night to bother people; the *characotel* has hypnotic power to make someone ill.

chupa: booze.

circular: an enclosure of the cemetery with a three-meter-high, stone-hewn fence.

citación: summons, or call.

cofrade(s): member(s) of a *cofradía.*

cofradía(s): religious brotherhood(s).

c'o jotz: aromatic leaves.

colegio(s): secondary school(s).

comadre: coparent; female friend; godmother.

comadrona empíricas: midwifery.

comedor: small restaurant; diner.

comisario: commissary.

compadre: ritual coparent; male friend; godfather.

compañeros: companions, friends.

concejales: councilmen.

contadores: electric meters.

copal: incense.

corte(s): native skirt(s).

cortesía: present, gift.

costumbre(s): custom(s); ritual(s); ceremony(ies).

coyote: coyote; guide; illicit smuggler of migrants.

cuadra(s): linear measure(s) of 275 feet.

cuadrilla: crew.

cuarta: portion, plot of land, dirt.

cuerda(s): measure(s) of 0.178 acre.

curandera(o): female (male) curer.

desconocido(s): unknown(s).

directiva: board of directors.

dueña(o), dueñas(os): female (male) owner(s).

dueño del santo mundo: owner, lord of the sacred world, earth.

educación primaria urbana: primary education in city schools, as opposed to rural schools.

finca(s): farm(s).

finqueros: owners or administrators of *fincas.*

Flor Infantil: Flower Child.

fresco: cool or soft drink.

fuego simbólico antorcha: symbolic fire on a torch.

galera: a large shed that has benches and an altar in front.

gotero: the edge of the roof from which the rain- and dew drops fall.

guardia de hacienda: semimilitary border patrol, armed treasury police.

guardia municipal: municipal guard.

guardián: watchman.

guaro: liquor.

Guatemalteco(s): person (people) of Guatemala.

guerrilla: guerrilla movement.

guindana: a roll of special thread or yarn weighing one pound that is used to tie strands around the weaving thread to keep the dye from penetrating, thus leaving figures or patterns; when untied, they are called *labores* (figures or patterns) *de jaspe.*

güisquil(es): climbing plant(s) whose fruit is the size of an orange; an edible fruit with a spiny outer membrane.

hermanos: friends or brothers.

Hombres de maíz: Men of Corn.

huesito: little bone.

huipil: traditional blouse.

indígena(s): indigene(s), Indian(s), native inhabitant(s).

instituto básico: secondary school similar to junior high.

intestado: dying without leaving a valid will.

izote: a plant with multiple erect stems that has a white flower that is edible and tasty.

jaspe(s): tie-dyed figure(s) or design(s) in thread or yarn.

jícaras: cups made of gourds.

jornalero(s): day laborer(s).

Joseña(s), Joseño(s): woman (women), man (men), person (people) of San José.

juez (jueces): judge (judges); vice-*alcalde(s)* in *cofradías.*

juicio: trial, action.

juntos: together; living as common-law husband and wife.

juzgado: court.

labores de jaspe: works or adornment of tie-dyed thread or yarn.

lámina: pieces of sheet metal for roofing.

las posadas: guest houses; the ceremony of taking out the images of José and María in their *ranchitos* before Christmas.

lengua: Mayan language, tongue.

licenciado: counselor, licensed person, graduate.

listado nacional: a list of congressional deputies not elected by a town but appointed by Congress or the Executive Branch.

locura: madness, insanity, craziness.

madres de familias: mothers of families.

magisterio: teaching staff or assembly.

Mala Hora del Mundo: Bad Hour of the World.

manteles: tablecloths.

manzanilla: Matricaria chamomilla, chamomile.

Martinero(s): man (men), person (people) of San Martín.

masa: corn dough.

más o menos: more or less; not good or bad but average.

mayor(es): superior(s).

mayordomo: low ranking officer of a *cofradía.*

M'hijo: Mi hijo, my son.

militar ambulantes: roving military police.

ministerio: ministry.

misterio: a local, older word used to express going to the church to worship God, which is now equivalent to *rosario.*

mojados: "wetbacks," illegal immigrants.

mozo(s): helper(s), servant(s).

municipios: municipalities, districts, towns.

mozo(s): helper(s), servant(s).

muchacha(s): girl(s), young woman (women).

muchacho(s): boy(s), young man (men).

mundo: world, earth. See also *santo mundo.*

municipios: municipalities, districts, towns.

nagual: spirit and animal forms of humans, especially witches; soul.

natural(es): native(s), Indian(s).

naturista: naturist.

Nicodemos: young men named after Nicodemus (Nicodemo), who lowered the body of Jesus from the cross.

Niña Independencia: Child of Independence.

niño: small boy.

nixtamal: kernels of corn softened and hulled by boiling in limewater to make hominy, which is easy to grind into dough for tortillas.

novenario: nine days of praying, saying the rosary with hymns, and signaling with *bombas* and firecrackers that the arrival of the patron saint is near. The *novenario* ends on 1 July, the day that the image arrives in the new *cofradía.*

novia: girlfriend.

novios: lovers.

ocote: pine with resin.

octavo: an eighth of a liter.

oro: gold; name given to coffee beans that have been thoroughly cleaned, or husked, but unroasted.

pacayas: palm fruit whose flowers are also edible.

padrino(s): coparent(s); godparent(s); teacher(s) selected by the students as the most liked or helpful.

panteón: vault, aboveground tomb.

papel sellado: official paper.

párvulos: preprimary school, similar to kindergarten.

Pastor del Mundo: Pastor of the World.

pataxtes: white cacaos.

patín: tomato paste

patín con pescaditos: small fish in tomato sauce or paste.

patojos: youngsters.

patrullaje: news patrol; periodic news for the day.

Patrullaje Informativo: Informative Patrolling.

patrulleros de autodefensa civil: civil defense patrolmen.

pergamino: See *café pergamino.*

perito contador: qualified accountant.

piedra de moler: grinding stone.

pita: maguey fibers.

pisto: money.

policía ambulante: roving police.

policía de asuntos criminales: judiciales, or judicial police, criminal police.

primer zajorín: primary, first shaman.

principal(es): elder(s).

profesor: teacher; professor.

protestantes: protestants.

pulique: beef seasoned with salsa of corn or bread, tomato, garlic, onion, *apazote,* and salt.

pulique de res: dish of meat with chili.

quintal(es): measure of weight, one hundred pounds; one-hundred-pound units.

quinto año magisterio: fifth year of teacher training.

ranchito(s): small ranchos.

rancho(s): hut(s), rustic dwelling(s), ranch(es).

registro de rentas: registry of revenue, department of revenue.

retrasados: nongraduates; held back.

Ronda del Mundo: Round of the World, or Earth.

ropa antigua: traditional costume.

rosario: rosary.

Sábado de Gloria: Easter Saturday.

salón: lounge, sitting room, assembly hall.

salud: health.

Sanjoseños: See *Joseños.*

Santísimo: See *Santísimo Sacramento.*

Santísimo Sacramento: Holy Sacrament, Eucharist.

Santo Día: Holy Day.

santo mundo: sacred world, or earth.

Santo Rosario cantado: Holy Rosary that is sung.

secreto: sacred or magical act.

seguridad: security.

Señor de Esquipulas: Lord of Esquipulas.

servicio: service.

sexto año magisterio: sixth year of teacher training.

símbolo de entrega de título: symbolic degree.

sitio: place; homesite.

Sololatecos: people of Sololá.
splendor: halo.
suerte: luck, ability.
supernación: self-improvement.
supervisor núcleo: central supervisor.
sute: head cloth.
tablón(es): raised plot(s).
tamalitos: little tamales.
tapesco: cane bedframe.
tareas: jobs, pieces of work, amount that can be done in one day.
temascal: sweat house.
Tepotzlanecos: people of Tepotzlán.
texel(es): low-ranking female member(s) of a *cofradía.*
tienda(s): small store(s).
tragos: drinks, shots.
traguitos: little drinks.
tun: big drum, drum.
Uspantanecos: people of Uspantán.
útiles: school supplies.
vara(s): linear measure(s) between 32 and 33 inches.
Visión Mundial Cristiano: World Christian Vision.
Xocomil: strong wind.
zajorín(es): shaman(s).

References Cited

Aceituno, Luis
1999   "Entrevista a Arturo Taracena sobre Rigoberta Menchú: Arturo Taracena rompe el silencio," pp. 1–7. [Cited 17 September 1999]; available from http://ourworld.compuserve.com/homepages/rmtpaz/Mensajes/ 0990110.html.

Anzueto, Alfonso
1999   "Guatemalan Prosecutor Flees: Abandons Case of Bishop's Death." *The Arizona Republic,* 9 October, p. A25.

Aznárez, Juan Jesús
1999   "Los que me atacan humillan a las víctimas." El País (Mexico City), 24 January, pp. 6–7. [Cited 27 September 1999]; available from http:// ourworld.compuserve.com/homepages/rmtpaz/Mensajes/e990124.html.

Associated Press
1999a   "Guatemalan Rebel Apology." *New York Times,* 14 March, p. 17.
1999b   "Guatemalans Ignore History in Election." *The Arizona Republic,* 25 December, p. 27.

Beverly, John, and Marc Zimmerman
1990   *Literature and Politics in the Central American Revolution.* Austin: University of Texas Press.

Burgos, Elisabeth
1999   "The Story of a Testimonio." *Latin American Perspectives* 26, no. 6 (November):53–63.

Burgos-Debray, Elisabeth, editor
1984   *I Rigoberta Menchú: An Indian Woman of Guatemala.* London: Verso.

Burt, Jo-Marie, and Fred Rosen
1999   "Truth-Telling and Memory in Postwar Guatemala: An Interview with Rigoberta Menchú." *NACLA Report on the Americas* 32, no. 5 (March/ April):6–10.

Central America Report
1999a   "Guatemala: Country Reeling from Truth Commission Report." 5 March, pp. 1–3.
1999b   "Guatemala: Xamán Verdict Sparks Outrage." 20 August, pp. 1–3.
1999c   "Guatemala: FRG Comes Close but Fails to Win in First Round." 12 November, pp. 1–3.

Cholbál Qíj Agenda Maya
1998   Guatemala City: Editorial Cholsamaj.

Daily, Charles A.
1971   *Assessment of Lives: Personality Evaluation of Lives in a Bureaucratic Society.* San Francisco: Jossey-Bass.

Darling, Juanita
2000   "Guatemala Sees Organized Crime as Security Threat." *Los Angeles Times,* 31 December, p. A3.

Dewart, Tracey, and Michael Eckersley
1988   "Guatemala's Giron: Good Shepherd or Pied Piper?" *NACLA Report on the Americas* 22(2):6–8, 11.

Dudley, Steven
1999   "David Stoll on Rigoberta, Guerrillas and Academics." *NACLA Report on the Americas* 32(5):8–9.

Dyk, Walter
1938   *Son of Old Man Hat: A Navajo Autobiography.* Recorded by Walter Dyk. New York: Harcourt, Brace and Company.

Edgerton, Robert B., and L. L. Langness
1974   *Methods and Styles in the Study of Culture.* San Francisco: Chandler and Sharp.

Garvin, Glenn
1999   "Guatemalan Murder Case Drags on 18 Months after Bishop's Killing." *Miami Herald,* 5 December. [Cited 6 December 1999]; available from http://www.herald.com/content/today/news/americas/digdocs/053487.html.

Gordon, Max
1983   "A Case History of U.S. Subversion: Guatemala, 1954." In *Guatemala in Rebellion: Unfinished History,* ed. Jonathan L. Fried et al., pp. 45–69. New York: Grove Press.

Katel, Peter
1988   "Priest Shielded by Bodyguards as He Leads Land-Reform Fight." *The Arizona Republic,* 14 February, AA13–14.

Kennedy, John G.
1977   *Struggle for Change in a Nubian Community: An Individual in Society and History.* Palo Alto: Mayfield Publishing Company.

Kovaleski, Serge F.
1999   "Runoff Expected in Guatemala's Presidential Election." Washington Post Foreign Service, 9 November. [Cited 4 December 1999]; available from http://www.washingtonpost.com/wp-s...te/1999-11/09/0681-110999-idx.html.

Langness, L. L.
1965   *The Life History in Anthropological Science.* New York: Holt, Rinehart and Winston.

Latin American Caribbean & Central America Report
1999a   "URNG Becomes Party." 19 January, p. 3.
1999b   "Guatemala/Cocaine Bust, Crime Report." 30 March, p. 4.
1999c   "Portillo Just Short of Outright Victory." 7 December, p. 3.

Latin America Regional Reports Mexico & Central America
1982 "Guatemala: Army Steps Up Action against Guerrillas." 12 February, p. 3.

Lewis, Oscar
1951 *Life in a Mexican Village: Tepoztlán Restudied.* Urbana: University of Illinois Press.

Lovell, George W.
1988 "Surviving Conquest: The Maya of Guatemala in Historical Perspective." *Latin America Research Review* 23:25–57.

Ly-qui-Chung
1970 *Between Two Fires: The Unheard Voices of Vietnam.* New York: Praeger.
Monsanto, Pablo
1983 "The Foco Experience: The Guerrillas' First Years." In *Guatemala in Rebellion: Unfinished History,* ed. Jonathan L. Fried et al., pp. 262–64. New York: Grove Press.

New York Times
1999 "Peace Winner Admits Discrepancies." 12 February, p. 12. [Cited 17 September 1999]; available from http://archives.nytimes.com.

Payeras, Mario
1983 "The Tiger of Ixcán." In *Guatemala in Rebellion: Unfinished Business,* ed. Jonathan L. Fried et al., pp. 264–69. New York: Grove Press.

Perera, Victor
1993 *Unfinished Conquest: The Guatemalan Tragedy.* Berkeley and Los Angeles: University of California Press.

Prensa Libre
1989 "Asesinaron al artista Juan Sisay." Guatemala City. 23 April, pp. 1, 4, 38.

Redfield, Robert
1930 *Tepoztlán: A Mexican Village: A Study of Folk Life.* Chicago: University of Chicago Press.

Rohter, Larry
1982 "Guatemala: No Choices." *Newsweek,* March 1, p. 24.
1999 "Guatemalan Commission's Report Is Searing Indictment on Military." *New York Times on the Web.* [Cited 4 December 1999]; available from http://www.nytimes.com/library/wor...ericas/022799guatemala-report.html.

Sexton, James D., Editor
1985 *Campesino: The Diary of a Guatemalan Indian.* Tucson: The University of Arizona Press.

1990 *Son of Tecún Umán: A Maya Indian Tells His Life Story.* Prospect Heights: Waveland Press. (1st ed. The University of Arizona Press, 1981)

1992 *Ignacio: The Diary of a Mayan Indian of Guatemala.* Philadelphia: University of Pennsylvania Press.

1999 *Mayan Folktales: Folklore from Lake Atitlán, Guatemala.* Albuquerque: The University of New Mexico Press. (1st ed. Anchor Doubleday, 1992).

Sexton, James D.

1972   *Education and Innovation in a Guatemalan Community: San Juan
       la Laguna.* Latin American Studies Series, vol. 19. Los Angeles: University
       of California, Los Angeles.

1978   "Protestantism and Modernization in Two Guatemalan Towns."
       American Ethnologist 5:280–302.

1979a "Modernization among Cakchiquel Maya: An Analysis of Responses
       to Line Drawings." *Journal of Cross-Cultural Anthropology* 10:173–90.

1979b "Education and Acculturation in Highland Guatemala." *Anthropology
       and Education Quarterly* 10:80–95.

2000   "Environmental Determinants of Folkloric Content in Guatemala."
       Latin American Indian Literatures Journal 16:1–17.

Sexton, James D., and Ignacio Bizarro Ujpán

1999   *Heart of Heaven, Heart of Earth and Other Mayan Folktales.* Washington
       and London: Smithsonian Institution Press.

Sexton, James D., and Clyde M. Woods

1977   "Development and Modernization among Highland Maya: A Comparative
       Analysis of Ten Guatemalan Towns." *Human Organization* 36(2):156–72.

1982   "Demography, Development and Modernization in Fourteen Highland
       Guatemalan Towns." In *Highland Guatemalan Historical Demography,*
       ed. Christopher Lutz, Robert Carmack, and John D. Early, pp. 189–202.
       Albany: SUNY, Institute for Mesoamerican Studies, Pub. 6; distributed by
       the University of Texas Press.

Sherman, Amy

1997   *The Soul of Development: Biblical Christianity and Economic Transformation
       in Guatemala.* New York and Oxford: Oxford University Press.

Simmons, Leo W., editor

1942   *Sun Chief: The Autobiography of a Hopi Indian.* New Haven: Yale
       University Press.

Simons, Marlise

1983   "Guatemala: The Coming Danger." In *Revolution in Central America,* ed.
       Stanford Central American Action Network, pp. 127–34. Boulder:
       Westview Press.

Sklodowska, Elbierta

1991   *Testimonio hispanoamericano: historia, teoría, poética.* New York: Peter Lang.
1996   "Spanish American Testimonial Novel: Some Afterthoughts." In *The Real Thing:
       Testimonial Discourses and Latin America,* ed. George M. Gugelberger,
       pp. 84–100. Durham and London: Duke University Press.

Smith, Carol, and Jeff Boyer

1987   "Central America since 1979." In *Annual Review of Anthropology*
       16:197–221.

Stoll, David
1993 *Between Two Armies in the Ixil Towns of Guatemala.* New York: Columbia University Press.
1997 "I, Rigoberta Menchú." *Brick,* no. 57 (Fall):31–38.
1999a *Rigoberta Menchú and the Story of All Poor Guatemalans.* Boulder: Westview Press.
1999b. Personal Communication.

Tedlock, Dennis
1996 *Popol Vuh: The Definitive Edition of the Mayan Book of the Dawn of Life and the Glories of Gods and Kings.* New York: Simon and Schuster.
The Arizona Republic
1999 "Lawyer Elected in Guatemala." 28 December, p. A16.

Tomuschat, Christian, Otilia Lux de Cotí, and Alfredo Balsells Tojo
1999a "Conclusions I: The Tragedy of Armed Confrontation." In *Guatemala: Memory of Silence,* pp. 1–16. CEH Online Report, American Association for the Advancement of Science and the United Nations Office of Project Services. [Cited 3 December 1999]; available from http://hrdata.aaas.org/ceh/report/english/conc1.html.
1999b "Conclusions II: Human Rights Violations, Acts of Violence and Assignment of Responsibility." In *Guatemala: Memory of Silence,* pp. 1–11. CEH Online Report, American Association for the Advancement of Science and the United Nations Office of Project Services. [Cited 3 December 1999]; available from http://hrdata.aaas.org/ceh/report/english/conc2.html.
1999c "Caso Ilustrativo No. 86." In *Guatemala: memoria del silencio,* pp. 1–9. [Cited 30 December 1999]; available from http://hrdata.aas.org/ceh/mds/spanish/anexo1/co11.no86.html. United Nations
1998 *Guatemala: los contrastes del desarrollo humano,* Edición 1998. Sistema de las Naciones Unidas en Guatemala. Guatemala City: United Nations.

U.S. Department of State
1999 "Guatemala Country Report on Human Rights Practices for 1998." [Cited 4 December 1999]; available from http://www.state.gov/www/global/hu . . . ghts/1998_hrp_report/guatemal.html.

Welker, Glenn
1998 "Homage to Rigoberta Menchú Tum, Quiche Mayan." [Cited 17 September 1999]; available from http://www.indians.org/welker/menchu.html.

Wilson, Richard
1995 *Maya Resurgence in Guatemala: Q'eqchi' Experiences.* Norman and London: University of Oklahoma Press.

Woods, Clyde M.
1975 *Culture Change.* Dubuque, Iowa: W. C. Brown.

Woods, Clyde M., and Theodore D. Graves
1973 *The Process of Medical Change in a Highland Guatemala Town.* Latin American Studies Series, vol. 20. Los Angeles: University of California, Los Angeles.

World Factbook
1999   Central Intelligence Agency. [Cited 19 January 2000];
        Available from http:/www.odci.gov/cia/publications/factbook/gt.html.

Yúdice, George
1996   "Testimonial and Postmodernism." In *The Real Thing: Testimonial Discourse and Latin America,* ed. George M. Gugelberger, pp. 42–57. Durham and London: Duke University Press.

Zimmerman, Marc
1992   "El otro de Rigoberta: los testimonios de Ignacio Bizarro Ujpán y la resistencia indígena en Guatemala." *Revista de Crítica Literaria Latinoamérica* 6:229–43.

1995   *Literature and Resistance in Guatemala: Textual Modes and Cultural Politics from El Señor Presidente to Rigoberta Menchú.* Monographs in International Studies, no. 22. Athens: Ohio Center for International Studies.

Acknowledgments

I WISH TO THANK my research assistants David Ortiz, Anne Manning, Victoria Spencer, Mauricio Rebolledo, Lorenzo Sotelo, and Charles Wright for helping me to translate and edit specific sections of this book. My research assistants Lisa Hardy and Christina Getrich read the entire manuscript and made numerous worthwhile suggestions. Mark Middleton prepared the prints from my slides, and James Tate produced the two maps. My wife, Marilyn, read portions of this manuscript and gave me valuable feedback. I especially want to thank my son, Randy, for carefully reading the final draft of the entire manuscript and providing numerous constructive suggestions for improving the clarity and style of the prose. David Stoll kindly read the whole manuscript and gave me many insightful suggestions. I also thank the anonymous reviewer for the University of New Mexico Press who gave me useful suggestions. Sheila Berg's sharp eyes found numerous ways to improve the clarity and consistency of the book. My nephew Michael Brooks graciously gave me intellectual property counsel. Finally, I am appreciative for my Regents' Professor research funds, which made it possible for me to return to Guatemala in 1992, 1994, 1995, and 1998.

Index

mourning, after massacres, 162
Movimiento de Acción Solidaria (MAS, Movement of Solidarity of Action), 100, 173; candidate, 176
Movimiento de Liberación Nacional (MLN, Movement of National Liberation), 41, 65, 176
MR-13 (13 November Movement), 7–8
municipal administration, 90–93
municipal service, 195
murder cases, 226–29
music, All Souls' Day, 241; marimba music, 41, 93, 101, 118, 233; *tun* drum, 263

nagual, cures according to, 47
naming babies, 55–56, 279n14
National Association of Peasants for Land, 279n16
National School of Rodolfo Juan García, 132
National Security Doctrine, 11
nervous breakdown, 264–65
New Year, 194–95
Nicodemos, 247
Niña Indepencia, selection, 143–44
nixtamal, 263
Nobel Peace Prize, 14, 17, 20, 277n7
North Americans, Mormons drowned, 129–30
novenarios (nine days of prayer and song), 233–34, 237

occupations, 278n9
Oliva y Oliva, Juan, 246
Operation Guatemala, 8
Operation Phoenix, 8
Orantes Vájera, Mario (Father), 271–72, 286n76
Organización del Pueblo en Armas (ORPA, Organization of the People in Arms), 9
Ortiz, Diana, 125

pacaya leaves, 242
Pachavac, 169
Pachichaj, 27–29
painters, 115
Pantzay, Ciro (Father), 82, 124–25
Partido de Avanzada Nacional (PAN, National Advancement Party), 13
Partido Democratico de Cooperación Nacional (PDCN, Democratic Party of National Cooperation), 90, 176
Partido Guatemalteco de Trabajo (PGT, Guatemalan Labor Party), 6, 8–9
Partido Revolucionario Guatemalteco

(PRG, Guatemalan Revolutionary Party), 65
Partido Socialistica Democrático (PSD, Social Democratic Party), 65, 176
Pastor del Mundo [Pastor of the World], 79–80
patterns of speech, 4
Patzilín, 116, 174
Patzunoj, 202–4; land disputes, 205–8
Paz Tejada, Carlos, 8
peace, elusive, 185
peace, poverty related to, 20
peace accords, 10, 253–57, 255 fig.
peace talks, 185–86
peasant committees, 20–21
peasants, work as campesinos, 46
San Pedro the Apostle Day, 186
Peña, Benjamín, 32
Peña, Juan (Father), 234–35
Peña Cholotío, Benjamín, 72–73, 90–96; anonymous letters, 220; military interrogation, 255–56; space for private school, 127
Penados del Barrio, Próspero (archbishop), 67, 115
Pérez, Catarina, 80–82
PID (Partido Institucional Democrático, Institutional Democratic Party), discredited, 40–41; Ignacio in, 22; young people on, 40–41
place names, 275n1
Poco Barreno, José María, 145
Polaz Bizarro, Santiago, 246
policemen, 158–59; Joseño, 172; kidnapping suspects, 170–72; refusal to serve in restaurants, 167
political parties, advantages, 41; campaign promises, 151–53. *See also individual parties*
politicians, 21; promises, 22–23, 141–42; as vampires, 24
Pop, Juan, 139
population, 12
Portillo, Alfonso, 12–13
posadas celebrations, 243–45, 285n65
poverty, 6, 12, 115, 185; Ignacio's family, 123–24, 143–44; inflation, 123; malnutrition, 123; peace accord effects, 256
pox lak' flowers, 232
premonitions, 158
presidential elections, 173
priests, 124, 238, 269. *See also individual priests*
prison, 39
private schools, 126–27, 130–33